RESEARCH HIGHLIGHTS IN SOCIAL WORK 37

# The Changing Role of Social Care

*Edited by Bob Hudson*

Jessica Kingsley Publishers
London and Philadelphia

First published in the United Kingdom in 2000 by
Jessica Kingsley Publishers Ltd
116 Pentonville Road
London N1 9JB, England
and
325 Chestnut Street
Philadelphia, PA 19106, U S A
*www.jkp.com*
Copyright © 2000 Robert Gordon University, Research Highlights Advisory Group,
School of Applied Social Studies

**Library of Congress Cataloging in Publication Data**
The changing role of social care / edited by Bob Hudson.
      p.  cm. -- (Research highlights in social work ; 37)
    Includes bibliographical references and index.
    ISBN 1-85302-752-9 (alk. Paper)
    1. Social service--Great Britain. 2. Public welfare--Great Britain.
    I. Hudson, Bob, research fellow. II. Series.
    HV245.C583    1999
    361.941--dc21                                99-41651

**British Library Cataloguing in Publication Data**
The changing role of social care. - (Research highlights in social work ; 37)
1. Public welfare - Great Britain 2. Public welfare - Great Britain - Management 3. Social legislation - Great Britain
I. Hudson, Bob
362.9'41

ISBN 1 85302 752 9

Printed and Bound in Great Britain by
Athenaeum Press, Gateshead, Tyne and Wear

# Contents

## Part II: Working Across Boundaries

## Part III: Comparative Perspectives

# CHAPTER I

# Introduction and Overview

*Bob Hudson*

The last major reorganisation of what used to be termed 'the personal social services' was over 30 years ago in the wake of the Seebohm Report of 1968 (Seebohm 1968). This resulted in the creation of one unified department in each relevant local authority with responsibility for 'local authority social services'. Every such authority was to have a new social services committee which would take over a range of responsibilities which had previously been fragmented between departments responsible for children, health and welfare. Seebohm argued that a large and prestigious department of this kind would attract senior local politicians who would ensure a higher profile for this relatively neglected area of activity. The subsequent legislation also made it a requirement to appoint a local director of social services or, as Scotland preferred to describe it, director of social work.

The new departments got off to a lively start, with major pieces of legislation being implemented (such as the 1969 Children and Young Person's Act and the 1970 Chronically Sick and Disabled Person's Act) and some early years of financial plenitude. By the end of the 1970s, notwithstanding the beginnings of financial rectitude, social services departments appeared to have successfully grafted themselves onto the established structure and system of local government. Now, as the new millennium dawns, the very existence of these departments is under question. From the 1980s onwards, both social services departments in particular, and local government in general, began to change in important respects. These changes in turn had substantial implications for other organisations whose role had hitherto been limited. Foremost amongst these changes has been the division between providing and purchasing roles, the consequent growth of independent sector providers, the growing emphasis upon 'partnership', the changing role of social work as a profession, the shifting balance between central and local government, and the emergence of users and carers from the role of passive recipients.

The cumulative impact of these and other changes has been so great that the 'social services department' envisaged by Seebohm is now unrecognisable, if not extinct. The publication of the new White Paper, *Modernising Social Services* (Department of Health 1998), effectively puts an end to the Seebohm era and identifies an approach thought to be better suited to the next century. It is surprising that this remarkable and relatively short period in the history of social care has rarely been scrutinised and analysed – an omission which will be made good by this volume, both for the purpose of looking back and reflecting upon change, and using this reflection to think about the future.

The book is in three parts. Part I examines the changing role of social care over the past 30 years, particularly the changes associated with the introduction of the 'quasi-market' in the 1990s. Part II looks at interagency relationships. The crucial relationship between social care and health care is such an integral part of so many of the chapters in this book that it would have been repetitious to examine it discretely, but three other crucial intersections are covered – those with housing and social security, and the broader relationship between central and local government. In Part III the opportunity is taken to go beyond an English focus, with chapters looking at the position in other parts of the United Kingdom and beyond. Finally, the new social care White Paper is analysed.

The picture which is built up through the contributions fits together in a coherent way to chart some of the most significant social policy changes at local government level in the post-war period. In Chapter 2, John Stewart puts the discussion in the broad context of change in local government. The 'personal social services' have by no means been the only aspect of local government to change in recent years – indeed, to a large extent the changes in social care have simply been a reflection of changes going on elsewhere in the nature, process and structure of local government. Stewart unpacks the concept of 'the enabling authority', showing how it challenged traditional ways of working and thinking, and then goes on to explore new ideas about 'local governance' which underpin the local government White Paper, *Modern Local Government*

(Department of the Environment, Transport and the Regions 1998). It is an essential starting point for the rest of the volume, for the changes in social care cannot be understood in isolation from the wider changes in the role of local government.

The other chapters in Part I cover the key stakeholders in local social care services: the statutory sector with its combination of purchasing and providing roles; the private and voluntary sector providers; the frontline staff who are delivering care; and those who are receiving support – users and carers. In Chapter 3, Nirmala Rao looks at changes in the statutory sector, particularly those fundamental changes associated with the 1989 White Paper, *Caring for People* (DoH 1989). She focuses upon two ostensibly contradictory imperatives, those of competition and collaboration respectively. On the one hand, the opening up of the 'purchaser–provider split' had the potential of setting up provider agencies against one another in the pursuit of contracts, whilst the purchasers of care seemed to have an opportunity to work together collaboratively through 'joint commissioning'. Rao examines both the intentions and achievements of this crucial period in the history of statutory social care agencies. She takes a sceptical view of what can be achieved by grand political design, pointing to some of the enduring features of organisations and professions which can serve to neuter broad policy shifts.

In Chapter 4, Brian Hardy and Gerald Wistow examine in detail one part of the purchaser–provider split – the growing and changing role of private sector providers of residential, nursing and domiciliary care. The growth of private sector care is the most striking manifestation of the ways in which the Seebohm model of state planning, state funding and state provision has been challenged, and it is also the most controversial. The authors trace and explain this social policy phenomenon, and draw upon much of their own extensive research in this field to tease out some of its political and moral aspects. Private provision of social care is something which arouses strong feelings, particularly where it is associated with a shift from free NHS care to means-tested local authority support, and the authors show how perceptions and misconceptions have shaped the contours of care. They conclude that the hardened attitudes of many local authorities in the early 1990s have now softened, and that private provision is now so entrenched that its dominance in residential, nursing and even domiciliary care is both unchallenged and irreversible. The other, more junior, partner among the 'independent' providers is the voluntary sector, and this is explored in Chapter 5 by Jeremy Kendall. Using voluntary sector care for older people as his focus, he describes historical and recent evolution, teasing out what makes these services different from those provided by other sectors. Such care has traditionally been seen as 'trustworthy' by local public purchasers and – in some contexts – has apparently charged relatively low prices. However, Kendall also uses research in which he has been involved to conclude that at least some voluntary provision appears to be socially exclusive, relatively costly in some contexts and sometimes only securing cost advantages through 'cost-shunting' to other providers.

Chapter 6, by Sue Balloch and John McLean, also has the advantage of drawing upon research conducted by the authors, in this case into human resources in social care. Whereas Chapters 4 and 5 concentrate upon the enormous changes which have taken place in provision by *sector*, this chapter focuses upon the consequences of these changes for the *staff* who are organising and delivering care. It examines similarities and variations amongst staff in different sectors on such matters as employment conditions and work experiences. Although reassuringly able to identify a picture of a highly committed, mature and stable workforce, Balloch also warns of some dangerous sources of pressure – workplace stress, abuse and violence from service users and relatives, racism from service users and colleagues, and changes in the workplace. This, as she points out, has some important consequences for recruitment and training which will need to be carefully addressed in the wake of the social care White Paper.

In the final chapter of Part I – Chapter 7 – Julia Twigg reviews the changing role of users and carers. It is probably true to say that at the time of the Seebohm Report in 1968, it would not have seemed appropriate to include such a chapter, for the needs of users and carers would have been assumed to coincide with whatever services and support professionals provided for them. Indeed, it is unlikely that carers would even have been recognised to have any needs! As this chapter notes, radically different ideas which began within the Disabled Living Movement in the 1970s have now become the received wisdom of academic and policy discourse, although there remains resistance at the level of practice.

Twigg refines the discussion by looking at the differences in approach and perspective of the main user groups – those with physical disabilities, learning disabilities, mental health problems and older people – as well as those associated with carers. However, the whole debate about incorporating these groups has been informed by two very different general models, those of empowerment and consumerism respectively, and these are also explored. She concludes that 'conceptual gains' have not always been translated into real gains in the lives of disabled, frail or troubled people.

Part II looks at some key aspects of working across interagency boundaries. Three intersections are specifically examined: that between social care agencies and housing agencies; the implications of social security policy for social care; and the balance between central and local government. The critical intersection with health care has not been separately examined, but forms a prominent feature of many chapters in this book, most notably Chapters 3, 4, 10 and 13. In Chapter 8, Murray Hawtin analyses a relationship which has grown in importance over the past 20 years or so, that between social care and housing. He outlines the legislative context within which community care and housing has operated, noting that the backlash to the Griffiths Report (suggesting that the housing role should be confined to 'bricks and mortar') has resulted in a flurry of official guidance which now recognises that housing is a mainstream element of community care policy. However, his review of the research shows that progress has been at best slow, and in many respects disappointing, and the chapter looks at some of the factors that may lie behind this situation.

Like housing, the relationship between social care and social security has not always been accorded the significance it merits. In the UK, the benefit system amounts to a complex set of interactions between the contributory and means-tested provision, and with some benefits (especially those for disabled people) which fall into neither category. As Geoff Fimister notes in Chapter 9, the benefits system is simultaneously a practical question of day-to-day survival for millions of people, and one of the most technically complex areas of public policy. Most people accordingly find it all very baffling, and this is as likely to apply to most professional staff as to claimants themselves. Fimister's chapter draws out some of the key issues, places them in their historical context and looks for some pointers to the future in this rapidly changing policy context.

The most significant impact of the social security system in recent years has been upon the growth of private sector residential and nursing homes, and Fimister traces the ways in which 'the rosy glow of spreading privatisation gave way to the clanging of alarm bells' as benefit costs soared. However, the debate goes far beyond the institutional sector, to cover the 'middle range' area of supported accommodation and its interaction with the housing benefit system. The complexity and interdependency between the two systems has continued to trouble the Labour government, and in this respect the position with retirement benefits and benefits paid in respect of sickness and disability is examined. Drawing upon his long experience as an adviser to the Local Government Association and its predecessors, Fimister is in an ideal position to give an insider view of the chequered relationship between social care and social security.

The final chapter in Part II, by Melanie Henwood, looks at the balance between central and local government in health and social care – or, as she describes it, the changing balance between direction and discretion. As her starting point she takes the ways in which the 1989 White Paper, *Caring for People*, sought to establish a new framework for collaboration based upon shared vision, the allocation of lead roles, the use of incentives and rewards, and a clearer pattern of accountability. It is only in the area of hospital discharge and continuing care, she suggests, that all four of these elements could be seen to be relatively well developed and coherently expressed, and she therefore uses this as the basis for  investigating of the relationship between the centre and localities. It is a crucial area of policy which has dogged both Conservative and Labour governments, and the key strategies, along with an assessment of their effectiveness, are considered. Henwood concludes that since 1989 the management of community care in general, and of health and social care collaboration on this issue in particular, has become increasingly centralised – a conclusion which is explored further by Bob Hudson in Chapter 13. However, she sees the reliance upon accountability and performance management, rather than also providing incentives and rewards, as a continuing weakness.

Finally, Part III takes a brief comparative perspective with contributions from Alison Petch and Michael Hill. In Chapter 11, Alison Petch looks mainly at variations across Scotland and Wales at a time when the two countries have established their own legislatures. She examines the historical and continuing factors which have contributed to differences in policy and practice and which will inform the approaches of the new assemblies, while at the same time showing how the 1990 NHS and Community Care Act – the first major piece of social care legislation to embrace all three countries – has led to some similarities. Differences in approaches to two client groups (learning disability and mental health) are explored alongside some relating to process (assessment and care management and the mixed economy of care). As far as the future is concerned, Petch concludes that it is very much a case of wait and see as the new parliaments determine their priorities for social care.

Michael Hill's remit in Chapter 12 is rather different. His examination of 'international perspectives' does not attempt to provide a country-by-country comparison, but rather explores some of the issues that need to be taken into account if effective comparative models for the study of social care are to be developed. As he argues, before getting into the business of policy *borrowing* there is a need to look very carefully at policy *context*. The two key elements of his model revolve around answers to the questions 'who pays?' and 'who provides?' and involve looking at diverse responses across the world. He suggests that whilst in the study of social security in particular, and in the study of health services to some extent, there are now various ways in which the policies of different countries may be meaningfully compared, this is not the case with social care. Differences relate to the role of the state, assumptions about the role of family members, the place of means-tested versus universal approaches, and the contribution of individualistic insurance based entitlements. He concludes that there remains a need for careful comparative work which establishes exactly who gets what under what circumstances in various countries.

In the final concluding chapter, Bob Hudson looks in detail at the 1998 White Paper, *Modernising Social Services*, the most significant official publication on social care since the Seebohm Report. He describes the key proposals in the White Paper and considers in what ways this might constitute a 'third way' for social care. Comparisons are made between the aims and principles of the 1989 and 1998 White Papers, suggesting that in important respects there are similarities, but that in one respect – the degree of centralisation – there is real change. Centralising features are identified around six themes: the 'national-isation' of local authority social services; the circumscription of local discretion; the expectation of greater efficiency; the enhancement of protection; the pursuit of professionalism; and the promotion of partnership. He concludes that social services will in future be subject to an unprecedented degree of central command and surveillance with far-reaching consequences for their very existence, let alone their direction.

The contributions to this volume chart a period in the history of social care which began with consolidation and expansion, but soon began a roller-coaster ride of shifting ideology and policy. The Seebohm settlement was challenged in several respects: by shifts in the roles of different purchasers and providers of care; by changing and often confusing relationships between social services and other agencies; by a changing perception of the legitimate role of users and carers; and by a repositioning of the roles of central and local government. Now, with the publication of *Modernising Social Services*, the kaleidoscope looks set to be turned yet again. As the Editor concludes in his closing chapter: 'The only certainty about local authority social services in the new millennium is uncertainty.'

## References

Department of the Environment, Transport and the Regions (1998) *Modern Local Government: In Touch With the People.* London: The Stationery Office.

Department of Health (1989) *Caring for People: Community Care in the Next Decade and Beyond.* Cm 849. London: HMSO.

Department of Health (1998) *Modernising Social Services: Promoting Independence, Improving Protection, Raising Standards.* Cm 4169. London: The Stationery Office.

Seebohm Report (1968) *Report of the Committee on Local Authority and Allied Personal Services.* Cm 3703. London: HMSO.

PART I

# The Changing Role of Social Care

# CHAPTER 2

# New Approaches
# to Local Governance

*John Stewart*

The role of local authorities in community governance is being emphasised within local authorities and the policies of central government. It is recognised that many issues facing local communities can only be resolved by the action of many agencies and organisations and the involvement of local people. The phrase 'community governance' recognises that the process of government at local level depends upon the interaction of those agencies and organisations and their communities and citizens. The local authority, as the elected body, can have a lead role in community governance, but that requires a challenge to past roles and past ways of working.

### From local government to local governance

The role of local authorities has traditionally been regarded as the delivery of a series of services as required by national legislation. That conception of the role has underlain the patterns of organisation and management in local government. Local authorities have been structured with committees and departments focusing on particular services, with the boundaries between them determined more by legislation and professional territory than by decisions of the authority. This role is reflected in a number of assumptions about the ways in which local authorities have traditionally operated. Dominant amongst these has been the assumption of self-sufficiency: that when a local authority was given a responsibility, it would discharge that responsibility itself and employ all the staff required. Although modified occasionally, direct provision of a service was the assumed necessity, with joint action between authorities only entered into with reluctance. This was a factor in determining the size of authorities, which had to be large enough to employ the necessary professional staff. It was as if an authority gained its identity from the services provided rather than the community served.

Associated with the assumption of self-sufficiency is a set of assumptions determining the way of working. The assumption of *uniformity* meant that services were provided on a common basis throughout the area, and the assumption of *direct control* reinforced that uniformity in the detailed work of committees and through the hierarchies built into the workings of the organisation. The formal structures of the authority were built on the assumption of *accountability upwards*, rather than to users of the service.

In the 1980s and the 1990s this conception of the role of local government was challenged as a result of the policies of the Conservative government. In its first two terms the policies of the government were mainly directed at securing financial control of local government expenditure in order to secure the reductions in expenditure at which they were aiming, but in the third term a new emphasis emerged. Policies were directed at restructuring the process of service delivery, particularly that of reducing the role of local authorities in the direct delivery of services. Through compulsory competitive tendering local authorities were required to submit services to competition. Originally focused on such manual work operations as refuse collection, highways maintenance and school cleaning, it was extended first to leisure management and housing management and then to a wide range of professional services. In education, local management of schools was introduced and schools were given the opportunity to opt out of local authority control. In social services the government's policy was to encourage a mixed economy of care. In housing, apart from the sale of council houses, policy increasingly emphasised the role of housing associations in the provision of social housing.

These changes can be seen as reflecting a redefinition of the role of local authorities, expressed in the phrase 'the enabling authority'. The clearest expression of that role was in the pamphlet by Nicholas Ridley, published when he was Secretary of State for the Environment and entitled *The Local Right: Enabling Not Providing.*

> The role of the local authority will no longer be that of the universal provider. But it will continue to have a key role in ensuring that there is adequate provision to meet needs, in encouraging the various providers to develop and maintain the necessary services, and where necessary in providing grant support or other assistance to get projects started, and to ensure that services are provided and affordable for the clients concerned. (Ridley 1988, p.17)

This conception of the role of local authorities challenged traditional conceptions and the organisational assumptions that underlay their ways of working. The assumption of self-sufficiency was challenged by the emphasis on alternative ways of working. Assumptions about direct control reinforced by hierarchy were challenged by the development of control of contracts reinforced by divisions between client and contractor or between purchaser and provider. At the same time, the government was emphasising accountability to the customer, rather than to the council. William Waldegrave, in *The Reality of Public Accountability*, argued that the government had made 'public services directly accountable to the customer' (Waldegrave 1991, p.15).

The enabling role was not uncontested. Many Labour authorities defended the role of local authorities in direct service provision. There was, however, another challenge. Clarke and Stewart, while accepting the need to reconsider the role, proposed an alternative and wider meaning to the phrase 'the enabling authority':

> The local authority will be about enabling the community to define and then to meet the needs and problems it faces. It neither requires the direct provision of services or prescribes it. The local authority will act in a wide variety of ways accepting that direct provision of services is one means of providing for the community among many. It will produce some services itself. It will work with and through other organisations in the public, private and voluntary services – aiding, stimulating and guiding their contributions. It will provide the means by which people can meet their needs directly. It will regulate and control, inspect and advise, support and provide grants. It will act within its sphere of statutory responsibility but it will also have a concern for anything which is the concern of local people. It will work to promote the health of its community. (Clarke and Stewart 1990, p.4)

In their research, Ennals and O'Brien distinguished between this wider view and the narrow view which they say is 'about getting arms-length agencies, especially the private sector, to provide on the authority's behalf what it has hitherto provided itself, with its own staff, directly to the public' (Ennals and O'Brien 1990, p.3). Their conclusion was that:

> Most local authorities see themselves as enablers, whatever their political control. They express the idea in a variety of different ways, but the common thread is that under its enabling role the authority seeks to meet the needs of the community in the most effective way, not necessarily by direct provision. Not only do most authorities see themselves as enablers but their definition of the role is closer to the wider version than the narrower one, even though they may not necessarily have fully developed the role themselves. (Ennals and O'Brien 1990, p.5)

The challenge posed by the government's policies had led an increasing number of authorities to reconsider their role. While not generally accepting the narrow conception of the enabling role, they were developing conceptions of the role that challenged the traditional conception of the authority as first and foremost an agency for the provision of a series of services. The services remained important, but could be seen as one – but only one – means of meeting community needs. This new view of the role of local authorities led to a reconsideration of the relationship of local authorities to the whole system of community governance, involving the complex of agencies and organisation that are part of the government of local communities. It also led to reconsideration of the relationship of the local authorities to the communities which they are concerned to meet. As a result the debate has moved on. Certainly the language has changed. No longer is the debate about the enabling role. The dominant phrases are 'community governance', 'community leadership' and 'the role of local authorities in community government'. The debate focuses now on the whole issue of the relationship between government and local communities and the place of local authorities within it.

This emerging issue should be seen as much more than a response to the policies of central government, although those policies have had an important part to play, as will be shown later in this chapter. The issue of the local authorities' role in community governance can and should be seen as a response to changes in the polity and as a product of two forces, or drivers, which can be described as:

- the growing recognition of issues confronting local communities which cannot adequately be dealt with by traditional ways of working
- the recognition of the diversity of local communities, many of which are alienated from the process of government.

## The challenge to community governance

### *The issues faced*

The first driver derives from a recognition of the range of issues that confront the government of local communities. Many of these have been called 'wicked issues'. These include:

- the environmental issue and the aspiration to sustainable development
- problems of crime and the aspiration to community safety
- discrimination and the aspiration to an equitable society
- social exclusion and the aspiration to social justice.

Wicked issues can be distinguished from 'tamed issues', as both such problems were named by the American authors who developed the phrases (Rittel and Webber 1973). A tamed problem is a problem well understood to which solutions have been worked out. Staff can be trained to provide the necessary response, and responsibility for handling the problem can be clearly allocated within the system of government to an organisation and to a department within it.

Wicked issues, on the other hand, are problems to which solutions are not clear, often because the problem is imperfectly understood and its causes have not been clearly identified. Because of this, wicked issues cannot be managed as tamed issues are managed. It is uncertain what responses are required and hence what organisations are involved. There will be ideas, but no certainty as to the right solution. A learning style is required which recognises that the existing pattern of organisational responsibilities may be challenged by the complexity of the issues. Thus if one considers the environmental issue it is clear that many organisations, both public and private, and at many levels are involved.

Responsibilities, even if divided up cannot be clearly allocated, but have to be resolved in interaction.

Over and above these issues, many towns and cities are confronted by the transformations of our times. The traditional industries on which they are based have disappeared or ceased to be a major source of employment. The commercial role of town centres is challenged by out of town development. Economic challenge creates social costs and they are not evenly borne, creating new lines of division in society. The physical infrastructure requires renewal. The ease of communication which has been the asset of urban life is undermined by choked transportation systems. The challenges to rural life are as great. Changing patterns of agriculture combine with environmental concerns and with the demands of tourism. Village life has to accommodate commuters and second homes. Rural deprivation can be as deep or deeper than urban deprivation. Lack of transport marks a deep divide.

National policy has a contribution to make to these challenges. It can create a framework which will enable them to be met, but central government has to recognise they cannot be met at national level. Each area has its own problems and its own opportunities. New roles have to be developed and they will inevitably differ from area to area. Some cities see themselves with an international role. Others can be regional or cultural centres. New mixtures of industry are sought or service centres are developed. Such transformations require far more than economic change. Social change, educational development, environmental change and physical renewal are all involved. Local authorities have an important part to play in this process, but they cannot carry it through alone. Many agencies – both public and private – are involved. Yet the local authority can have a role in leadership in working with others in building a sense of direction for local communities. Social services cannot stand apart from this changing agenda.

### The structure of community government

The wicked issues and the transformations of urban and rural life have to be faced in a fragmented system of community government. That reality is often hidden by describing some authorities as unitary authorities, as if they embraced all the functions of government in the locality. The reality is very different. If one asks in a metropolitan district how the area is governed, to say 'by the local authority' is totally inadequate. Amongst the many public bodies one can mention are the health authority, the health trusts, the training and enterprise council, the boards of further education colleges, the police authority, the joint boards for fire, public transport and waste disposal. That is without emphasising the private and voluntary sectors who have been given increased public roles, just as housing associations have undertaken an increasing role in social housing.

This system of community governance is not described as fragmented because it is divided into different organisations. Any system of government has to be divided into parts, just as any organisation is divided into departments or divisions. It is not fragmented because of necessary differentiation. It is fragmented because it has lacked a capacity for integration. An effective system of governance, like an effective organisation, has to recognise the need for differentiation, but also the need for integration. The driver for community governance is then the need to achieve integration in relation to the problems and issues faced by local communities. That is a task for which the local authorities have the legitimacy as a result of elections to provide a leadership role – but that role is only justified if the local authority is close to the communities within.

### The diversity within

It is a mistake to regard the local authority, or indeed other agencies, as concerned with a single community. Within the area of any local authority there are many communities with diverse interests and concern. In the past that has been too little recognised because of an assumption of uniformity, which has sometimes meant that services have been directed at what was assumed to be a homogenous society. More recently, the needs of different ethnic groups, the impact of gender and the requirements of the disabled have begun to be recognised. There are communities of place, of background, interest or concern. Society is not divided on class lines alone, but in many ways; lines of conflict and cooperation mark out the space that constitutes the area of the local authority. This means that a key task within community governance is to seek to reconcile different interests and aspirations and, if that task is impossible, to balance the different demands in political judgement.

*The alienation to be confronted*

Local authorities, it has been argued, have the legitimacy that comes for local election. But local elections also reveal the weakness of local democracy. The turnout in local elections has averaged about 40 per cent. More recently, turnout has fallen even lower. Too often low turnout has been regarded as a fact of life to be accepted rather than an issue for concern. Yet turnouts in local elections in the United Kingdom are on average at least 30 per cent below most countries in the European Union. Turnout should, however, not be regarded as the problem but rather as a part and a symptom of a wider problem – the weakness of local democracy. It reflects an apathy or even alienation from the local political process. If citizens felt involved in the process of local government then turnout would be likely to reflect that reality. The second driver, then, to a redefinition of the local authorities' role in community governance, is the need to build a new relationship with communities and the citizens that constitute them. The two drivers are linked. Only if the local authority is representative of the communities within it, can it justify a leadership role in community governance.

*The principles of community leadership*

Local authorities' role in community leadership can take many forms. Communities vary and local government is the government of difference, reflecting that in a diversity of response. In the two-tier system, different issues will be faced by county and district, although the district will be likely to provide the main building block. Yet certain principles can be stated.

- A local authority has concerns that extend beyond the services provided. It has an overall concern for the economic, social and environmental welfare of the area. This does not mean the local authorities services are unimportant. They represent its particular contribution to the system of community governance.

- In expressing that concern it will work with other agencies to identify problems and issues and directions for action. The aims will be to build up a shared understanding against which all concerned with the area will act and to form partnerships for action where it is required.

- The aim will be to realise the potential of community resources to the full in meeting needs. The analysis of the resources of different agencies in meeting shared problems is the starting point, allowing discussion between agencies as to how they are used.

- A local authority will recognise the wide range of alternative ways of acting in its role in community governance. It will provide services directly, but also through other organisations. It will form partnerships and nurture self-help. It will regulate, network, influence and advocate. The analysis of alternative ways of acting – neglected in the past – will now be at a premium.

- The role of local authorities in community leadership is justified by, and gains strength from, closeness to the communities within and to its citizens. This requires innovation in democratic practice as a local authority reaches out to involve communities and citizens in the process of community governance.

- Within any area there are many communities with different needs, different interests and different aspirations. It is the role of elected representatives to appreciate those differences, to reconcile them where that is necessary and possible and, in the final resort, to balance them in and through political judgement.

Within these principles a tension has to be recognised that derives from the two drivers. It is the tension between a focus at the macro or authority-wide level, and a focus at the micro level or the communities within. The first is concerned mainly with the relationship between the authority and other organisations. The second is concerned with the relationship between the authority and its publics. Different emphases can be given. An overemphasis on the former could lead to the danger of an enclosed elite of organisations. An overemphasis on the latter could lead to the frustration of involvement without influence. The correct response must be to recognise that the macro-focus must be informed by the insights of the micro level and that action at the macro level must sustain action at the micro level.

*The Labour government's policy*

In its consultation paper, *Modernising Local Government – Democratic Renewal and Community Leadership* (Department of the Environment, Transport and the Regions 1998), the Labour government sets out a concept of the role of local government in community leadership. At the start of the chapter entitled 'Councils leading their community', it is stated that 'The Government believes that councils, with their democratic mandate, their tax raising powers, and wide range of responsibilities, have a unique role to interpret the priorities and aspiration of local people. In short, leadership is at the heart of modern local government' (p.35). This role involves:

- developing a vision for the locality; taking action to deliver that vision, themselves and in partnership with others; and

- guaranteeing quality services for all.

These requirements give expression to the principles of community governance focused at the macro level. However, the government see the link between community leadership and democratic renewal and set out proposals for 'involving local communities'. The link is more logically presented in the equivalent Welsh Office paper, which opens with the concept of community leadership and then shows its requirement for community involvement (Welsh Office 1998), whereas the DETR paper reverses the presentation. In both papers the concepts are linked, however, focusing attention on the macro level and on the micro level.

The government proposes to lay a new statutory duty on local government 'to promote the economic, social and environmental well-being of an area'. In this proposal the role for local authorities in community leadership is asserted. Local authorities have always been concerned over specific events affecting their area, such as the closure of a local hospital, but it has been a spasmodic concern. What is proposed is very different. Local authorities' role in community governance is being redefined not as an option, but as a duty.

Related to the new duty is a widening of the powers, avowedly based on the government's view 'that councils should have complete discretion in how they discharge the duty' (DETR 1998, p.37), although rather inconsistently the next paragraph suggests that there could be restrictions on that discretion. Generally, however, the government proposes to give local authorities greater freedom to play their role in community leadership forming partnerships with other agencies and organisations.

The main means proposed for community leadership is through community planning which is seen as the way in 'which local stakeholders can be brought together to identify the needs and aspirations of local communities and improve service provision in response to these needs and aspirations' (DETR 1998, p.36). The government is not proposing legislation for English local authorities, preferring to see the development of community planning on a voluntary basis. In Wales they are, however, proposing it be made 'a specific function' of local authorities (Welsh Office 1998).

While community planning gives expression to the macro level focus on community governance, the consultation papers give recognition to the need for a micro level focus on the communities within. 'The prize is an even closer match between the needs and aspirations of communities and the services secured for them by their local authority, better quality services, greater democratic legitimacy for local government and a new brand of involved and responsible citizenship; in short reinvigorated local democracy' (DETR 1998, p.23). To achieve this there is a need for innovation in democratic practice, innovation that is already taking place (Stewart 1997) in a number of authorities. New forms of public meetings are being developed. Citizens' juries and deliberative opinion polls seek out the informed views of citizens. Community forums have been established providing settings for the voices of communities of place and of communities of background or of concern. Public conferencing has brought together stakeholders in local communities to develop futures. In a variety of ways communities are being involved. The government considers that over and above the particular initiatives 'there may be value in authorities regularly reviewing and setting out their strategy for consultation and public participation' (DETR 1998, p.23). There is a danger that preparation of such a strategy could become a routine and a constraint where initiative and innovation is required. It would, however, represent a commitment to community involvement.

*Changes in local authorities*

The developing interest of local authorities in community governance will be reinforced by government policies. That will require change in the ways of working of local authorities. Traditional models of the organisation and management of local authorities are inadequate to the challenge. The local authority's leadership role in community government challenges the assumptions of self-sufficiency – it is the essence of community leadership that a local authority cannot act alone, but needs to work with others. It follows that many of the activities with which a local authority will be concerned will not be under its direct control, or subject to the requirements of management hierarchies and committee decisions.

A focus on the communities within an authority in their diversity challenges assumptions of uniformity. The services provided by the local authority have to be based on a recognition of that diversity and the need to involve communities and citizens means that accountability cannot merely be seen as upward to the elected representatives. This need not be threatening to councillors, if they themselves recognise the need for community involvement and provide the lead in redefining accountability as a continuing relationship.

The local authority's role in community leadership also challenges the narrow concept of the enabling role. Within that version of the enabling role, a local authority was still largely concerned with the delivery of a series of services, albeit through other agencies. The emphasis was on a single way of approaching the decision on how to deliver services. Compulsory competitive tendering, for example, was enforced upon local authorities, denying them the management responsibility of analysing and evaluating alternative ways of meeting needs.

The development of local authorities' role in community governance therefore requires new ways of working. In particular it requires:

- the development of community planning in which local authorities will require the ability to work with other agencies in developing a shared understanding of needs and problems and the ability to work in partnership with them in realising community resources to the full

- a readiness to involve communities and citizens in the process of government, recognising that this will require innovation in democratic practice

- the analysis and evaluation of alternative ways of working.

Such developments will challenge existing structures and processes – not least at the political level. The government has emphasised the need to separate 'the executive and representational role of councillors which are so easily confused in the traditional committee' (DETR 1998, p.30) leading them to support proposals for elected mayors or cabinets as political executives. This is not an adequate response to the challenge of the local authority role in community government. It focuses on the macro level and ignores the micro level. There is a need to find ways of responding at both levels. The government is right to emphasis the need to review existing structures, but wrong to prescribe the results of the review. The development of the role in community government places an obligation for learning of new ways of working. It should not be assumed the lessons have already been learnt. The challenge of the role has still to be fully appreciated.

## References

Clarke, M. and Stewart, J. (1990) *The General Management of Local Government.* London: Longman.

Department of the Environment, Transport and the Regions (1998) *Modernising Local Government – Democratic Renewal and Community Leadership.* London: The Stationery Office.

Ennals, K. and O'Brien, J. (1990) *The Enabling Role of Local Authorities.* London: Public Finance Foundation.

Ridley, N. (1988) *The Local Right: Enabling Not Providing.* London: Conservative Political Centre.

Rittel, H. and Webber, M. (1993) 'Dilemma in a general theory of planning.' *Policy Sciences.*

Stewart, J. (1997) *More Innovation in Democratic Practice.* Birmingham: School of Public Policy, Birmingham University.

Waldegrave, W. (1991) *The Reality of Public Accountability.* London: Public Finance
    Foundation.

Welsh Office (1998) *Modernising Local Government – Democratic Renewal and Community
    Leadership.* Cardiff: The Stationery Office.

# CHAPTER 3

# Changes in the Statutory Sector

## Nirmala Rao

The current community care initiative originated in the Barclay Report and Norman Fowler's 1984 Buxton speech in which he proposed a strategic role for social service departments (SSDs): to mobilise all sectors to provide a full range of care to the local communities. The Griffiths Report, *Community Care: Agenda for Action*, proposed a lead role for SSDs as purchasers of social care, but largely relinquishing the role of direct providers (Griffiths 1988). By the time the government's community care White Paper *Caring for People* appeared (DoH 1989a), the concept of a purchaser-provider separation was already well developed in the NHS. The NHS White Paper *Working for Patients* (1989b) set out a vision of an internal market with health authorities purchasing services on behalf of patients, an approach which was to be directly transferred to the social care sector. In *Caring for People* the government set down the role of the SSD as:

> determining clear specifications of service requirements, and arrangements for tenders and contracts; taking steps to stimulate the setting up of 'not-for-profit' agencies; identifying areas for their own work which are sufficiently self contained to be suitable for 'floating-off' as self-managing units; [and] stimulating the development of new voluntary sector activity. (Department of Health 1989a, para 3.4.6)

SSDs would be required to assess needs and arrange the provision of suitable packages of care, observing a clear split between their own purchaser and provider functions. They would manage a consolidated budget for social care, in which the greater part of new funding was to be spent in the new sector. New powers to monitor and inspect the quality of care provided was central to the conception.

Collaboration was at the heart of the new arrangements. The Act (section 46) required SSDs, district health authorities and Family Health Services Authority(ies) (FHSAs) to prepare and publish joint plans for community care, covering common goals for particular client groups, funding agreements, agreed policy on key operational areas and agreed contract specifications for securing joint working between service providers. The community care initiative thus represented the fourth attempt to bring together health and personal social services under a national programme for coordination following the health and welfare plans of 1962, the personal social services plans of the 1970s and the health authorities'/SSDs' joint planning arrangements.

This chapter focuses on two key aspects of post-1990 developments in the statutory sector: the purchaser–provider split in SSDs and joint working between them and health authorities. It assesses progress and considers some of the difficulties that stand in the way of achieving the aims of the initiative, and concludes by highlighting present uncertainties as to whether the future of social care will be one of continued fragmentation or institutional integration.

## Planning and implementation

The full implementation date for the operation of these plans was set for 1 April 1993. The government's second thought was to phase implementation in stages. Inspection units were to be in place by April 1991; by April 1992 community care plans were to be published and preparations made for unified assessment and case management. By April 1993, funds transfer of Department of Social Security (DSS) funds was to begin. The government's rationale for phasing implementation was that it had no confidence in the capacity of local authorities to implement community care in one go: local authorities needed longer 'to come to terms with the need to discharge their duties efficiently' and at an affordable cost. Its postponement for two years, however, increased the level of uncertainty and did little to encourage planning for change (Wistow *et al.* 1992).

SSDs were to work towards a development of markets capable of responding to policy needs over time. These responsibilities were described as simultaneously 'managing down' residential and nursing home markets and 'managing up' the markets for domiciliary and other services. Given the requirement that a smooth transition should be achieved, and the recognition that markets for certain types of care were a long way from achieving maturity, it could hardly be expected that dramatic progress would be visible within a short space of time.

Nor did the world stand still. After 1993 several factors emerged to shape implementation and to complicate further the change programme. FHSAs and district health authorities merged and a number of districts joined together to increase greatly the size and strength of the commissioning bodies. At the same time, primary health care increased in importance with a shift of resources to the community setting increasing the power of the GPs and bringing them (fundholders and non-fundholders) into the purchasing process. The requirement to consult on local health plans has been a further development deriving from EU requirements (Balogh 1996). The Carers' Recognition and Services Act 1995 ensured a place for carers within the community care process by giving statutory effect to their needs. A Framework for Local Community Care Charter was published in 1994, requiring SSDs to provide information about community care services and set performance standards.

In March 1997 the then government published *Social Services: Achievement and Challenge* (Cm 3588). The Conservatives promised further legislation to separate more clearly assessment of need and commissioning from the provider and regulator roles. This amounted to an acknowledgement that their efforts hitherto had been only partly successful in terms of diminishing the role of statutory agencies. Permanent arrangements would be made to promote the development of the independent sector, and legislation would be introduced to promote greater choice of care. A key statement of principle placed the issues in context:

> Social care is the care which the very large majority of people are able to provide for themselves or for their family, friends and neighbours. The principal responsibility for social care rests on individual members of society and society's own networks of mutual support. It believes that responsible individuals should plan to meet their own needs, and that every encouragement should be given to family and friends who are willing to act as carers of those quite unable to provide for themselves ... The role of statutory social services is to act as a support to those who are meeting social care needs in these ways, and

as a commissioner of care to support those for whom these networks fail.
(para 1.7)

While the Labour government which came to office in May 1997 gave high priority to health and social care issues, its response was primarily administrative, with no immediately comparable statement of principle. The new government acted quickly to fulfil its promises on the abolition of the NHS internal market and to replace GP fundholding. In December 1997, its proposals were published in a White Paper, *The New NHS – Modern, Dependable*. GPs and community nurses are to be grouped into 500 primary care groups, with average catchment areas of 100,000 patients, and will take on a greater part of purchasing and commissioning. The primary care groups will take account of social services and health authority boundaries and will work to promote integration. SSDs will have a role in the management of these groups and are expected to work towards joint planning and delivery. Action on joint working is expected to be accelerated by the placing of new statutory duty of partnership on local authorities and health bodies. Health authorities are required to prepare health improvement programmes to which SSD staff will make a direct input.

Reactions to these further changes were cautious, as it was far from obvious how the government's emphasis on cooperation was to be put into practice. One source of concern was the extent to which social workers would be involved in the GP-led primary care groups. More fundamental was a healthy scepticism as to whether this latest collaborative initiative can work without pooling of care budgets on the part of separate agencies (George 1998). In the meantime, the statutory sector had continued to move ahead, if somewhat unevenly, with the implementation of the key features of community care. It is possible, five years after 1 April 1993, to take stock of the extent to which actual structures and operations have changed. One effect of the community care initiative has been to open up a new debate on how its aims could best be achieved. There has been new thinking about needs, entitlements and rights. But in terms of action to produce an integrated programme of care in the community, less progress is discernible.

## Purchasers, providers and the managed market

Under this new initiative, local authorities were expected to 'take all reasonable steps to secure diversity of provision'. One of the government's objectives was to 'promote the development of a flourishing independent sector' by which was meant both voluntary (non-profit) and private (for-profit) providers. The SSDs were to retain their ability as direct service providers only if other provision was 'unforthcoming or unsuitable'. They were obliged to make use of private providers 'wherever possible' and to otherwise 'stimulate such activity'.

The means by which these were to be achieved was by instituting a purchaser–provider split within the SSD itself. In this way it would be possible to engineer a shift from provider-led to needs-led services; from provision dominated by the public sector to a mixed economy of care; and from providing care in the institutions to doing so, as far as possible, in the client's own home. It seemed to be an article of faith that a clear purchaser–provider split would in itself bring about the shift from a service-led to a needs-led approach. Such an effect is central to the theory of quasi-markets in public services, although in the real world the more immediate results have been increased uncertainty and confusion, and rising costs.

When the government in its draft guidance on community care legislation suggested a functional split, initial reactions were not favourable. The Association of Metropolitan Authorities insisted that local authorities should avoid making a rigid purchaser–provider split, and instead focus on redefining the form of partnership. Subsequent policy guidance issued in 1991 modified the earlier concept and concluded that the new relationship should best be conceived as 'being a contract culture involving close on-going relationships with providers'.

Such studies as were carried out in the early years of implementation underlined the complexity of the split and pointed to the difficulty of making definitive judgements about effectiveness, highlighting the different experiences of planners, providers, users and carers (Henwood, Wistow and Robinson 1996; Lewis *et al.* 1996). SSDs often found difficulty in separating purchasing and providing roles, with internal critics fearing that the split could produce a counterproductive tension within the department through an overemphasis on organisational structures and on the contracting process at the expense of the service. The risk of procedural changes becoming an end rather than means was one to which the Audit Commission itself had drawn attention (Audit Commission 1992).

In any case, despite the agonising over the purchaser–provider split, it has not been pushed forward with great vigour by the government, and while the policy was accompanied by copious government guidance there has been 'relatively little hard prescription as to implementation' (Lewis, Bernstock and Bovell 1995, p.90). According to Norman Warner the government was reluctant to press a purchaser–provider split in children's services out of deference to the professional jealousies of social workers (Warner 1997).

No doubt the values implicit in the purchaser–provider split and the emphasis on managing up the market for private sector provision ran counter to the deeply embedded ethos of SSDs. Such foreseeable resistance may have been exacerbated by the occasional tendency of social service managers to intellect-ualise organisational problems, by the lack of credence given to the notion that yesterday's client could become today's authentic consumer, and by a reluctance to accept a horizontal split between two professionals – one concerned to assess needs, and the other to provide care (Downes, Ernst and Smithers 1996). There is something more at stake here than mere professional jealousies.

However, the whole point of the purchaser–provider separation was to bring about 'a mixed economy of care'. Evidence suggests that such a mixed economy has emerged, but gradually and unevenly across the country. A sample of 25 SSDs surveyed in 1993 found private sector provision to be the largest, and voluntary sector the smallest, share of total provision outside London. These proportions are reversed in the capital itself where a strong tradition of working with the voluntary sector exists. Overall, the pattern of provision of residential care shifted markedly between 1983 and 1993, with local authority provision falling from well over 50 per cent to under 30 per cent, the balance being almost wholly taken up by the expansion of the private sector. The voluntary sector's share of provision declined nationally slightly over this period (PSSRU/ Nuffield 1994).

What were the forces driving this shift to the mixed economy? Demographic pressures, early hospital discharges and expenditure limits all appear to have played a part. But by far the most powerful factor cited by English directors of social services was the requirement (absent elsewhere in the UK) that 85 per cent of the social security transfer element of the STG be spent in the independent sector.

Of course, the fact that a gradual intersectoral shift is occurring does not in itself prove the existence of a managed market. It is notable, moreover, that the loss of the provider role to the non-statutory sector has been progressive throughout the 1990s, suggesting that the 1990 legislation gave expression to and reinforced a trend that was already under way independently of the Community Care Act. It has been argued that the assumption that SSDs would be able to manage the markets for social care was overoptimistic. Sectoral changes were predicated on existence of a substantial, competent and nationally distributed non-market sector of providers; in reality it would take time for new providers to begin to enter the market. Nor did SSDs generally have the kind of information needed to manage markets effectively (Forder, Knapp and Wistow 1996).

## Joint commissioning since 1990

The current emphasis on joint working and joint commissioning flows from a number of developments over a period of years. The shift from institutional to community care and from secondary to primary care inescapably involves a wider range of organisations in more complex care packages. The trend to deprofessionalisation enables tasks to be performed by a wider range of less qualified staff in agencies other than those with traditional 'ownership'. There is now (due in part to the Griffiths Report) a greater recognition of the interdependence of the problems that people experience. Finally, the universal drive to more efficient resource use encourages the reduction of duplication through joint action and sharing.

But if joint working lies at the heart of the community care initiative, there is little in the past experience of health authorities and SSDs to justify this 'act of faith' that obstacles will be overcome (Hudson 1992, p.193). Nevertheless, some of the new requirements are specifically designed to overcome interagency rivalries. Joint action is required in care planning, contracting and purchasing, inspection and registration, needs analysis and training. The practice of joint commissioning has been advanced by a DoH project group, which has sought to encourage SSDs and health authorities to pool their resources in a common approach. In 1995 the DoH published two guidance papers, one introducing the concept of joint commissioning and the other providing practical advice (DoH 1995a, 1995b). The guidance papers set out the different forms of joint commissioning and explain the importance of developing effective mechanisms and involving key stakeholders. Since then, the inducements to joint working have been increased, the new government offering a renewed emphasis on partnership as an alternative to Conservative competition.

So what is commissioning, and when is it joint? Commissioning has been defined as 'a strategic activity of assessing needs, resources and current services and developing a strategy as to how to make best use of available resources to meet needs'. It is, then, a higher level activity than mere purchasing, which is itself broader than contracting with particular service providers for specific services. Joint commissioning involves two or more agencies taking a co-ordinated view and accepting joint responsibility for achieving better outcomes for users and carers.

That said, the term has provoked considerable debate as to the true meaning of jointness (Hudson 1995). Clarity is important, for, as one advocate of joint working acknowledges, euphemistic terms

> have no effect on the real differences and contradictions that do exist between health and social services agencies, and it is only through the painful process of identifying and facing these issues that effective resolution and real joint working becomes possible. (Gostick 1994, p.3)

So, the term 'joint' itself is shrouded in ambiguity. Gostick considers the claims of cooperative commissioning and integrated commissioning as more helpful terms, and offers 'collaborative commissioning' to refer to 'agencies working harmoniously together on the basis of shared understanding of their respective roles, responsibilities and objectives' (p.3). However, as head of the DoH project team, he acknowledges that many agencies are unclear even about the distinctions between commissioning, purchasing, contracting and providing. As the demands upon joint working multiply with concurrent reforms of health and social services, it becomes still less credible that linguistic contortions will in themselves solve the problems of interagency coordination.

So much for terminology. What then of the outcomes? Gareth Thomas MP, Vice-Chair of the All-Party Panel on Personal Social Services, gave a pithy summary:

> The concept of joint working between health and social services has been around for a long time, yet despite thousands of column inches, numerous seminars, and the many speeches devoted to the subject, growing partnership between these two key branches of care has remained an elusive elixir – to the frustration of most in the field. (Thomas 1998, p.12)

That there would be problems in joint working was recognised in the Audit Commission's 1993 report, *Their Health, Your Business: The New Role of the District Health Authority.* Since then, the general difficulties of working across sectors have been highlighted by the report on Scottish implementation by the House of Commons Scottish Affairs Committee. Service providers and users alike provided the committee with evidence of ineffective coordination and poor cooperation between local authority social services and the NHS. The circumstances are special to Scotland, where NHS trusts were unable to offer social care services and so maintain the sharp distinction between health and social care.

While the new government is consulting on the development of closer working relationships in Scotland, experience there highlights the continuing problem: that while human needs are indivisible, agency missions, cultures and accountabilities are all too clearly divided. Charging regimes, regulations on user choice and rules relating to the transfer of funds differ between agencies. Local authority care services are means tested, whereas NHS care is provided free at the point of delivery (Kay 1998). Health authorities emphasise cost-volume contracting, and SSDs a user-focused spot purchasing process. For SSDs, the assessment of clients is seen as integral to the care management process, while in the NHS assessment lies mainly with the provider through clinical diagnosis. These operational differences present considerable barriers to a close alignment on which joint commissioning rests (Hudson 1998).

Many of those who were called upon to work jointly experience a sense of diversion from their primary task of managing the agency's own services. 'We could without difficulty', wrote one community health trust chief executive, 'fill our working lives with activities linked to relationships with services outside the service we are paid to manage ... If we use significant portions of our time in joint working, it is time which could have been used to improve our own organ- isations, performance and services to people'. Joint working requires sacrifices: 'the time and energy needed for joint working may be at the expense of other activities which turn out ... to be the ones which are judged more important in appraisal of performance' (Haggard and Ormiston 1993, pp.80, 83).

It should be no surprise that joint working is thought more effective at the (sometime vacuous) level of planning than at the operational level where people have to work together to achieve things. A survey of clinical directors, trust managers, health commissioners and social services managers showed widely varying assessments of the actual success of joint planning and operations (Shepherd 1997). Working at agency boundaries can be a thankless task. Practitioners in one service may be reluctant to accept the authority of another professional operating in a care manager role (Henwood 1995). This 'grit within the machine' leaves service users and carers 'as frustrated spectators in the unsavoury disputes that exist between agencies' (Jones 1995, p.119).

The period of implementation of community care has been one of great change in the statutory services, and other preoccupations, not least other reorganisations, can readily displace involvement and commitment in making joint working a success. Agencies, then, are naturally inward looking and driven by their particular concerns. An unusually stable and consensual environment is required to make joint working practicable; the experience since 1990 has been that these preconditions are notably lacking.

Effective interprofessional collaboration is based on mutual respect, characteristics which cannot be conjured up by administrative fiat (Hudson *et al.* 1997, p.30). These are subtle, even slippery, qualities. They cannot be wished into existence. Instead, the fault lines that run between agencies and professions require an adequate analysis of the prerequisites of cooperation. Problems of implementation arise when the interests and values of those agencies responsible for implementation are directly threatened by the consequences of actions they are required to take (Wistow *et al.* 1992, p.43). Effective partner- ships depend on bringing about a convergence of those interests so that the parties come to work through a structure of incentives that binds them together in an implicit contract which serves the interests of both (Domberger, Farago and Fernandez 1997), conditions which seem to be scarcely met in social care.

So much for theory. Can collaboration actually bridge the fault lines? Can it do so at acceptable cost? Hudson judges that

> there is no substantial evidence to suggest that joint consultative committees, joint care planning teams, joint finance, community care plans, joint commissioning or other collaborative mechanisms have been anything other than marginal in their impact. (1997, p.2)

Indeed, the rise of the self-governing trust and of the independent fundholding practice represent moves towards greater competition:

> there is some contradiction between the principles of collaborative working and collective responsibility, and the fostering of a quasi-market based upon the principles of competition and individual responsibility. (Hudson 1995, p.246)

Moreover, the emerging styles of 'the new public management' encourage a competitive expansionism and cost-shunting on the part of individual managers, qualities which are not conducive to the compromises, reconciliation and mutual understanding required of collaboration. For the individual manager, competition has become both cheaper and more rewarding than collaboration. Can these trends, so vigorously promoted during the 1990s, be readily reversed?

**Where next?**

Exhortations to coordinate and cooperate assume an essentially stable universe. The reality today is of continuing struggles between centre and locality, between profession and profession, and between professionals and managers, all of which are played out in a continually changing landscape of care provision (Charlesworth, Clarke and Cochrane 1996). The 1990s brought a wave of distinct but simultaneous changes in the style and scope of SSDs. Each of these changes had knock-on effects for other aspects of the department's work, making the implementation of purchaser–provider split something that would be fraught with uncertainty. These uncertainties were equally antithetical to managing markets, to successful contracting, and to interagency collaboration.

It is in this context of shortfall on grand aims that issues of organisational integration are likely to raise their heads again, for the present alignments are not immutable. The problems of collaboration between health and social services can be traced back to the missed opportunities of the post-war settlement, when Aneurin Bevan effectively drove a wedge between health and social care provision. The post-war history has been one of successive attempts to bridge that gap. While joint commissioning purports to span the divide between agencies, it could come to be no more than a transition to full integration with the planning, commissioning and purchasing responsibilities being placed with one agency.

However, there is considerable scepticism as to the desirability and, most certainly, the likelihood of this happening. There are those who see fundamental problems in integrating services under any single agency, not least, differences in boundaries and in charging regimes (Poxton 1997). The NHS Confederation not surprisingly argues that the case for local authorities taking over the health commissioning role is 'seriously flawed' and

> would undermine the NHS, fragment its organisation and the delivery of care, to the detriment of patients, the public, those working in the service and, indeed, the tax payer. Local authority discretion in purchasing would be an illusion, unless some of the finance was raised locally. This in turn would endanger the equity of the NHS. (Vellenowet 1997, p.8)

Instead, the confederation places its faith in joint commissioning as 'the most pragmatic and realistic approach'. Pragmatic it may be but it is becoming ever clearer that the delivery of community care in the spirit of the Griffiths Report is impeded by the present pattern of interagency working. The past Conservative government flirted with the idea of unification under health authorities. Might a Labour government give more serious consideration to integration under elected local authority control?

# References

Audit Commission (1992) *Community Care: Managing the Cascade of Change.* London: HMSO.

Balogh, R. (1996) 'Exploring the role of localities in health commissioning: A review of the literature.' *Social Policy and Administration 30*, 2, 99–113.

Charlesworth, J., Clarke, J. and Cochrane, A. (1996) 'Tangled webs? managing local mixed economies of care.' *Public Administration, Spring,* 67–88.

Department of Health (1989a) *Caring for People: Community Care in the Next Decade and Beyond.* Cm 849. London: HMSO.

Department of Health (1989b) *Working for Patients.* Cm 555. Department of Health.

Department of Health (1995a) *An Introduction to Joint Commissions.* London: Department of Health.

Department of Health (1995b) *Practical Guidance on Joint Commissioning.* London: Department of Health.

Department of Health (1997) *Social Services: Achievement and Challenge.* Cm 3588. Department of Health.

Department of Health (1997) *The New NHS – Modern, Dependable.* TSO. Department of Health.

Domberger, S., Farago, S. and Fernandez, P. (1997) 'Public and private sector partnering: A reappraisal.' *Public Administration 75,* winter, 777–87.

Downes, C., Ernst, S. and Smithers, M. (1996) 'Maintaining the capacity for concern during organisational restructuring for community care.' *Journal of Social Work Practice 10,* 1, 25–40.

Forder, J., Knapp, M. and Wistow, G. (1996) 'Competition in the mixed economy of care.' *Journal of Social Policy 25,* 2, 201–21.

George, M. (1998) 'Mixed reception.' *Community Care,* January 22–28, 21–2.

Gostick, G. (1994) 'Joint commissioning: Issues and objectives.' *Management Issues in Social Care 1,* 1, 3–6.

Griffiths, Sir R. (1988) *Community Care: Agenda for Action. A Report to the Secretary of State for Social Services by Sir Roy Griffiths.* London: HMSO.

Haggard, L. and Ormiston, H. (1993) 'Joint commissioning and joint working in South Derbyshire.' *Community Care Management and Planning 1,* 3, August, 77–85.

Henwood, M. (1995) *Making a Difference? Implementation of the Community Care Reforms: Ten Years On.* London: Kings Fund Centre.

Henwood, M., Wistow, G. and Robinson, J. (1996) 'Halfway there? Policy, politics and outcomes in community care.' *Social Policy and Administration 30,* 1, March, 39–53.

Hudson, B. (1992) 'Community care planning: Incrementalism to rationalism?' *Social Policy and Administration 26*, 3, September, 185–200.

Hudson, B. (1995) 'Joint commissioning: Organisational revolution or misplaced enthusiasm?' *Policy and Politics 23*, 3, 233–49.

Hudson, B. (1997) 'Local government and the NHS.' In *The Future Organisation of Community Care: Options for the Integration of Health and Social Care.* London: King's Fund.

Hudson, B. (1998) 'Prospects of partnership.' *Health Service Journal*, 16 April, 26–7.

Hudson, B., Hardy, B., Henwood, M. and Wistow, G. (1997) 'Working across professional boundaries: Primary health care and social care.' *Public Money and Management*, October–December, 25–30.

Jones, R. (1995) 'Spanning the divide: Joint commissioning of health and social services.' *Community Care Management and Planning 3*, 4, August, 112–19.

Kay, A. (1998) 'Community care reforms: Challenges which remain after five years of implementation.' *Integrate News 69*, April, 7–10.

Lewis, J., Bernstock, P., Bovell, V. and Wookey, F. (1996) 'The purchaser/provider split in social care: Is it working?' *Social Policy and Administration 30*, 1, March, 1–19.

Lewis, J., Bernstock, P. and Bovell, V. (1995) 'The community care changes: Unresolved tensions in policy and issues in implementation.' *Journal of Social Policy 24*, 1, 73–94.

Poxton, R. (1997) 'Time to experiment.' In *The Future Organisation of Community Care: Options for the Integration of Health and Social Care.* London: King's Fund.

PSSRU/Nuffield (1994) *The Mixed Economy of Care Bulletin 3.* Leeds: Nuffield Institute for Health.

Ross, F. and Tissier, J. (1997) 'The care management interface with general practice: a case study.' *Health and Social Care in the Community 5*, 3, 135–61.

Shepherd, J. (1997) 'Joint resolutions.' *Health Service Journal*, 10 April, 30–1.

Thomas, G.R. (1998) 'Will the walls come tumbling down?' *Professional Social Work*, February, 12–13.

Vellenowet, C. (1997) 'Strengthening collaboration in community care.' In *The Future Organisation of Community Care: Options for the Integration of Health and Social Care.* London: King's Fund.

Warner, N. (1997) 'Muddled thinking.' *Community Care*, 27 February–5 March, 25.

Wistow, G. (1990) *Community Care Planning: A Review of Past Experiences and Future Imperatives.* London: Department of Health.

Wistow, G., Knapp, M., Hardy, B. and Allen, C. (1992) 'From providing to enabling: Local authorities and the mixed economy of social care.' *Public Administration 70*, 1, 25–45.

# CHAPTER 4

# Changes in the Private Sector

*Brian Hardy and Gerald Wistow*

## Introduction

The private sector has become firmly established in the late 1990s as the dominant provider of residential and nursing home care and has been rapidly moving to a position of similar dominance in the domiciliary sector. Perhaps the most significant measure of the current changes is that, until 1980, private residential provision was the minority player, smaller not only than local authority provision but also that of the voluntary sector. Indeed, it is worth remembering that when social services departments came into existence in 1971 one of the basic assumptions of welfare services was that they would be both state funded and state provided. At that time non-statutory provision was marginal, being confined to relatively small-scale 'specialist' services for 'minority' client groups such as people with physical or mental handicaps. Public funding of the private sector was then 'barely conceivable' (Wistow 1996): the profit motive was widely perceived to be incompatible with the provision of care for vulnerable people; and the expansion of non-statutory services, if not completely an anathema outside its specialist areas, was considered retrogressive.

As remarkable as the explosive growth in residential and nursing home provision – mainly private sector – is the fact that this expansion, from the mid-1970s especially, took place despite an apparent policy intention to shift the balance of care from institutional to home-based services. Whilst that balance of care has begun to be reversed, notably in the last five years, the dominance of the private sector as a provider of residential and nursing home care is undiminished and continues to grow. Indeed, so established is private provision in these sectors that its dominance is virtually unchallenged and apparently irreversible.

In the case of domiciliary care, although the latest official figures (for 1997) show the local authorities continuing to be the dominant provider, the pace of change in this sector since 1993 has been so rapid and the local authorities' historic position of dominance so eroded that it may have ceased to be the majority provider by the time the 1998 statistics are published. In what follows, we look behind these trends to identify the nature of, and reasons for, the private sector's growth. In addition, we identify some of its principal impacts on the structure and shape of provision. We then examine policy reactions and responses to the growth in private sector provision in the 1970s and 1980s and its growing role as set out in *Caring for People* (Department of Health 1989) and the 1990 NHS and Community Care Act. Finally, we look at current purchaser–provider relationships between the public and private sectors before anticipating prospects for the latter in a predominantly local authority-managed market.

### The growth of the private sector

The growth of the private sector as a provider of residential care in the last 25 years is shown in Tables 4.1 and 4.2. These tables demonstrate how the level of private provision overtook (in 1989) that supplied by local authorities and, by 1998, was almost three times the scale of the latter (180,000 compared with 64,000 places). By contrast (Table 4.1), the growth of voluntary sector provision has been substantially more modest (53,000 places in 1998 as compared with 40,000 places in 1970), while the overall level of local authority services has actually fallen by 41 per cent. The result of these changes has been that the private sector's share of the market has risen from 13 per cent in 1975 to 32 per cent in 1985 and 61 per cent in 1998. During the same period, the local authority share fell from 65 per cent in 1975 to 22 per cent in 1998. The same time series data do not exist for private nursing homes and the number of private and voluntary places are not separately available until 1987. However, they show (Table 4.3) a pattern of remarkable growth for the second half of the 1980s onwards.

## Table 4.1 Residential home care for elderly, chronically ill and physically disabled people, places by sector, UK 1970–98 (000s)

| | Sector | | | | | | | |
| | Local authority | | Private | | Voluntary | | Total | |
| Date | No. | % change | No. | % change | No. | % change | No. | % change |
|---|---|---|---|---|---|---|---|---|
| 1970 | 108.7 | | 23.7 | | 40.1 | | 172.5 | |
| 1975 | 128.3 | +18 | 25.8 | +9 | 41.0 | +2 | 195.1 | +13 |
| 1980 | 134.5 | +5 | 37.4 | +45 | 42.6 | +4 | 214.1 | +10 |
| 1985 | 137.1 | +2 | 85.3 | +128 | 45.1 | +6 | 7.5 | +25 |
| 1990 | 125.6 | -8 | 155.6 | +82 | 40.0 | -11 | 321.2 | +20 |
| 1991 | 117.4 | -7 | 161.2 | +4 | 41.9 | +5 | 320.5 | +0.2 |
| 1992 | 105.2 | -10 | 162.4 | +1 | 46.9 | +12 | 314.5 | -2 |
| 1993 | 94.6 | -10 | 165.8 | +2 | 52.4 | +12 | 312.8 | -1 |
| 1994 | 85.8 | -9 | 168.4 | +2 | 55.7 | +6 | 309.9 | -1 |
| 1995 | 80.0 | -7 | 169.3 | +1 | 56.7 | +2 | 306.0 | -1 |
| 1996 | 77.2 | -4 | 172.7 | +2 | 57.5 | +1 | 307.4 | +1 |
| 1997 | 68.6 | -11 | 177.8 | +3 | 55.5 | -3 | 301.9 | -2 |
| 1998 | 64.1 | -7 | 180.1 | +1 | 53.2 | -4 | 297.4 | -2 |
| | | -41 | | +656 | | +13 | | +72 |

*Source: Laing and Buisson (1998) Care of Elderly People, Market Survey 1998. Suffolk: Laing and Buisson (from Table 2.2. p.19).*

**Table 4.2 Residential home care places for elderly, chronically ill and physically disabled people, market share by sector, UK 1970–98**

|  | Sectoral share (%) | | |
|---|---|---|---|
| *Date* | *Local authority* | *Private* | *Voluntary* |
| 1970 | 63 | 14 | 23 |
| 1975 | 66 | 13 | 21 |
| 1980 | 63 | 17 | 20 |
| 1985 | 51 | 32 | 17 |
| 1990 | 39 | 48 | 13 |
| 1991 | 37 | 50 | 13 |
| 1992 | 33 | 52 | 15 |
| 1993 | 30 | 53 | 17 |
| 1994 | 28 | 54 | 18 |
| 1995 | 26 | 55 | 19 |
| 1996 | 25 | 56 | 19 |
| 1997 | 23 | 59 | 18 |
| 1998 | 22 | 61 | 17 |

*Source: Based on figures in Table 4.1. Statistics (1997).*

| | Sector | | | | | |
|---|---|---|---|---|---|---|
| | Private | | Voluntary | | Total | |
| Date | No. | % Change | No. | % Change | No. | % Change |
| 1970* | | | | | 20.3 | |
| 1975* | | | | | 24.0 | +18 |
| 1980* | | | | | 26.9 | +12 |
| 1985* | | | | | 38.0 | +41 |
| 1990 | 112.6 | | 10.5 | | 123.1 | +224 |
| 1991 | 135.2 | +20 | 12.1 | +15 | 147.3 | +20 |
| 1992 | 152.8 | +13 | 13.7 | +12 | 166.5 | +13 |
| 1993 | 172.1 | +13 | 15.8 | +15 | 187.9 | +13 |
| 1994 | 184.3 | +7 | 17.2 | +9 | 201.5 | +7 |
| 1995 | 193.4 | +5 | 17.9 | +4 | 211.3 | +5 |
| 1996 | 201.9 | +4 | 18.3 | +2 | 220.2 | +4 |
| 1997 | 205.8 | +2 | 18.4 | +1 | 224.2 | +2 |
| 1998 | 205.6 | -0.1 | 18.4 | 0 | 224.0 | -0.1 |

**Table 4.3 Nursing home care for elderly, chronically ill and physically disabled people, places by sector UK 1970–98 (000s)**

*No breakdown of figures by sector available.

Private sector and voluntary sector nursing homes together provided only 24,000 places in 1975 and 38,000 places in 1985; a figure that had risen to 123,100 in 1990 and 224,000 in 1998. Growth in the private sector alone was 295 per cent between 1987 and 1998. Over the period 1970 to 1993 the number of long-stay hospital places fell by 18 per cent and by a further 36 per cent between 1993 and 1998, demonstrating a major shift from publicly provided care, free at the point of delivery, to private sector care funded by user payments. The dominance of the private sector in the nursing home market is underlined in Table 4.4 below: its market share has been 92 per cent for the last eight years.

| Table 4.4 Nursing home care for elderly, chronically ill and physically disabled people, market share by sector, UK 1990–98 | | |
|---|---|---|
| | Sectoral share (%) | |
| *Date* | *Private* | *Voluntary* |
| 1990 | 91 | 9 |
| 1991 | 92 | 8 |
| 1992 | 92 | 8 |
| 1993 | 92 | 8 |
| 1994 | 92 | 8 |
| 1995 | 92 | 8 |
| 1996 | 92 | 8 |
| 1997 | 92 | 8 |
| 1998 | 92 | 8 |

Compared with residential and nursing home services, the growth in the private sector in domiciliary care (both volume and market share) has been much more recent. As late as 1992, the independent sector's share of the local authority-funded market (Table 4.5) amounted to 2.3 per cent, of which 1.9 per cent was purchased from the private sector.

| Table 4.5 Local authority purchased home care, market share by sector, 1992–97 | | | |
|---|---|---|---|
| | Sectoral share (%) | | |
| *Date* | *Local authority* | *Private* | *Voluntary* |
| 1992 | 98 | 1.9 | 0.4 |
| 1993 | 95 | 4 | 1 |
| 1994 | 81 | 16 | 3 |
| 1995 | 71 | 26 | 3 |
| 1996 | 64 | 32 | 34 |
| 1997 | 56 | 39 | 5 |

Source: *Compiled from Government Statistical Service (1998), Community Care Statistics 1997.*

The effect of the community care changes, implemented in 1993, has proved to be dramatic. As Table 4.6 shows, both the number of hours overall and, more especially that provided by the private sector, has grown significantly.

| Table 4.6 Local authority purchased home care by sector No. of hours (000s) and % change per annum, 1992–97 | | | | | | | | |
|---|---|---|---|---|---|---|---|---|
| | All sectors | | Local authority in-house | | Private | | Voluntary | |
| *Year* | *No. hours* | *% change* | *No. hours* | *% change* | *No. hours* | *% change* | *No. hours* | *% change* |
| 1992 | 1687 | | 1648 | | 32 | | 7 | |
| 1993 | 1781 | +6 | 1694 | +3 | 70 | +118 | 16 | +129 |
| 1994 | 2215 | +24 | 1787 | +5 | 366 | +420 | 62 | +288 |
| 1995 | 2396 | +8 | 1689 | -6 | 629 | +72 | 78 | +26 |
| 1996 | 2487 | +4 | 1586 | -6 | 805 | +28 | 96 | +23 |
| 1997 | 2638 | +6 | 1485 | -6 | 1013 | +26 | 140 | +46 |

Source: *Government Statistical Service (1998), Community Care.*

Thus, the total volume of home care hours provided by the private sector has grown by 3065 per cent between 1992 and 1997, while its share of the market has increased from 1.9 per cent to 39 per cent. By contrast, the volume of local authority provision has been falling since 1994 and its market share fell from 98 per cent in 1992 to 56 per cent in 1997.

## Principal provider characteristics

The principal characteristics of the independent sector residential, nursing home and domiciliary care markets are their fragmentation (in terms of ownership), their relative immaturity (especially in domiciliary care) and their dependence on public funding of clients. The majority of private sector providers are independent small businesses. In the case of residential and nursing home care, for example, by the end of 1997 major providers (i.e. those operating three or more care homes) owned or leased only a quarter (26%) of all for-profit nursing, residential and dual registered beds in homes for elderly and physically handicapped people in the UK (Laing and Buisson 1998a and b). In the case of domiciliary care the sector is also very young: in 1997 11 per cent had been in business for ten years or more, while 70 per cent had been in business for less than five years. Most of the industry is also small-scale, with 82 per cent of providers in 1997 delivering under 5000 hours of service a month. Even more significantly, 23 per cent of providers delivered less than 500 hours per month (Hardy 1998).

Independent sector providers are highly dependent on local authority funded clients. This is especially so in domiciliary care: 69 per cent of respondents in the most recent UKHCA survey (reflecting the position at the end of 1997) were dependent on local authorities for all or most (i.e. 60% to 80%) of their clients (Hardy 1998). In the care home sector 46 per cent of independent sector residents were local authority funded; 22 per cent were still in receipt of income support, being preserved rights cases from April 1993 (Laing and Buisson 1998). Across all sectors, therefore, private providers are heavily dependent on publicly funded clients (more than two-thirds) rather than privately funded clients (less than one-third).

## The history of private sector growth

The principle explanation for both the rapid growth in the private residential and nursing home sector – and also the more recent growth in private domiciliary care – is to be found in the changing nature of public funding for such care. Most importantly, the decline in public provision was not primarily associated with reductions in public sector expenditure. Indeed, the reverse was the case. As one of us has argued elsewhere, 'much of the growth in private ... homes has been funded through social security payments which were linked to institutional but not domiciliary care, and which were payable following a test of individual income/assets but not of their need for care' (Wistow 1997). Between 1982 and 1993 the number of residents in private and voluntary residential and nursing homes supported by the Department of Social Security rose from £39 million to £2.57 billion (House of Commons 1997). Indeed, by 1993 64 per cent of such residents had their fees supported by means-tested social security payments (Laing and Buisson 1994) compared with 44 per cent in the mid-1980s and 14 per cent in 1979. This growth in means-tested payments at least in part was substituting for care which might previously have been expected to be provided by the NHS. Of the 194,000 nursing home residents in 1994 (compared with 27,000 in 1980), only 5 per cent were funded by the NHS and thus not exposed to means-testing.

The dramatic growth in social security support to the independent sector as a whole was unplanned and took place despite a series of attempts to check its growth (House of Commons Social Security Committee 1991; House of Commons Health Committee 1993). The ready availability of such demand-led payments for one sector of care contrasted strongly with the tight cash limits on local authority spending. With no equivalent social security support for domiciliary care, the effect of these funding arrangements was seriously to constrain the development of the latter and to focus service development on institutional services. As a result, the number of residential and nursing home places grew more rapidly than the population of older people, while the reverse was the case for domiciliary services. Thus, by 1991, an estimated 27 per cent more older people were living in long-term care institutions than would have been predicted if per capita levels of provision had remained constant (Laing and Buisson 1995). By contrast, the supply of domiciliary care services failed to keep pace with demographic growth. By 1984/85, for example, the number of home help hours and meals had fallen by 14 per cent and 15 per cent respectively, from their 1977/78 levels of head of population aged 75 and over (Wistow 1987). Similar reductions took place between 1986/87 and 1992/93, with 10 per cent and 13 per cent reductions, respectively, taking place for the same services over that period (Wistow 1996). One consequence of the pattern of growth in the private sector before 1993, therefore, was that service systems developed in ways which were inconsistent with the core policy objective of community care in terms of shifting the balance of care from institutional to domiciliary services.

Since 1993, however, this pattern of development has begun to be reversed: the growth of residential and nursing home services has levelled out (Table 4.3) and in 1997 fell for the first time (Laing and Buisson 1998). In addition, as we have already noted, domiciliary care began a period of very high growth rates the same year (Government Statistical Service 1998). It is worth emphasising that unlike the developments in the late 1970s and the 1980s, the more recent trends have been systematically planned and were given statutory force by the 1990 NHS and Community Care Act which was fully implemented from 1993 onwards. This legislation specifically required local authorities to: make access to any form of publicly funded care dependent on an assessment of individual need; provide care wherever possible in people's own homes (or in homely settings in local communities); and stimulate the growth of independent providers especially in the field of domiciliary care (DoH 1989).

These requirements amounted to an explicit transformation of the role of local authorities so that they would increasingly become purchasers rather than providers of care. In this respect, the legislation was following Griffiths' recommendation that local authorities should in future become

> the designers, organisers and purchasers of non-health care services and not primarily [be] direct providers, making the maximum possible use of voluntary and private sector bodies to widen consumer choice, stimulate innovation and encourage efficiency. (Griffiths 1988, para. 1.3.4)

In Griffiths' view, 'the onus in all cases should be on social services authorities to show that the private sector is being fully stimulated and encouraged, and that competitive tenders or other means of testing the market are being taken' (1988, para 24). It is important to recognise that local authorities initially had considerable reservations about this changing role. Whilst there was widespread support for the principle of needs-led services focused, wherever possible, on home-based care, they had considerable misgivings not only about the introduction of markets into social care in general, but about the role of the private sector within those markets in particular (Wistow *et al.* 1994).

### Reactions to an expanding private sector

At the time of the introduction of the community care changes in the early 1990s the prevailing local authority attitude to what many perceived as the 'privatisation' of care created a potentially serious implementation problem for the centre. The perceived risk was that local authorities would take advantage of their newly constituted role as monopoly purchasers to favour their own direct provision: and their reluctance to support the private sector would threaten the viability or survival of many businesses. It was largely to counter this risk of market collapse within the private sector that the government introduced a range of measures: first, the 'so-called' '85% rule'; second, the 1992 Direction on Choice; and third, the 1993 Direction on consultation of the private sector in the community care planning process.

The first of these measures (applicable only in England) was the most significant and substantial. With the implementation of the 1990 Act local authorities were to have transferred to them the money previously spent on residential and nursing care through the social security system. The transfer was made by a partially ringfenced special transitional grant (STG) amounting to £1.568 million in the three financial years from 1993/94. In order to safeguard the position of the private and voluntary sectors local authorities were required to spend 85 per cent of the sums transferred on the services of independent sector providers. Thus the price of receiving these substantial additional sums was that the local authorities would sustain and develop the private and voluntary sectors. Even more particularly it meant that the expansion of domiciliary services would largely have to be within the independent sector.

The second measure introduced by the government was the National Assistance Act 1948 (Choice of Accommodation) Directions 1992 –

commonly referred to as the Direction on Choice. Under the terms of this Direction individuals have the right to be cared for in the residential or nursing home of their choice after 1 April 1993. Although individuals were given the right to choose a place in a home more expensive than the local authority would normally expect to purchase, this would necessitate payment of the difference by some third party. It is important to note that the Direction on Choice was, and is, limited to residential and nursing care and does not extend to non-residential services.

As regards the third measure, analyses of the first round of community care plans in April 1992 had highlighted a discrepancy between the extremely limited involvement of private sector providers in plan production and the much more extensive involvement of voluntary sector agencies (Wistow, Leedham and Hardy 1993). The Department of Health commissioned KPMG Management Consultants to examine such limited private sector involvement. Following KPMG's report (1992) the secretary of state issued a statutory Direction in 1993 requiring not only that the private sector be fully involved, but that local authorities specify in future plans how this was to be achieved (DoH 1993).

### Relations between private sector providers and local authority purchasers

In view of the scale of the private sector's dependence upon local authorities' funding of their clients, relations with local authority purchasers have an important effect upon providers' entry into and development within local care markets. As we have made clear elsewhere (Wistow *et al.* 1994, 1996), the legacy of the 1980s was a relationship between local authorities and private sector providers characterised by suspicion and mistrust. The belief amongst local authorities was that home owners in the private sector were often motivated purely by profit maximisation. This motivation was widely thought to be inappropriate in view of the general perception amongst local authorities – under whatever political control – that 'social care is different' (Wistow *et al.* 1994). As such, market mechanisms, and especially the pursuit of profit, were widely regarded not only as inappropriate, but as unacceptable. And yet the task for local authorities post-1993 was to stimulate a diversity of supply and generate competition between independent sector providers and between such providers and their own in-house services.

The mutual mistrust was of two kinds: competence trust (i.e. trust in an organisation's ability to deliver care efficiently and cost-effectively) and goodwill trust (i.e. trust in an organisation's 'caring credentials'). On the part of local authority purchasers there was a mistrust of the managerial ability of some voluntary organisations and some of the smaller private sector providers. There was generally high goodwill trust in voluntary sector providers (reflecting a belief that they broadly shared the same values, service principles and ethos as their public sector counterparts) but generally low goodwill trust in private, for-profit, providers due, as indicated above, to their profit orientation being seen to conflict with a public service ethos. For their part, many independent sector providers had low competence trust in local authorities faced with commissioning tasks which were not only technically demanding but of which they had little experience. There was also, amongst many providers, little goodwill trust in the local authority: amongst private sector providers this was based on the widespread suspicion that they were being discriminated against, primarily to the benefit of local authorities' own direct providers and also of voluntary sector providers.

It was against this general legacy of mutual misunderstanding and mistrust that we have conducted three detailed studies of independent sector providers – of residential care in 1994 and 1996/97 (see Wistow *et al.* 1997) and of domiciliary care in 1995/96. In such a context the findings of these studies are notable. In the first of these studies we found a significant proportion of private sector residential home owners (representing three-quarters of the sample of providers), far from being 'red in tooth and claw' profit maximisers, espoused the same caring values and service principles as their voluntary sector or public sector counterparts: indeed most placed little emphasis on profit making, let alone profit maximisation. This, of course, is precisely the response that might be expected of providers simply asked to describe their motivations; what was significant, however, was that their observed behaviour in terms of admissions procedures, service provision and, most notably, pricing policies, was consistent with such claims. Even those who described financial goals as important typically saw these as subsidiary to meeting the needs of elderly people. One important explanation was that most private sector providers had worked previously as caring professionals in the public sector (see Wistow et al. 1996, Chapter 6). These findings are echoed by our subsequent studies and by others. Taylor, Langan and Haggett (1995), for example, found evidence that profit was not the only imperative motivating so-called for-profit organisations and that caring values were as prevalent in the for-profit as in the not-for-profit sectors (see also Leat 1993).

Given these findings, in order to shape and manage their developing local markets successfully, local authority purchasers need to recognise the diversity of motivations and behaviours – especially amongst private sector providers – and acknowledge the dangers of developing purchasing relationships on the basis of ill-informed stereotypes (Wistow *et al.* 1996). They also need to move away from the sort of contractual relations they developed initially with private sector providers – short-term, adversarial, arms-length relationships character-ised by low-trust, classical contracts – towards longer term, collaborative relationships based upon higher trust, relational forms of contracting (Wistow *et al.* 1996).

The language of cooperation and partnership between local authority purchasers and independent sector providers had, in fact, been used by the previous Conservative government even before the full implementation of the community care changes. In 1992 the then Minister for Health, Dr Mawhinney, spoke of the need for local authorities 'to work closely with the private and voluntary providers of care' (Mawhinney 1992). Similarly, the government-established Community Care Support Force in April 1993, immediately prior to the implementation date, argued forcefully that local authorities should recognise the dangers of behaving as 'immature' purchasers:

> sometimes when private sector mechanisms are applied to the public sector, services managers in the public sector behave in the way they imagine the private sector behaves, rather than how it behaves in practice. Some early approaches to social care contracting, and the relationships between purchasers and providers, suggest distance, friction and simplistic price competition [whereas] comparisons with high quality private sector contracting emphasise effective partnerships between purchasers and

providers to develop and deliver high quality services. (Department of Health Community Care Support Force 1993a, para. 72)

The evidence is that adversarial attitudes and behaviour, rather than cooperation or partnership, were indeed the defining characteristics of public–private sector relationships before and immediately after 1993. According to a recent Audit Commission report this remains the case: 'Social Services Departments (SSDs) typically have adversarial relationships with the independent sector' (Audit Commission 1997, p.66). Our evidence is that this may now be too sweeping a generalisation, describing attitudes and behaviour which have changed considerably since 1993 and which are still changing. Even by 1995/96 local authorities had travelled an enormous distance in terms of understanding, acceptance and competence in developing and managing the emerging quasi-markets. There was a growing recognition of the range and motivations amongst independent sector providers and a transformation in the degree to which local authority members and officers acknowledged the need to establish collaborative relationships with independent sector providers – in the private as well as the voluntary and not-for-profit sectors. We concluded that such broad misunderstandings and mistrust of the motivations of many (especially small, private) providers had diminished significantly (Audit Commission 1997). The principal exception was the larger corporate for-profit providers (and some specialist voluntary providers) in relation to which a good deal of mistrust or misgivings remained.

## Future prospects

A recent study of residential home owners, in 1996/97, found much support for the view that local authority attitudes had changed significantly, but also widespread pessimism about local market conditions and the future prospects for home owners (Forder *et al.* 1999). There was much talk of simply 'digging in' and of fighting to retain a place in the market, and for many owners the prospects were either so bleak or they were so weary that they were planning to leave the market altogether. Such weariness was borne largely, but not entirely, of continuing cost pressures. Across all care sectors private sector providers are heavily reliant on local authorities as the funders of clients. And whilst local authorities' resources are constrained there is also limited scope in many localities to expand the number of private payers. Of growing concern to providers are problems of staff recruitment and retention in highly competitive local labour markets – especially in the case of domiciliary care (see Hardy 1998) – and the impact of both the national minimum wage (from 1 April 1999) and the Working Time Directive (which came into force on 1 October 1998). Providers' estimates are that the national minimum wage will add between £90m and £100m per annum to care costs; and that, in the case of domiciliary care, the working time regulations will increase operator costs by 8 per cent per annum (Laing and Buisson 1999). Provider concerns are not about the national minimum wage and working time regulations *per se* – in principle they will aid recruitment and retention – but about the threats to businesses if the changes are not properly funded by the government and by local authorities.

Such concerns in part reflect the long-held view that local authority (and Department of Social Security) fee levels significantly fail to meet providers' costs (see, for example, Laing 1998). The immediate effects of such disparities are deficits being 'made up from providers' charitable funds or from "cross-subsidisation" by self-payers' (Laing 1998). The longer term effects may be 'private sector home operators being discouraged from investing in good quality stock for clients dependent entirely on state funding' (Laing 1998).

Notwithstanding such gloom (see also Laing and Buisson 1998) there is a growing recognition that many local authorities are now working much more as partners with independent sector providers. There is now much less mutual suspicion, or 'goodwill mistrust', than previously. There are, however, some concerns about local authorities' sensitivities to the vulnerability of smaller home providers. Some owners expressed fears of having their business squeezed too tightly by the twin pressures of continuing local authority financial constraints and the growth of the large corporate providers. According to the most recent market surveys (Laing and Buisson 1998a and b) the trend is for increased market concentration via mergers and acquisitions in both the domiciliary care and the residential and nursing home markets. As a result of the latter the number of publicly quoted care home companies, for example, fell from 15 at the end of 1995 to 7 at the end of 1998. And although the average size of residential homes (20 places in 1997) makes them still accessible to small home owners, the average size of nursing homes has risen from 25 to 37 places over the decade to 1997; thereby making them increasingly accessible only to the larger care home organisations (Laing 1998). The threat to smaller homes has long been a concern for local authorities themselves. But they face a dilemma if they attempt to forestall the growth of the larger corporate providers – with what in any case are the limited powers at their disposal. On the one hand they risk being accused – not only by users and carers but by district auditors, on the grounds of both quality and cost – of limiting the choice of care homes. On the other hand, if local authorities are entirely passive in the face of such expansion they risk being accused of jeopardising the survival of the smaller homes, the proprietors of which are particularly vulnerable to fluctuations in referral patterns, small changes in occupancy levels and pressures on prices. The difficult task for local authorities is to determine under what circumstances, if any, they should help sustain the latter providers by, for example, the payment of quality premiums or through block contacts.

Under current 'best value' disciplines – as underlined by *Modernising Social Services* (Department of Health 1998) – authorities are forced to be transparent about the rationale for any differential payments amongst homes, whether on the basis of sector (local authority or independent sector) size or location. The payment of such differentials is not in itself new: local authorities have long paid providers of specialist care user-based premiums for particular levels of dependency or complexity. The task for local authorities, across all services (residential, nursing and domiciliary care), will be to develop relationships and contracts (with what, in many cases, will be a smaller number of 'preferred' providers) which ensure such providers some stability but which simultaneously ensure some competitive edge. Without sufficient stability few private sector providers will undertake the investments in the business required to enhance service quality – whether by, for example, capital improvements or staff training. Equally, such providers can neither be guaranteed future local authority business nor be protected from alternative providers wanting to enter or to expand within local markets who can compete on quality and price.

The private sector's share of the publicly funded social care market – in residential, nursing and domiciliary care – has grown dramatically in the last two decades and seems unlikely to be significantly changed. There will continue to be concern about the size of these markets and about cost pressures and operating margins in a context of continuing resource constraint upon local authorities and increasingly competitive local labour markets. One important change affecting future prospects, however, is that the private sector's position will be underpinned by a national framework of commissioning and regulating which treats them no differently from their provider counterparts in the voluntary and public sectors.

## References

Audit Commission (1997) *Take Your Choice.* London: Audit Commission.

Department of Health (1993) *Community Care Plans (Consultation) Direction 1993.* 25 January 1993. London: Department of Health.

Department of Health Community Care Support Force (1993a) *Reviewing Community Care Contracts.* London: Department of Health.

Department of Health (1989) *Caring for People: Community Care in the Next Decade and Beyond.* London: HMSO.

Department of Health (1998) *Modernising Social Services: Promoting Independence, Improving Protection, Raising Standards.* Cm 4169. London: The Stationery Office.

Forder, J., Hardy, B., Kendall, J., Knapp, M. and Wistow, G. (1999) *Residential Care Providers in the Independent Sector: Motivations, Pricing and Links with Purchasers.* Report to Department of Health. London: Personal Social Services Research Unit, London School of Economics; Leeds: Nuffield Institute for Health.

Government Statistical Service (1998) *Community Care Statistics 1997.* Statistical Bulletin 1998/13. London: Department of Health.

Griffiths, R. (1988) *Community Care: Agenda for Action.* London: HMSO.

Hardy, B. (1998) *Domiciliary Care Markets: Growing and Growing Up.* Report of the 1997 Survey of UKHC Members. Carshalton: UKHCA.

House of Commons Social Security Committee (1991) *The Financing of Private Residential and Nursing Home Fees.* 4th Report. Session 1990–91, HC421. London: HMSO.

House of Commons Health Committee (1993) *Community Care: The Way Forward.* London: HMSO.

KPMG Management Consultants (1992) *Implementing Community Care: Improving Independent Sector Involvement in Community Care Planning.* London: Department of Health.

Laing, W. (1998) *Disparities Between Market Rates and State Funding of Residential Care.* York: Joseph Rowntree Foundation.

Laing and Buisson (1995) *Care of Elderly People Market Survey 1995,* 8th edition. London: Laing and Buisson.

Laing and Buisson (1998) *Disparities Between Market Rates and State Funding of Residential Care.* York: Joseph Rowntree Foundation.

Laing and Buisson (1998a) *The Homecare Market 1998: From Home Help to High-Tech Health Care.* London: Laing and Buisson.

Laing and Buisson (1998b) *Care of Elderly People Market Survey 1998,* 11th edn. London: Laing and Buisson.

Laing and Buisson (1999) *Community Care Markets News.* December 1998/January 1999, 158.

Leat, D. (1993) *The Development of Community Care by the Independent Sector.* London: Policy Studies Institute.

Mawhinney, B. (1992) *Speech to IHSM/ADSS Conference,* 10th July. London: Department of Health.

Taylor, M., Langan, J. and Haggett, P. (1995) Encouraging Diversity: Voluntary and Private Organisations in Community Care. Aldershot: Ashgate. (1995) 'Non-profit organisations in the institutional environment: Does sector matter?' Paper presented to ISTR Inaugural Conference, Pecs, Hungary, July.

Wistow, G. (1987) 'Increasing private provision in social care: Implications for policy.' In R. Lewis (ed) *Care and Control: Personal Social Services and the Private Sector.* Discussion Paper 15. London: Policy Studies Institute.

Wistow, G. (1996) 'Community Care in the Twenty First Century: Choice, Independence and Community Integration.' Paper presented to St Anne's Housing Association Conference, 6 December. Leeds: Nuffield Institute for Health.

Wistow, G. (1997) 'Funding long-term carers.' In E. Bransdon and M. May (eds) *Social Policy Review No. 9.* London: Longmans.

Wistow, G., Leedham, I. and Hardy, B. (1993) *A Preliminary Analysis of a Sample of English Community Care Plans.* London: Department of Health.

Wistow, G., Knapp, M., Hardy, B. and Allen, C. (1994) *Social Care in a Mixed Economy.* Buckingham: Open University Press.

Wistow, G., Knapp, M., Hardy, B., Forder, J., Kendall, J. and Manning, R. (1996) *Social Care Markets: Progress and Prospects.* Buckingham: Open University Press.

Wistow, G., Knapp, M., Hardy, B., Forder, J., Kendall, J. and Young, R. (1997) 'Purchasing home care: how independent sector providers see the developing market.' *Evidence No.2.* Leeds: Nuffield Institute for Health; London: Personal Social Services Research Unit, London School of Economics.

# CHAPTER 5

# The Voluntary Sector and Social Care for Older People

## From Origins to the Mid-1990s

*Jeremy Kendall*

## Background

Up until the twentieth century and the consolidation of the modern Welfare State, voluntary organisations were the primary conduits of formally organised care, supplementing the informal support provided by family, friends and neighbours. This situation changed during the course of the first half of this century, as the state increasingly became involved in welfare activities. Most dramatically, in the aftermath of World War II, the voluntary sector's erstwhile role as the dominant provider of both income maintenance (through the friendly societies and private charity) and health care (through the voluntary hospital network) was almost extinguished. With a small number of exceptions, these activities were fully nationalised and brought fully under central state ownership and control, where they have remained, to a significant extent, to this day.

However, a third important welfare function traditionally led by the voluntary sector, and from which older people were, and are, a highly significant group of beneficiaries – *personal social services* – was treated differently. These services were made the responsibility of local rather than central government under the post-war settlement, and voluntary providers, for the time-being, remained at the core of service delivery. As with other human service fields, the *intention* was certainly to expand the ambit of (local) state controlled provision in a general climate of pro-state beliefs and attitudes, but social care services were a relatively low spending priority in the years after the war, and so investment in this area was initially relatively limited. Moreover, the 1948 National Assistance Act and subsequent legislation specifically empowered local authorities to meet the needs of their elderly populations not only through building up their own residential and community services, but also by funding voluntary organisations to do so. For example, much of the residential care provided by traditional charities, including the Anglican and Catholic sisterhoods and the Salvation Army, was applauded as exemplary (Kendall and Knapp 1996, pp.212–14). In the non-residential care field, an example of the voluntary sector's resilience would include its position as the principal provider of day care provision at least up until the late 1970s (Carter 1981).

Voluntary sector social care and housing for elderly people was also given added impetus from within the sector between the 1940s and the 1970s, with the formation of new national specialist voluntary organisations and federations. These were distinguishable from the providers with deeper historical roots – including many denominational activities, and those based around particular professional, occupational and ethnic identities – by their founding orientation towards older people in general. Major players in this category include Age Concern, the Abbeyfield Society, Anchor Housing, Help the Aged and Crossroads (for carers, predominantly but not exclusively, of elderly people), which often worked particularly closely at the local level with local authorities in developing both institutional and community care.

However, in the 1960s and the early 1970s, as more public funding was made available reflecting the climate of 'welfare optimism' (George 1996), local authorities in general tended to develop care services on behalf of their electorates by expanding directly run public services rather than through providing financial support for independent suppliers. Moreover, this course of action generated relatively little resistance. Professionals and volunteers in the voluntary sector, as much as the community in general, largely welcomed this development as wholly consistent with the consolidation of the Welfare State; they tended to see their role as local authorities saw it: primarily that of pioneers, supplementers and niche market specialists.

At least from the 1960s onwards, greater emphasis was also being given to community-based options for elderly people in response to their own preferences, professional opinions, voluntary groups' lobbying efforts, and considerations of cost (Tinker 1992). There was a broad acceptance here that as public funds became available for non-residential services, expansion should be achieved *primarily* through the direct services route. Voluntary organisations and volunteers were still recognised as key players in these forms of care – as often representing a way of securing appropriate community-based care, independent living and also pursuing more general community development (Brenton 1985). Yet while voluntary organisations were sometimes given financial support to enable them to provide a range of care services in line with the recommendations of various official committees (Seebohm 1968; Wolfenden 1978; Barclay 1982), it does need to be emphasised that the vast bulk (well over 90 per cent) of social service departments' expenditure on non-residential services still tended to be deployed to fund local authorities' own services.

While local authorities' expenditure on their own residential care fell dramatically during the years of 'welfare pessimism' from the mid-1970s to the late 1980s (George 1996), this was not because of a large-scale switch to local authority funding for independently provided care. Rather, it represented a combined response to a reduction in central government funding for local government as the former sought to rein in public expenditure overall, and an internal reallocation of funds towards (overwhelmingly still in-house) community care (Evandrou, Failkingham and Glennerster 1990, p.218). At the same time that local authority investment in residential care in particular was highly constrained by these influences, publicly funded independently provided care was growing – but fuelled by the availability of central rather than local government funds. Through central government's social security system, relatively generous cash payments were available to elderly people, provided they satisfied a means test and entered residential care, but not if they stayed at home – regardless of their needs (Audit Commission 1986; Griffiths 1988). During the 1980s, these state resources effectively acted as residential care-specific 'vouchers', ensuring elderly people had the ability to pay for at least a certain level of residential care. However, these 'vouchers' were *not* sector-specific, so elderly people were able to choose between private, voluntary and public sector residential care – provided, of course the suppliers were there in the first place.

In fact, it was the private sector and not the voluntary sector, which responded to this phenomenal surge in publicly funded demand (see Chapter 4). Voluntary sector residential provision remained almost unchanged, and thus accounted for a dwindling market share as the market expanded. Although it is hard to identify patterns because data on the voluntary sector cannot be disaggregated, most religious, professional and occupational charities were probably relatively unresponsive to the changing conditions, and may even to have declined in absolute terms. Growth appears to have been confined to national specialist providers, and to new consortia and hybrid arrangements, often involving non-profit housing associations. These sought creatively to combine different sources of local and central government funds with user charges (Morton 1990). Outside of the residential sector, little is known in concrete terms about the relative contributions of the private and voluntary sectors, but the latter certainly continued to fulfil its historic role as the major independent player, sometimes funded by local authorities and sometimes not, but almost always dwarfed by municipal provision as far as publicly funded care was concerned.

The most consequential reform in the Welfare State in the post-war era as far as services for older people has been concerned did not materialise until John Major become prime minister in 1990. The 1990 NHS and Community Care Act, with full implementation from 1993 onwards, is currently having far-reaching implications for all providers of social care, having introduced the most sweeping legislative reforms in the field since the 1940s. This includes the restyling of local authorities as 'enabling' purchasers on behalf of older people, involving the transfer to them of the funds which otherwise would have been spent by central government, as described above (see Wistow *et al.* 1994 and 1996 for details). For our purposes, it is particularly important to note that on the supply side, one of the primary intentions of the Act was to enhance the role of *both* the private and voluntary sectors through the deployment of contractual and quasi-contractual agreements, and through the creation of 'not-for-profit' providers to manage floated off services formerly directly run by local authorities.

A range of influences lay behind these reforms. The New Right central government's enthusiasm for markets and consumer-led services, and a rather indiscriminate ideological prejudice against all forms of municipal direct service provision, was one factor. A second was the desire to shift political blame for apparent 'underspending' and scandals involving client neglect or abuse entirely on to the shoulders of local government (see Klein 1995, for a discussion of the concept of decentralisation of blame in the context of the National Health Service). Yet these arguments were *not* carried through to their logical conclusion since the 1990 Act suggested that 'good quality public services' would continue to have a major, albeit reduced, role to play.

There was certainly some resistance from within the voluntary sector to the extension of the contracting out element of the reforms. This came particularly from those who either saw this aspect of the reforms as a 'stalking horse' for withdrawal by the state from core welfare state financial responsibilities in the future, or regarded the (further) involvement of independent – and especially private sector – providers, as inherently incompatible with care processes and user welfare.

However, the overall reform package was certainly not purely the outcome of pro-market ideology and fraught relations between central and local government. Its other aspects – including the emphasis on the desirability of independent living and the imperative of sensitivity to users' needs and preferences – commanded much greater support. From at least the 1960s onwards, professional opinion and many voluntary sector organisations themselves had vocally supported precisely these principles. Moreover, during the 1980s, there was a steady build up of evidence from academic research and official reports that the *status quo* involved extensive unmet or inappropriately met needs and ineffective use of resources (Baldock and Ungerson 1993). Inasmuch as the reforms sought to alter this situation to secure more appropriate use of taxpayers' money, their broad thrust was broadly welcomed – notwithstanding the doubts about the long-term repercussions of contracting out.

**Personal social services for older people in the 1990s: evidence on the relative scope and contributions of voluntary organisations**

If measured purely in terms of overall financial or paid human resource terms, the voluntary sector is very much ranked third behind the public and private (for-profit) sectors. This is both for personal social services across all client groups, and specifically in care for elderly people. Yet the voluntary sector's contribution is a crucially important ingredient to the mixed economy of care in ways which might get lost by concentrating on aggregated indicators of this kind. For example, the previous section suggests that voluntary sector personal social services provision may be distinctly layered in terms of resourcing and structure, and it is important to find some way of capturing this variety. Box 5.1 shows a typology which attempts to do this, building on Smith and Lipsky (1993) and Mocroft and Thomason (1993) by incorporating two further categories – national specialists and not-for-profit trusts – with the particular history of provision for elderly people in the UK in mind. The choice and diversity these layers engender are a key aspect of the sector's role in care for elderly people.

Cross-cutting this typology are the different forms of care that the voluntary sector provides. Residential care *financially* dominates the voluntary sector's activities (Kendall and Knapp 1996, Chapter 6), but the voluntary sector is also heavily involved in providing social care outside old people's homes, including domiciliary services, day care services and social/luncheon clubs, and this is where its *volunteer* efforts are concentrated. The latter is relatively rare in residential care settings across all provider sectors (Ernst and Whinney 1986; Local Government Management Board and Central Council for Education and Training in Social Work 1997b). The estimated 3 per cent of the adult population who were volunteering in 1997 in the UK through formal organisations on behalf of older people (Davis Smith 1998) – many of them elderly themselves – are concentrated outside old people's homes. Popular activities undertaken by volunteers, sometimes alongside paid staff, include care, quasi-care and support tasks such as the delivery of meals, laundering, shopping and cooking and providing transport. Fundraising and participating on committees, and the provision of advice and counselling, are other important activities. The simple provision of companionship may be a particularly important benefit to older people from the involvement of volunteers (Waddington and Henwood 1996), and this clearly cuts across and interweaves with the various care and support activities described.

---

### *Box 5.1 Major types of voluntary organisation providing for elderly people*

- Generalist social service agencies with services for elderly people operating alongside services for other people in need. Typically with pre-World War II origins, these tend to be either directly or indirectly connected to religious denominations or based around occupational, trade or professional groupings with a wide variety of structures. Mixed funding, but Smith and Lipsky (1993) emphasise that many traditional providers of this sort may have substantial endowment income and accumulated financial reserves.

- Specialist providers for elderly people, typically founded from around World War II onwards, and often with federal structures. Mixed funding.

- New social entrepreneurship organisations founded and/or expanded from the 1960s onwards, but most extensively in the 1980s in direct response to the availability of public funds, particularly for community care, training and housing programmes. These may or may not specialise in providing care for elderly people, can develop national structures from typically local or regional origins, and often remain heavily reliant on public funding and user contributions.

- Community and self help groups not covered in the above categories. Mixed funding.

- Not-for-profit trusts operating homes formerly run directly by local authorities from whom they have been 'floated off'. Typically funded almost entirely by direct authority funding and user contributions.

---

A good deal of this activity is independently funded – through charges to users, private giving, or drawing upon income from organisations' own resources, especially in the case of what is referred to in Box 5.1 as generalists, specialists and community groups. However, significant chunks of these organisations' activities are now supported by local government through combinations of grants and (increasingly) contracts. Moreover, as the box also suggests, the more recent wave of not-for-profit trusts and social entrepreneurship agencies tend to be more dependent on the public sector. The net result has been that in recent years the sector as a whole has become markedly more reliant on local government financial support (see Kendall with Almond 1998).

Existing data allow us to put the contribution of the sector as a whole to local authority-funded activity in residential, domiciliary and day care in context, although it unfortunately does not allow us to disaggregate it according to the provider types that we have identified. Figures 5.1 to 5.3 therefore show how changing levels of local authority-funded activities only (in England) are split between the three formal sectors in the case of residential, domiciliary and day care respectively over the period 1992–96. The following three key stylised facts emerge from this data.

- In *residential care*, after a long period of relative decline (1970–90), during which it provided an almost unchanged number of places in a rapidly expanding overall market, the voluntary sector's market share has begun to recover (Figure 5.1).

- In *domiciliary care*, the voluntary sector's contribution is relatively small and lags far behind the contribution of the public and private sectors.

- In *day care*, the voluntary sector has retained a strong position in recent years, and is the only field of the three in which it ranks ahead of the private sector, and approaches the scale of in-house services.

The remainder of this section reviews the most important sources of empirical evidence on the relative contribution of voluntary sector providers to each form of care. Unfortunately, this evidence is heavily concentrated in just one form of care – residential homes – but an attempt will be made to extract as much as possible from research undertaken in other forms of care.

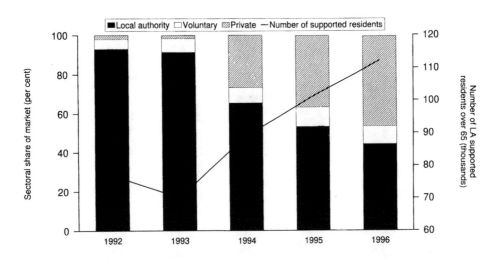

*Figure 5.1 Local authority funded residential care for elderly people, 1992–96: supported resident numbers*

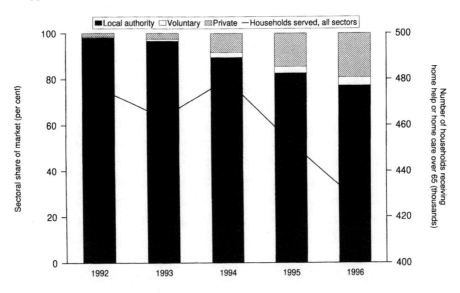

*Figure 5.2 Local authority funded domiciliary care for elderly people, 1992–96: households served*

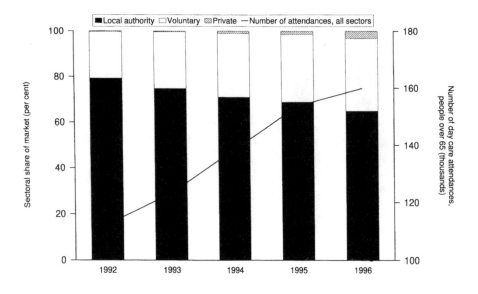

*Figure 5.3 Local authority funded day care for elderly people, 1992–96:average number of attendances*

### Shared features of the voluntary sector's contribution to residential, domiciliary and day care

First, there is perhaps one important generalisation that can be made about how the voluntary sector systematically differs from the private sector, and two concerning how it differs from both the public and private sectors across all three forms of care. The first is the relative prevalence in the voluntary sector of *multi-field organisations*, which distinguishes it sharply from the private sector in which isolated small businesses are the norm. Second, and perhaps most obvious, on average voluntary sector providers have been operating much longer than either local authority providers or private sector providers. This reflects the *historical rootedness* of many voluntary establishments and organisations as described in the opening section. This strong voluntary sector track record, together with the extent to which it operates under a non-distribution constraint and a number of other factors to which we return below, have traditionally fuelled a belief amongst local authority purchasers that providers in the voluntary sector in general are more trustworthy than private organisations.

Third, the *average dependency of elderly people has typically been relatively low in the voluntary sector.* The effect is most obvious in residential care where surveys throughout the 1980s and 1990s have repeatedly shown that the average dependency in terms of incontinence, mobility, mental frailty and so on, of both existing residents and new admissions, is much lower in voluntary homes than in local authority or private homes. In domiciliary care, hours per client is the only proxy for dependency available across all three sectors. These data suggest that, since 1992, the private sector has consistently catered for relatively dependent elderly people compared with the voluntary or local authority sector. The voluntary sector on average provides slightly more hours per client than the local authority sector, which could be indicative of slightly more dependent clients in the former sector, although the difference is quite small. Finally, the study of day care in the early 1980s found that attendees at voluntary sector facilities were considerably less dependent than those who attended public sector facilities.

There are, nevertheless, at least three ways in which evidence suggests that the nature of the voluntary sector's contribution varies according to the type of care. First, *voluntary sector care agencies provide a qualitatively different service, but the way in which this difference is apparent varies according to the type of care.* In their analysis of residential care, Wistow *et al.* (1995) first of all considered internal employment patterns. They found that staff:resident ratios differed systematically between sectors, with more full-time staff but fewer part-time staff per resident in the voluntary sector. And although voluntary sector homes tended to have fewer care staff with a social work qualification per resident than private sector homes, they had more qualified nursing staff and ancillary staff per resident.

Research has also been undertaken on the array of external services offered to care home residents. Voluntary sector facilities are more likely than private sector homes to arrange day/evening outings, social evenings and (most significantly different) a range of 'other activities' for their clients (Darton, personal communication, 1997); moreover, analysis of a large-scale survey of care home residents showed that those in the voluntary sector homes were actually taking up the wider social and recreational opportunities made available to them, with greater attendance at day centres and social clubs than residents of the private sector and residents in public sector facilities (Kavanagh and Knapp 1997). Finally, there appear to be differences between the private and voluntary sector in admissions policy and client selection: voluntary sector homes are significantly more likely to restrict admissions to clients from particular professional, ethnic or religious backgrounds, leading to a different environment or ethos for elderly people in those homes (Wistow *et al.* 1995). Interestingly, however, voluntary sector homes are not significantly more likely than private sector homes to discriminate formally through an admissions policy on the grounds of dependency. We might speculatively reconcile this with the earlier observation concerning the lower average rates of dependency in the voluntary sector reported above either by positing that voluntary sector homes are more likely to operate a covert, informal admissions policy in favour of less dependent clients, or by suggesting that clients may choose, or tend to be referred, into voluntary residential care when they are less dependent.

Evidence outside residential care is unfortunately very limited, but it is perhaps worth reporting that in the case of (local authority-funded) domiciliary care, voluntary providers appear to be considerably less likely to offer some services, most noticeably day sitting, night sitting, night sleeping and live-in services, than their counterparts in the private sector. Similarly, in day care, Carter's (1981) study found that the voluntary sector was providing more limited physical treatment for users, this time in comparison with public sector provision (cited in Knapp and Missiakoulis 1982, p.342). These patterns are of course likely to be connected to the systematic variation in client dependency by sector to which we have referred, and this has to be taken into consideration when comparing the costs of provision according to sector (see below).

Second, and most obviously, there is a distinction as between the use of unpaid labour: *volunteering is not evenly distributed across the different forms of care.* To be more specific, it can be estimated that in 1995, only around 1.5 per cent of all people volunteering to work on behalf of elderly people were working internally within residential care homes. Unfortunately, however, there appears to be no reliable way of determining how those of the 98.5 per cent rump of volunteers that are involved in direct service provision are distributed as between day care, domiciliary care or other services. There is, however, some case study and anecdotal evidence to suggest that (at least as far as state-funded care is concerned), volunteer supply is heavily concentrated in day care and relatively sparse in domiciliary care. Gaskin and colleagues, in an evaluation of volunteer programmes, have reported that:

> projects (across client groups) primarily provided day care or activities based in centres (58 per cent), while only a quarter offered domiciliary care. Recruiting volunteers to visit and support clients in their own homes, while not impossible, has been shown by the research to be inherently more difficult than centre-based activity ... this is especially true of a significant proportion of the volunteers are unemployed people looking for something to do and not initially committed to the client group. (cited in Robbins 1993, p.91)

Similarly, Ware's study of voluntary sector domiciliary care projects found that, while some schemes did involve volunteers, many did not. One reason for this, according to the organisations she studied, was that 'people prefer to volunteer to meet people and get out of their own homes and so volunteering to be alone with an elderly person in a domestic environment may not be popular' (1997, p.222). Gaskin *et al.* (cited in Robbins 1993) also imply that client dependency appears to affect the supply of volunteers, commenting that 'the more demanding the volunteer–client relationship, the fewer volunteers in the scheme'. Given that (on average) high levels of dependency are to be found in residential care, lower levels in domiciliary care and the lowest levels of all in day care, this observation is also consistent with volunteers' revealed preference for work in day care.

A third major difference follows at least in part from the first and second point, and is that the *voluntary sector's relative cost, and the causes thereof, vary according to the form of care, as well as its scale.* That is, the voluntary sector's relative costliness and pricing appears to depend on whether one focuses on residential, day or domiciliary care, and also on the size of the provider unit. The main limitation of this evidence is that it has not yet been possible directly to incorporate measures of 'final output' – the welfare of elderly recipients of care, their carers, and welfare-relevant external effects. Thus, it is *not* possible to comment definitively on the relative efficiency of the voluntary sector because no studies have yet combined measures of user welfare with comprehensive marginal social opportunity costings in the theoretically correct manner (Knapp 1984). Moreover, thorough cost and charging function analyses to date have been confined to comparisons of the private and public sectors in residential care – which have found the former to be less costly (Knapp 1984; Bebbington and Darton 1995); and a comparison of the public and voluntary sector in day care, to which we return below.

While less than ideal, there is nevertheless some evidence relating to the voluntary sector in the residential care field. Our own recent study was able to examine the relevance of sector on the charges made by sample of 63 independent residential care homes (Wistow *et al.* 1995). We found that, *ceteris paribus* (including having taken account of the lower dependency of clients in voluntary sector homes), voluntary homes' charges were significantly lower than those of private sector homes. Why was this the case? We have seen that voluntary sector homes receive very little input from volunteers; moreover, what is received is scarcely different from those received by private sector homes. In addition, private giving, the most obvious source of financial subsidy, appears to be a relatively unimportant source of income for them (Kendall 1996b). It therefore appears that cost advantages comes from other sources.

One possible explanation is suggested by considering how provider *motivations* vary systematically by sector. In an analysis of data collected in this same study, Kendall and Forder (1997) have shown how, if hypothetically presented with identical demand and cost conditions, voluntary sector providers, on average, would systematically behave differently from private sector providers, placing less weight on the pursuit of profit as an organisational objective and thus 'marking up' price for any given level of cost to a lesser extent. The paper also summarises evidence from face-to-face interviews that voluntary sector providers are more 'altruistic' than their private sector counterparts in the sense that they claim to be more motivated by a particularistic sense of duty and commitment – although this finding is less robust since it cannot be confirmed through inference.

Another contributory factor could be that voluntary providers do not, in fact, face the same cost structures as private firms, but for reasons other than differential access to volunteers or private giving, still have a cost advantage. Relative flexibility in the deployment of *paid* labour is one possibility, but there is in fact little or no evidence available in wage differentials. An exception is provided by recent sectoral analysis of the Quarterly Labour Force Survey, the main source of labour market data in the UK. Interestingly, this suggests that rates of pay in social care services – including those paid to the 'care assistants' who account for the bulk of the paid human resource input into residential care (Local Government Management Board and Central Council for Education and Training in Social Work 1997b) – are *higher* in the voluntary sector than the private sector, although less than in the public sector (Almond and Kendall 1998).

A cost difference may also stem from the different structural features and activities of providers which are outlined earlier in this section; relevant aspects are summarised in Box 5.2. These would appear to present them with, at least, more *opportunities* than private providers to keep prices relatively low; existing

---

**Box 5.2 Non-labour structural reasons why voluntary agencies may be positioned to charge lower prices in residential care**

- Access to income earned from endowments or through fundraising.

- Exploitation of the greater *potential* for *cross-field cross-subsidy* available to voluntary bodies, and the achievement of economies of scope.

- The achievement of economies of scale through voluntary agencies' larger size (although it could be that as size increases, scale diseconomies outweigh scale economies).

- Greater reliance placed on externally provided care could mean that these costs are not borne directly by the home, and therefore do not have to be factored into pricing. (If the costs are borne by the same organisation, which runs both the care home and provides the external care, then we have the cross-subsidisation referred to above, rather than cost-shunting.)

---

evidence does not allow us to ascertain the relative importance of these factors. Outside residential care, no work has yet been done, for example, to explore how motivations vary by sector. But in the case of day care, a thorough evaluation of the voluntary sector's relative cost effectiveness have been made, albeit in comparison with the public sector only (Knapp and Missiakoulis 1982). This study found that, after controlling for all relevant cost related factors, voluntary sector day care providers were more cost effective than their public sector counterparts, but that this effect was conditional on the relatively small size of the former's facilities. The cost functions suggested that voluntary sector facilities would quickly lose this advantage if run at high attendance levels, and the authors attributed the relative efficiency of small-scale voluntary sector provision to their comparative advantage in access to regular volunteers. This, it is argued, occurs both because their relative lack of formality and proportionately lower burden of management and care makes them relatively attractive environments in which to volunteer, and also because of limits to volunteer availability. With a fixed or inelastic supply of volunteers, homes seeking to expand would not, it is implied, be able to mobilise a proportionate increase in the scale of volunteering even if some way were found of retaining the informal character and low management and care burden of smaller scale operations.

Finally, a rather different picture again emerges if attention is focused on (local authority-funded) domiciliary care. As with residential care, the evidence is limited to prices rather than directly measured costs, but in this case, we find that *ceteris paribus*, voluntary sector providers' charges are significantly higher than those in the private sector, with multivariate analysis showing that, other things being equal, the mean price charged by voluntary sector providers was some 20 per cent *higher* than the mean charge made by private sector agencies. This could be connected to problems with volunteering for those organisations which deploy, as their involvement usually brings costs as well as benefits (Knapp, Koutsogeorgopoulou and Davis Smith 1995); motivational factors may be different than in residential care, although the analysis which might show this has yet to be undertaken; it could also be the case that voluntary organisations are not taking advantage of opportunities (see Box 5.2) to cross-subsidise this form of care to the extent that they may be cross-subsidising residential care. However, there are problems with these comparisons, partly because they have been unable to develop a shadow 'price' paid by purchasers for services provided under grant arrangements; and partly because the voluntary sector services often appear to be so completely different from their private sector counterparts. It may, therefore, be more appropriate to regard much voluntary sector provision as not just providing a qualitatively different service, but as operating in a completely separate market (Forder *et al.* 1996). An example here would be voluntary sector carers' organisations, which appear to have no equivalent in the private sector.

## Concluding comment: the UK voluntary sector in comparative context

This chapter has described the historical and recent evolution of the voluntary sector in the delivery of care services for elderly people, and sought to tease out what makes these services different from the bulk of care provided by the private and public sectors (alongside, of course, the massive fourth sector of households and informal care interactions). However, the voluntary sector's contribution is clearly of considerable importance in the mixed economy with its involvement bringing advantages and disadvantages to the system in which it operates. On the positive side, it has traditionally been seen (justifiably or not) as relatively trustworthy by local public purchasers; its existence has clearly expanded choice at least for those elderly people who meet its varied admissions criteria, offering an alternative peer group mix and ethos; it has apparently charged relatively low prices in some contexts, and enabled some cost savings to be achieved by public purchasers. It has also provided institutional expression for a range of motivations and behaviours for both managers and volunteers. More negatively, and in many ways the other side of the same coin, at least some voluntary provision appears to be socially exclusive, relatively costly in certain contexts beyond certain bounds of scale and, perhaps in some cases, only in a position to achieve any apparent cost advantages through 'cost-shunting' to other providers. It remains to see how this balance between costs and benefits will develop as the new system of contracting for care develops.

In fact, the UK voluntary sector plays a relatively minor role in the delivery of social care services for elderly people in comparison with many other parts of Europe. Perhaps three reasons can be suggested. First, in those countries institutional and ideological barriers to combining profit with care have played a major role in placing private sector care off limits as far as public sponsorship is concerned, so that practically all independent social entrepreneurship has occurred through the non-profit form. The UK's 'experiment' with what were effectively central government sponsored non-sector-specific demand-side 'vouchers' for residential care during the 1980s – which opened the door to the rapid expansion of social entrepreneurship in the *private* sector – was not paralleled in other countries.

Second, and related, the existence of the principle of subsidiarity in welfare in those countries has tended to privilege services delivered by the churches over the state and the market on the assumption that the former is necessarily more responsive to members' needs, even if the state has assumed responsibility for funding that care (Kendall with Almond 1998). Clearly, no such durable, guiding principle can be said to have animated public decision making across time and locales in the recent history of care for older people in the UK.

A third factor which distinguishes the UK sharply from other central European countries has been its lack of a minimum wage framework to protect low-paid workers until very recently. In particular, care workers are one of the most numerous categories of low-paid employees in service industries in Britain (Almond and Kendall 2000). Given the labour intensive nature of care for elderly people, the possibility of paying relatively low wages to these employees may have been an important ingredient in making social care a viable activity for private small business in the UK, but not in many other parts of the world.

## References

Almond, S. and Kendall, J. (2000) 'Low pay in the UK: The case for a three sector comparative approach.' *Annals of Public and Cooperative Economics.* Publication forthcoming.

Audit Commission (1986) *Making a Reality of Community Care.* London: HMSO.

Baldock, J. and Ungerson, C. (1993) 'Consumer perceptions of an emerging mixed economy of care.' In A. Evers and I. Svetlik (eds) *Balancing Pluralism: New Welfare Mixed in Care for the Elderly.* Aldershot: Avebury.

Barclay, P.M. (1982) *Social Workers: Their Roles and Tasks.* London: National Institute for Social Work/Bedford Square Press.

Bebbington, A. and Darton, R. (1995) 'Alternatives to long-stay hospital care for elderly people in London.' *Discussion Paper 1,* 139. Canterbury: Personal Social Services Research Unit, University of Kent.

Brenton, M. (1985) *The Voluntary Sector in British Social Services.* Harlow: Longman.

Carter, J. (1981) *Day Services for Adults.* London: George Allen and Unwin.

Darton, R. (1997) *Personal communication from Robin Darton,* Personal Social Services Research Unit, University of Kent at Canterbury.

Davis Smith, J. (1998) *The 1997 National Survey of Volunteering.* London: Institute for Volunteering Research/National Centre for Volunteering.

Department of Health (1997) *Community Care Statistics 1996: Day and Domiciliary Personal Social Services for Adults, England. Statistical Bulletin 1997/8,* Department of Health, London.

Ernst and Whinney, Management Consultants (1986) *Survey of Private and Voluntary Sector Residential and Nursing Homes for the DHSS.* London: Ernst and Whinney.

Evandrou, M., Failkingham, J. and Glennerster, H. (1990) 'The personal social services: Everybody's poor relation and nobody's baby.' In J. Hills (ed) *The State of Welfare.* Oxford: Clarendon Press.

Forder, J., with Knapp, M. and Kendall, J. (1996) *Purchasing Domiciliary Care: Provider Characteristics and Competition.* Provider Study II draft internal report to the Department of Health, London.

George, V. (1996) 'The future of the welfare state.' In V. George and P. Taylor-Gooby (eds) *European Welfare Policy: Squaring the Welfare Circle.* Basingstoke: Macmillan.

Griffiths, R. (1988) *Community Care: Agenda for Action.* London: HMSO.

Kavanagh, S. and Knapp, M. (1997) 'The costs of external services for elderly people living in institutions.' In A. Netten and J. Dennett (eds) *Unit Costs of Health and Social Care.* Canterbury: Personal Social Services Research Unit, University of Kent.

Kendall, J. (1996b) 'The scale and funding of voluntary provision: Care for elderly people in context.' *MEOC Bulletin Number 4,* 16–17. Canterbury: Personal Social Services Research Unit, University of Kent.

Kendall, J. and Forder, J. (1997) 'The Theory and Practice of Provider Motivation in Contracted Social Care Markets.' Unpublished manuscript, Personal Social Services Research Unit, London School of Economics and Political Science, London.

Kendall, J. and Knapp, M. (1996) *The Voluntary Sector in the UK.* Manchester: Manchester University Press.

Kendall, J. with Almond, S. (1998) *The UK Voluntary (Third) Sector in Comparative Perspective: Exceptional Growth and Transformation.* London: Personal Social Services Unit, London School of Economics.

Klein, R. (1995) *The New Politics of the NHS.* London: Longman.

Knapp, M. (1984) *The Economics of Social Care.* Basingstoke: Macmillan.

Knapp, M. and Missiakoulis (1982) 'Inter-sectoral cost comparisons: day care for the elderly.' *Journal of Social Policy 11,* 335–54.

Knapp, M., Koutsogeorgopoulou, V. and Davis Smith, J. (1995) *Who Volunteers and Why? The Key Factors which Determine Volunteering.* Voluntary Action Research Third Series Paper 3, Volunteer Centre UK, Berkhamsted.

Local Government Management Board and Central Council for Education and Training in Social Work (1997b) *Independent Sector Workforce Survey 1996.* London: LGMB and CCETSW.

Mocroft, I. and Thomason, C. (1993) 'The evolution of community care and voluntary organisations.' In S. Saxon-Harrold and J. Kendall (eds) *Researching the Voluntary Sector, 1.* Tonbridge: Charities Aid Foundation.

Morton (1990) *Packages of Care for Elderly People: How Can the Voluntary Sector Contribute?* Proceedings of an ageing update conference, 1 December 1989, University of London Students' Union, London.

Robbins, D. (ed) (1993) *Community Care: Findings From DH-funded Research 1988–1992.* London: HMSO.

Seebohm Report (1968) *Report of the Committee on Local Authority and Allied Personal Social Services.* Cmnd 3703. London: HMSO.

Smith, S. and Lipsky, M. (1993) *Nonprofits for Hire: The Welfare State in the Age of Contracting.* London: Harvard University Press.

Tinker, A. (1992) *Elderly People in Modern Society.* London: Longman.

Waddington and Henwood (1996) *Going Home: Report of an Evaluation of the British Red Cross Home from Hospital Scheme.* London: British Red Cross.

Ware, P. (1997) Independent domiciliary services and the reform of community care. Unpublished PhD thesis. Sheffield: Department of Law, University of Sheffield.

Wistow, G., Knapp, M., Hardy, B. and Allen, C. (1994) *Social Care in a Mixed Economy.* Buckingham: Open University Press.

Wistow, G., Hardy, B., Forder, J., Kendall, J. and Knapp, M. (1995) 'Provider Study 1: Independent Sector Providers of Residential Care: Activities, Motivations and Behaviour.' Draft internal report to the Department of Health, London.

Wistow, G., Knapp, M., Hardy, B., Forder, J. and Kendall, J. (1996) *Social Care Markets: Progress and Prospects.* Buckingham: Open University Press.

Wolfenden Report (1978) *The Future of Voluntary Organisations.* London: Croom Helm.

# CHAPTER 6

# Human Resources in Social Care

*Susan Balloch and John McLean*

## Introduction

In his retirement address to the Association of Directors of Social Services in April 1998, Sir Herbert Laming reflected on the fundamental changes that had taken place in social care services in recent years. Staff had been asked 'to assess, provide and arrange care for a much wider range of social care needs resulting from changes in health care, the transfer of funding for long term care, from the Department of Social Security and changes in the family'. As a result he noted 'very few people will go through life without having contact with social care either for themselves, a member of their family or neighbour. Fundamentally it is this change which underpins the large and growing social services and social care workforce.' The subsequent White Paper (Department of Health 1998) has also confirmed that social services are for all of us and do not just support a small number of 'social casualties' (p.5).

Over a million people are employed in social work and social care in the United Kingdom. The Labour Force Survey for Spring 1997 recorded 430,000 employed in the statutory sector, 227,000 in the voluntary sector and 316,000 in the private sector (Local Government Management Board and the Central Council for Education and Training in Social Work 1997). To paid staff should be added the many thousands of unpaid volunteers and an estimated 5.7m informal carers (Office for National Statistics 1995).

Paid staff are mostly women working in residential and home care. About half of these work part time. The Labour Force Survey recorded 84 per cent of women in the 'social work industry', and 47 per cent of all staff working part time. The gender distribution is uneven across statutory, voluntary and private sectors, with few men employed in the private sector. This is mainly because men are not attracted to residential or home care work, the areas in which private sector expansion has been concentrated since 1984. Men are, however, over-represented in senior management with only 28 per cent of senior women managers in 1997 (Local Government Management Board 1998). This is a mature workforce, with staff entering social work or social care at around the age of 30. Overall, it is also relatively low paid (Balloch, Fisher and McLean 1999).

Qualified social workers form only a small minority of this workforce. A survey of qualified social workers aged under 55 at the time of the 1991 Census suggested there were 53,000 resident in England, of which 80 per cent were working in social services, 13 per cent in other fields and 7 per cent not at all. Three-quarters of all qualified social workers were working for local authority social services departments. Of the rest, 11 per cent were working for the probation service and 8 per cent for voluntary organisations (Smyth 1996). This is a very different situation from, for example, that in the United States, where the majority of qualified social workers are employed by voluntary organisations and there is also a substantial group of freelance workers (Gibelman and Schervish 1996). Given the changes in service provision, we need to consider if, in due course, this pattern might increasingly be reflected here.

The social care workforce provides care and support for a wide range of service users. Expenditure by the statutory social services in England gives a reasonably accurate picture of the distribution of services, with 49.4 per cent of the total budget of £7,942.9 million spent on elderly people, 23.1 per cent on children, 13 per cent on people with learning disabilities, 7 per cent on those with physical disabilities, 5 per cent on those with mental illnesses and 2.4 per cent on other adults (Department of Health 1998).

The pattern of service provision, as described in previous chapters, is, however, changing rapidly. Although local authorities are still the main providers of services such as home care, day centres and meals on wheels, the increase of voluntary and private sector providers has been pronounced and these now employ two-thirds of social care staff (LGMB/CCETSW 1997). There has been striking growth in the independent provision of residential care. Local authorities now own only 12 per cent of places in residential and nursing homes (Department of Health 1997). The Independent Sector Workforce Survey 1996 represented the first detailed attempt at estimating levels of employment in residential and nursing homes within the independent sector. It showed 487,000 people working in residential and nursing homes in England in 1996 (LGMB 1997). While the domiciliary market has been slower to develop, almost half of local authority home care services are now contracted out to private providers (Department of Health 1999).

With provision growing in the voluntary and private sectors, and the retrenchment of local authority provision, the working conditions of staff are changing. Effects on service delivery and service users have still to be assessed, though many service users remain dissatisfied with the outcomes (Balloch 1998). Concerns have already been voiced about lower rates of pay in the independent sector and fewer benefits for staff (Clark, Dyer and Horwood 1998) and the employment of increasing numbers of agency staff in all sectors (Goodenough 1996; McCurry 1998).

Until recently, little was known about the working experiences of social services and social care staff in either statutory or independent voluntary and private sectors. While the latter two sectors remain relatively unresearched, more is now understood about the statutory sector as a result of a research programme carried out at the National Institute for Social Work (NISW) between 1992 and 1997. We will now turn therefore to the findings of these studies of the social services workforce in England, Scotland and Northern Ireland (Balloch *et al.* 1999).

## Human resources under pressure

The NISW workforce studies focused on four broad 'job types': managers, social work staff, home care workers and residential workers. Social services managers have remained curiously marginal to research on either social care or management (Balloch *et al.* 1999). Social work staff have been more extensively investigated with Smyth's study (1996) giving an overview of the social work labour force under 55 (in 1993), and providing valuable data on the career longevity of social workers (74% were then working as social workers and had always done so since qualification) and on the motivations of staff not currently in service. Using CCETSW employment survey data to explore longer term patterns in social workers' careers, Lyons has raised issues about, for example, the gender composition of this category of the workforce given the declining numbers of male recruits (Lyons, Valle and Grimwood 1995), and the 'Ready to Practise?' studies in England and Scotland conducted by Marsh and Triseliotis have examined a wide range of factors affecting the readiness to practise of newly qualified social workers (Marsh and Triseliotis 1996). Home care staff, the largest group of all care staff, have been least researched of all. Studies of residential workers have focused mainly on the quality of care in children's homes (Sinclair and Gibbs 1996), the low level of qualifications amongst staff (Lane 1994; Hills *et al.* 1997; Lane 1994; McLean and Andrew 1998) and the level of violence (Brown, Bute and Ford 1986; Norris and Kedward 1990; Joseph Rowntree Foundation 1995). However, the work experience of the majority of staff, care assistants in residential homes for older people, a workforce in many ways similar to home care workers, has not been the subject of the same level of investigation (Qureshi and Pahl 1992).

The NISW studies involved two waves of interviews, carried out between 1994 and 1996, with a sample which included 940 staff from five local authority social services departments in England, 317 staff from two social work departments in Scotland and 320 staff from the four health and social service boards and their trusts in Northern Ireland.

Strikingly similar employment conditions and work experiences were found across the three areas for each 'job type'. Nearly all men worked full time, but about half of all women worked part time. Almost all managers worked full time, as did between 80 and 90 per cent of social work staff, but, in contrast, most home care staff worked part time, except in one local authority in England which had a policy to employ only full-time home care staff. The widest variation between the three study areas was found among residential workers, with over a third in England working part time but only around 10 per cent in Scotland and Northern Ireland. The extent of part-time working is important because it is associated with lower levels of pay and restricted career development. However, new part-time workers, who are mainly qualified and experienced and become part-time through job sharing to, for example, raise children or take a degree, do have much higher pay and access to training and career development than 'old/traditional' part-time workers (Edwards and Robinson 1998, p.13).

As would be expected, managers and social work staff earned considerably more than residential and home care staff. There was some evidence of very low rates of pay for home care staff. Differences in pay were also found between men and women in full-time work, with men earning more than women in each job type. The differences between these 'professional' staff and the much larger group of home care and residential staff were marked. A majority of home care staff worked part time for low rates of pay, held few educational qualifications and virtually no professional qualifications. Residential staff were only slightly better paid and educated, with the exception of those in Northern Ireland, where a special programme had been put in place for residential child care staff to raise standards and reduce staff turnover. It is worth noting that direct care staff more often felt that their own life experiences rather than training were important, whereas professional staff more often sought formal training.

In spite of low pay, levels of satisfaction among home care staff were the highest of all those working in the social services. In their work they found rewards in the close nature of the caring relationship and from seeing direct results in return for their efforts. In fact, for all staff satisfaction was gained from the services delivered, marred mainly by the lack of necessary resources. What emerged from the studies was a picture of a highly committed, mature and stable workforce which placed value on the personal nature of social services work.

There were, however, warnings that staff were working under considerable pressure. Four major and interrelated features of this – workplace stress, abuse and violence from service users and relatives, racism from service users and colleagues, and change in the workplace – were identified and will now be considered in turn.

*Stress*

It has become so commonplace to talk about 'stress' that it is easy to forget that it is an inevitable component of any sort of stimulating experience, good or bad. In social services, recent court cases have highlighted the worst aspects of stress (North 1996) and have painted a dismal picture of some social workers' experiences. Findings from the workforce survey confirmed that experiences of stress were widespread in social services, affecting four out of five managers and field social work staff and about two-thirds of residential workers (McLean 1999). Although home care staff were less affected, up to half of English home care staff reported experiences of stress. Major sources of stress were the inability to provide service users with what they needed, having accountability or responsibility without power, and feeling out of sympathy with the way the service was run, frustration at game playing and office politics and uncertainty about the future. In line with other research findings (Ross 1993; Thompson *et al.* 1996) most stress was caused by aspects of work that were outside the individual's control.

Combining work and family responsibilities was another source of stress. The workforce studies showed that about a quarter of the workforce had caring responsibilities either for children or dependent adults. Staff with caring responsibilities, and especially those who were single parents with dependent children, experienced more overall stress in their lives than those without dependants (Ginn and Sandell 1997). The current insistence of central government on family friendly policies may break down employers' previous resistance to appreciating the complex interface between work and family life.

Levels of stress were measured using the 12-item General Health Questionnaire (GHQ12) at each interview. Mean scores for groups were calculated, with a score of 2.00 or over indicating possible psychological distress (Figure 6.1a). Figure 6.1b gives the mean GHQ12 scores for women and men. Stress levels were generally higher than those found in the British Household Panel Study (Buck *et al.* 1994) and seem to indicate that stress is higher for social services staff than for other occupational groups and that it may affect them differently from other workers (McLean 1999).

High levels of stress in a workforce are often associated with absence from work, or sick leave. In the workforce studies, social services reflected the pattern of sick leave in other sectors and in local government, as reported by the CBI and the Local Government Management Board (Norris 1995) with about 10 per cent or less having more than ten days off in a year. However, categories of staff with over ten days sick leave in a year showed higher mean GHQ scores, even though these staff reported little stress-related sick leave. There is a strong suggestion, therefore, that stress at work is directly linked to extensive absence

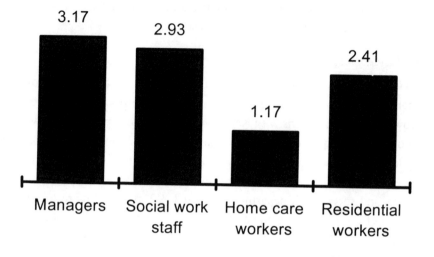

*Figure 6.1a Mean GHQ12 scores by job type*

*Figure 6.1b Mean GHQ12 scores for job type and gender*

from work. Given this, one might expect employers to have clearly established and well-managed procedures for helping staff to cope with workplace stress, but in social services, by and large, this is still not the case.

*Verbal abuse, threats and violence*

Previous studies have provided substantial evidence of abuse and violence experienced by those working in the social services, especially social workers (Brown *et al.* 1986; Norris with Kedward 1990). In both pilot interviews and responses to the questionnaire, those interviewed for the workforce studies confirmed such findings, showing that 'violence, threats of violence and verbal abuse are very much part of the working lives of those employed by social services and social work departments' (Pahl 1999, p.103). Figure 6.2 shows responses from staff in England and Scotland to a question asking if they had been attacked or physically abused, threatened, shouted at or insulted in their current job. Staff in residential homes were particularly at risk.

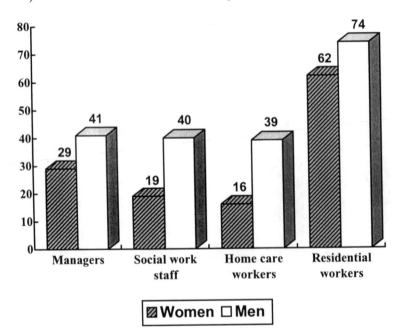

figure 6.2 *Responses to question 'Have you ever been physically attacked in your current job?'*

In general, men were more likely than women to have experienced any of these incidents. Overall in England a fifth of men had experienced physical attacks compared with a tenth of women. While this was partly because of the higher proportion of women in home care, the type of work in which staff are least likely to experience abuse or violence, the gender effect was clear among management, social workers and residential workers. The reasons for this are complex, but may stem from service users perceiving male staff as more threatening and female workers being more skilled at deflecting and defusing violence (Pahl 1999).

Asked about the most recent incident experienced, staff described these as most commonly occurring in the building where they worked, in a service user's home or in their office. Most incidents had taken place in the daytime, with late morning being the most typical time for the assault. Service users with mental health problems or learning difficulties were more likely to be physically violent than any other group, and children were the most likely to shout at or verbally abuse staff. In nearly a quarter of incidents, the person responsible for the abuse was not the service user but a relative.

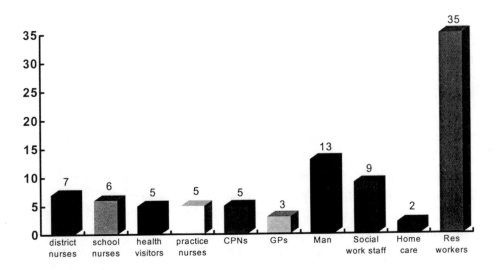

*Figure 6.3 Physical attacks in different occupations*

Pahl shows that working for social services represents a relatively dangerous occupational choice. As shown in Figure 6.3, comparison with nurses, health visitors and general practitioners reveals that 'Social care is more dangerous than any health service profession, in terms of violence and threats of violence, with the possible exception of community psychiatric nursing, and working in residential social care, particularly with young people, is much more dangerous, exposing the employee to even higher levels of physical violence and threats of violence' (Pahl 1999, p.103). As with stress, those interviewed in the workforce studies thought managers should be taking more steps to protect staff from violence and provide proper support when a violent incident had taken place.

It is in residential work that staff are most at risk of violence. While the evidence quoted above all relates to the statutory sector, it is likely that staff in the private sector have similar experiences too. Given the rapid growth of the independent residential sector, we need to feel concerned for those staff, especially if they are relatively young and inexperienced. In this context, central government's decision (*Guardian* 23 October 1998) to introduce a new programme of training and qualification for all residential workers is timely and appropriate.

*Racism*

Figures collected for the first time on the ethnicity of senior staff in England by the Local Government Management Board show 4 per cent of these staff from ethnic minorities (LGMB 1997). At the time of writing there is only one black social services director in England. The previous lack of ethnic minority monitoring in personnel records has meant that information about black, Asian and other ethnic minority workers in the social care workforce has remained patchy. It is generally established, however, that these are concentrated in the lowest grades, most commonly in residential work (Dutt 1992) with limited access to training and promotion (White 1998). This was confirmed in the workforce studies where, in England, at first interview only 6 per cent of black staff were managers while 43 per cent worked in residential care, compared respectively with 11 per cent and 27 per cent of white staff (Davey 1997). Black staff were also found to be significantly younger than their white colleagues, with nearly half of all black staff aged under 40 in comparison with less than a

users, unless provision is also made to protect staff in statutory, voluntary and private sectors from the stresses and strains this chapter has described.

## Conclusions

Since the Labour government came to power in May 1997 radical policy initiatives have continued to alter the landscape within which the caring services work, demanding 'partnership in action' to break down traditional barriers between professionals and services and meet the needs of service users and communities more holistically. This challenge to health authorities, social services and other agencies is closely linked to the fight against social exclusion and the search for a 'third way' in which to provide 'best value' welfare services. While in some respects social services have been marginalised in favour of health, education and employment agencies, their role in the provision of care services has been acknowledged and reaffirmed in the White Paper. 'Institutional change' it states, 'is essential to improve standards and public confidence and to give those working in social care a new status which fits the work they do' (p.85). We have to hope that change will also minimise the difficulties that those working in social care face on a daily basis.

## References

Balloch, S. (ed) (1998) *Outcomes of Social Care: A Question of Quality.* Social Services Policy Forum Paper No. 6. London: National Institute for Social Work.

Balloch, S., Fisher, M. and McLean, J. (eds) (1999) *Social Services: Working Under Pressure.* Bristol: Policy Press.

Beishon, S., Virdee, S. and Hagell, A. (1995) *Nursing in a Multi-Ethnic NHS.* London: PSI.

Brown, R., Bute, S. and Ford, P. (1986) *Social Workers at Risk: The Prevention and Management of Violence.* London: Macmillan.

Buck, N., Gershuny, J., Rose, D. and Scott, J. (1994) *Changing Households: The British Household Panel Survey 1990–1992.* Colchester: University of Essex.

Butt, J. and Davey, B. (1997) 'The experiences of Black staff in the social services.' In M. May, E. Brunsdon and G. Craig (eds) *Social Policy Review No. 9.* London: Social Policy Association.

Butt, J. and Mirza, K. (1996) *Social Care and Black Communities.* London: HMSO.

Clark, H., Dyer, S. and Horwood, J. (1998) *That Bit of Help.* Bristol: Policy Press.

Davey, B. (1997) 'The experiences of Black staff.' In Balloch *et al.*, *The Social Services Workforce in Transition.* London: National Institute for Social Work.

Davey, B. (1999) 'Discrimination at work.' In S. Balloch, J. McLean and M. Fisher (eds) *Social Services: Working Under Pressure.* Bristol: The Polity Press.

Department of Health (1998) *Modernising Social Services: Promoting Independence, Improving Protection, Raising Standards.* Cm 4169. London: The Stationery Office.

Department of Health (1998a) *Personal Social Services Current and Capital Expenditure in England: 1996–97, Bulletin 1998/22.* North Yorkshire: DoH.

Department of Health (1998b) *Personal Social Services Staff of Social Services Departments at 30 September 1997 England.* London: DoH.

Department of Health (1999) *Health and Personal Social Services Statistics England 1998.* Government Statistical Service.

Dutt, R. (1992) 'The harsh reality for care assistants.' *Community Care,* 26 October.

Edwards, C.Y. and Robinson, O. (1998) *'Better' Part Time Jobs? A Study of Part Time Working in Two Essential Services.* Kingston: School of Human Resource Management, Kingston Business School, Kingston University.

Evans (1998) 'User empowerment and direct payments.' In S. Balloch (ed) *Outcomes of Social Care: A Question of Quality?* London: National Institute for Social Work.

Ford, J., Quilgars, D. and Rugg, J. (1998) *The Domiciliary Sector's Employment Practice and Potential.* York: Joseph Rowntree Foundation.

Gibelman, M. and Schervish, P.H. (1998) 'Social work and public social services practice: A status report.' In *Families in Society: The Journal of Contemporary Human Services.* New York: Families International.

Ginn, J. and Sandell, J. (1997) 'Balancing home and employment: Stress reported by social services staff.' *Work, Employment and Society,* 413–34.

Goodenough, A. (1996) *Covering the Gaps: A New Form of Brokerage.* London: Central Council for Education and Training in Social Work.

Harding, T. and Beresford, P. (1996) *The Standards We Expect.* London: National Institute for Social Work.

Inman, K. (1998) 'The return of union power? *Community Care,* 1–7 October, 18–19.

Hills, D., Child, C., Hills, J. and Blackburn, V. (1997) *Towards Qualified Leadership of Residential Child Care.* Summary Report on the Evaluation of the Residential Child Care Initiative. London: Evaluation Development and Review Unit, Tavistock Institute.

Joseph Rowntree Foundation Findings (1995) *Job Satisfaction and Dissatisfaction Among Residential Care Workers.* Social Care Research, No. 69.

Joseph Rowntree Foundation (1998) *The Domiciliary Care Sector's Employment Practice and Potential.*

Lane, D. (1994) *An Independent Review of the Residential Child Care Initiative.* London: Central Council for Education and Training in Social Work.

Lane, D. (1998) 'A crisis of identity?' *Community Care,* 3–9 September, 20–21.

Local Government Management Board (1997) *Social Services Workforce Analysis Main Report 1996 Survey.* London: LGMB/ADSS.

Local Government Management Board (1998) *Social Services Workforce Analysis Main Report, 1997 Survey.* London: LGMB/ADSS.

Local Government Management Board and the Central Council for Education and Training in Social Work (1997) *Human Resources for the Personal Social Services.* London: LGMB/CCETSW.

Lyons, K., Valle, I.L. and Grimwood, C. (1995) 'Career patterns of qualified social workers: Discussion of a recent survey.' *British Journal of Social Work 25,* 173–90.

Marsh, P. and Triseliotis, J. (1996) *Ready to Practise? Social Work and Probation Officers: Their Training and First Year in Work.* Aldershot: Avebury.

McCurry, P. (1998) 'Just passing through.' *Community Care,* 10–16 September, 18–21.

McLean, J. and Andrew, T. (1998) *Residential Workers and Qualifying Training: A Preliminary Investigation into the Careers of Residential Workers who Become Qualified.* London: National Institute for Social Work.

Norris, D., with Kedward, C. (1990) *Violence Against Social Workers: The Implications for Practice.* London: Jessica Kingsley Publishers.

Norris, P. (1995) 'Stress in the Workforce and Absenteeism.' Conference paper, *A Force for the Future: Research and Planning the Social Services Workforce,* London.

North, S.J. (1996) 'Stress: Counselling services.' *Community Care,* 31 October–6 November, 20–21.

Office for National Statistics (ONS) (1998) *Informal Carers.* London: The Stationery Office.

Pahl, J. (1999) 'Coping with physical violence and verbal abuse.' In S. Balloch, J. McLean and M. Fisher (eds) *Social Services: Working Under Pressure.* Bristol: The Polity Press.

Qureshi, H. and Pahl, J. (1992) *Research on the Social Services Workforce.* London: National Institute for Social Work.

Residential Forum (1998) *Training for Social Care: Achieving Standards for the Undervalued Service.* London: National Institute for Social Work.

Ross, E. (1993) 'Preventing burnout among social workers in the field of AIDS/HIV.' *Social Work Health Care 18,* No. 2, 99–108.

Sinclair, I. and Gibbs, I. (1996) *Quality of Care in Children's Homes: Working Paper Series B., No. 3.* York: Social Work Research and Development Unit, University of York.

Smyth, M. (1996) *Qualified Social Workers and Probation Officers,* Office of National Statistics. London: HMSO.

Thompson, N., Stradling, S., Murphy, M. and Neill, P.O. (1996) 'Stress and organisational culture.' *British Journal of Social Work 26,* No. 5, 647–66.

Turner, M. (1997/98) Interim and final reports for the 'Shaping Our Lives' project available from the Policy Unit, the National Institute for Social Work.

White, C. (1998) 'Will the glass ceiling shatter?' *Community Care,* 17–23 September, 18–19.

# CHAPTER 7

# The Changing Role of Users and Carers

*Julia Twigg*

This chapter explores the changing role of users and carers in the care system, reviewing the dominant discourses in relation to the main user groups, and asking what impact these have had on the development of services in the field. The chapter starts with the four main user or client groups, together with the new quasi-client group, carers, and then turns to explore two general models for the incorporation of users: user empowerment and consumerism.

## Disability movement

The dominant force within thinking about disability in the last two decades has been the Disabled Living Movement. Old accounts of disability, dominated by medical discourse, emphasised functional failure and individual limitation, presenting disability as a personal tragedy. By contrast the social model of disability, promoted by Oliver, Finkelstein, Morris and others, adopts a social constructionist perspective, seeing problems as lying not in the individual but in the disablist assumptions of wider society (Oliver 1990; Morris 1991, 1993; Campbell and Oliver 1996). Early work emphasised the environmental and social barriers that limit the capacity of disabled people to control their lives and engage with society on an equal basis. As Lindow and Morris argue:

> Independence is not linked to physical or intellectual capacity
> to care for oneself without assistance; independence is created
> by having assistance when and how one requires it. (1995, p.11)

It is a civil rights approach that emphasises the rights of disabled people to achieve independence rather than their 'need' for support and care.

From this critique flow a number of principles governing the involvement of users in service provision: first, the need to reject segregated – and usually by virtue of that – poor quality and stigmatising forms of provision. Second, control over services needs to be wrested from the hands of professionals – all too often patronising in their approach and focused on their own self-interest through the aggrandisement of services. Assessments should concentrate on capacities and choices, not on deficits and standardised responses. The voice of disabled people should be heard at all levels of the service system. Voluntary sector associations should be 'of' disabled people not 'for' disabled people. Assistance should be provided on a rights basis rather than subject to individual scrutiny and discretion. Benefits and services should be provided on a universalistic not means-tested basis, otherwise disabled people will remain the pauperised recipients of charity rather than the beneficiaries of rights. Most important, support should be provided in the form of cash not care. Disabled people should have control over the forms of help they receive, making choices as to how and on what to spend the money that is currently controlled by professionals and managers. They should be free to recruit, train and manage their own personal assistants rather than accept services and staff provided by local and health authorities (Morris 1993; Lindow and Morris 1995; Campbell and Oliver 1996).

The impact of this agenda, at least at the level of ideas, has been considerable. In the last two decades, there has been a great flowering of disability studies in the academic world, such that the ideas of the movement have now achieved a form of intellectual dominance. This has in turn impacted on the policy discourse, where disability movement ideas are increasingly widely articulated. At the level of practice, however, there have been considerable resistances – less in the form of articulated opposition than of entrenched barriers. Lindow and Morris (1995) recount a number of these in their analysis of user empowerment. Professionals are reluctant to lose the status and power that goes with assessing and determining services. Sometimes they prefer to talk to the family rather than those in need of help. Agencies reduplicate the culture of the institution in what are meant to be community-based facilities. Money is short and high-quality, non-stigmatising services are expensive. The need to ration remains the priority of the system.

Some disability movement ideas have been translated into policy initiatives – most notably in the form of 'direct payments' whereby disabled people under pensionable age have been given money to purchase and manage their own care services. Kestenbaum's evaluation of the earlier independent living fund suggested that people were able to improve their situations through the direct control of care providers (Kestenbaum 1996). As yet, the use of direct payments is limited to those of non-pensionable age (although the intention is to extend the scheme to pensioners) and the majority of services for disabled people are still delivered through the conventional service system. It is not yet clear how many disabled people will elect to manage their own services, but the fragmentation of the service system through the purchaser–provider split and its growing privatisation are likely to encourage such developments.

Some concerns have been expressed about the potential for abuse of both user and worker in direct payments. Established services screen and monitor staff and take over the responsibilities of employment. On the worker's side, they provide standard terms of employment and in the past, through the commitment of local authorities to good practice, terms that have been better than those in the private sector. Much of the flexibility and cheapness of personally arranged services are achieved at the cost of reducing the conditions of careworkers (though this process is already underway within the privatised services purchased by the local authority). Ungerson has pointed out the potential for exploitation that comes from the personal character of carework (Ungerson 1997). In general, theorists of the disability movement do not accept these criticisms or they regard them of lesser significance than the gains that come from direct control (Morris 1997).

More recently, theorists of disability have questioned the dominance of the social model, arguing that its emphasis on the social construction of disability has consigned impairment (and with it the body) to the theoretical shadows, leaving a significant part of the experience of disability untheorised and conceptually invisible (Shakespere 1994; Hughes and Paterson 1997). New work on disability has begun to look at the disabled body, and this has opened up space in which to challenge more directly the cultural representation of disabled people and the use of demeaning practices in which disabled people have been made subject to public and medical gaze (Lonsdale 1990; Morris 1993).

The disability movement is led by young physically disabled people and its ideas reflect the aspirations of that group. The majority of people with disabilities are older and their impairments tend to result from the chronic conditions of later life, such as arthritis and heart disease. The ideas of the disability movement have had much to contribute to their situations, but the movement itself is less reflective of their views. Disability activists are confident and assertive, though often only as the result of considerable personal struggle. By contrast, the majority of disabled people remain locked in a world of relative poverty and limited expectations. For them there is a considerable gap between the aspirations of disability theorists and the realities of their lives.

## Learning disabilities

The dominant discourse in learning disabilities in the last two decades has been normalisation theory (Brown and Smith 1992). Originating in the work of Nirje and Bank-Mikkelsen in Scandanavia and developed further by Wolfensburger in North America, normalisation seeks to deliver a high quality of life to users, and one that reproduces the lifestyles of non-disabled people, particularly in relation to clothing and appearance, the rhythm of the day, the quality of housing and goods and access to income (Emerson 1992). O'Brien's account of key service accomplishments – in terms of being present in the community, making choices, developing skills and competences, being respected as part of society and able to participate in it – has been widely influential in the development of services in the UK (McGill and Emerson 1992).

Though there are debates among theorists of normalisation and some critiques of its ideas have developed, in broad terms the approach is predominant, at least at the level of discourse; there has been little overt challenge to its basic precepts (Brown and Smith 1992). Its impact has, however, been weakened in the field by a number of countervailing tendencies.

First, much service development for people with learning disabilities has taken place in the context of decarceration and the closure of the long-stay institutions (Ericsson and Mansell 1996). The transfer of staff from the old settings has sometimes meant the continuation of old attitudes and ways of working (Ward 1995). The full transfer of money from the hospital closures has not always taken place, and resources have been allowed to leach away into the health service. In certain areas, in order to retain revenue, trusts have developed new facilities on the old hospital sites, creating what Collins and others have characterised as mini institutions (Collins 1995).

Second, there are anxieties at the potential cost of the new service models, particularly for people with severe learning disabilities or with additional physical disabilities. Increasingly the preferred model among progressive service developers is supported living, whereby individuals live in ordinary housing and have support built around their individual needs (Fitton and Willson 1995). There is a tendency for trusts and local authorities, for reasons of conservatism and control as well as cost, to prefer the older models of specialist group living (Ward 1995).

Third, there is the influence of parents, many of whom are fearful of the new models of normalisation, which they present as being railroaded through by staff. They have seen policies and staff come and go and have little confidence in the continuity of service support (Tuvesson and Ericsson 1996). They can be particularly sceptical about the stability of long-term arrangements, and this is one of the reasons why many favour village communities, whose segregated provision is at odds with normalisation theory. Parents can certainly be overprotective, underestimating the potential of their son or daughter and maintaining them in an enforced state of childhood. Some parents also cling on to a relationship on which they have come to depend (Twigg and Atkin 1994). The area of greatest anxiety, however, is sexuality. The new models of normalisation support people in developing adult relations including adult sexual relations (McCarthy and Thompson 1995), and this can be threatening for parents. Some aspects of sexuality have, however, been a proper source of concern. Work by Brown has shown disturbingly high levels of sexual abuse among people with learning disabilities. Men and women are both at risk, and abusers are mostly men known to their victims – other service users, family members and staff (Brown and Craft 1989). Despite parents' fears, there is no evidence that abuse is more prevalent in the new, freer service models.

## Mental health problems

The policy agenda in relation to mental health is more ambivalent. Some of the themes that have been important in relation to physical and mental disability have been influential here also – normalisation and ordinary living models, for example, have been important in relation to the parallel process of deinstitutionalisation. Hostility to the dominance of professionals is, if anything, stronger in this field. Activists in relation to mental health regard conventional psychiatry with particular suspicion; the pressure group Survivors Speak Out, for example, describe themselves as 'survivors' of the mental health services, damaged by the processes of 'care' itself (Rogers and Pilgrim 1996).

Though care in the community has been the official policy since the 1960s, achieving that shift has been more difficult. During the 1980s and 90s a number of long-stay hospitals were closed, but the corresponding transfer of resources into community facilities did not take place. In 1994 two-thirds of the £1.8 billion spent on mental health (1992/93) still went on in-patient services (Audit Commission 1994). Social services have been slow to build up provision for this group. There has been a reluctance to see responsibility pass from doctors, with the result that people with mental health difficulties have remained largely within the orbit of health care, and social models remain weak. There are ambiguities in the post-1990 care arrangements, with the care programme approach reduplicating the local authority care management. Again, questions of racism have been particularly significant in the mental health field. Black people (particularly black men) appear to be treated in a more coercive way than whites, with greater use of compulsory detention and major tranquillisers, more often in depot form, and with less in the way of counselling and psychotherapy (Bhui and Christie 1996; Rogers and Pilgrim 1996).

The chief source of policy ambivalence comes, however, from issues of danger and risk. Though mental health service users encompass a great range of conditions, the policy agenda is driven by the issue of severe mental illness. Publicity given to a number of violent and tragic events in the 1990s, including the killing of Jonathan Zito, created a mood of anxiety among the general public. In 1994 a series of critical reports were published (Audit Commission, the Mental Health Foundation, the Ritchie Report, the House of Commons Select Committee). Pressure groups such as SANE pointed to deficiencies of the system, particularly in regard to emergency help, sustained and coherent community support and overpressurised services, especially in London. The press presented care in the community as a policy that had failed and politicians responded to this. The new Labour government has announced its commitment to reform. This is not set to disturb the long-established policy of care in the community, but new forms of coercion and control, particularly in relation to medication, are being proposed (Department of Health 1998).

## Older people

The debate in relation to older people is more diffuse, softer than that in relation to mental illness but less liberal and positive than in relation to learning disabilities. Although there are theories of ageing or of the position of older people, such as the political economy approach that stresses the structural factors that determine the situations of older people (Townsend 1986; Walker and Phillipson 1986), there is no corresponding ideological focus for service development to that provided by normalisation or disability theory. Some attempts have been made to extend these ideas to the situations of older people, but their impact has been inhibited by anxieties about numbers. Older people are the largest group of users, consuming the majority of social care resources. This means that policy makers and planners are nervous of extending positive models of service development to them. The deeply entrenched ageism of society supports this differential response (Bytheway 1995).

The dominant discourse of demography presents the growing proportion of older people in the population in largely negative terms. Pessimism about resources is openly expressed and in some countries, such as New Zealand or the United States, the concept of greedy elders consuming more than they deserve has entered the policy debate. Attempts have been made to emphasise the positive aspects of survival – the success it represents for society – and the fact that the majority of older people are self-caring. At the individual level of older people and their families these facts are well understood, but they do not necessarily get translated into political discourse at the national and media level. Walker has commented on the disjunction in the debate on intergenerational relations between the level of the family and informal care, where responsibilities continue to be assumed in a positive way, and that of national resources and responsibilities, where the tone is much harsher (Walker 1996).

Ageism is compounded by sexism. The fact that the majority of older people are women has subtly detracted from the status of older people as a group. The facts of gender have in the past often been played down by those wanting to enhance the situations of older people. New work emphasising the significance of gender has been influential in academic circles, but less so in the field (Arber and Ginn 1991, 1995). Again, in terms of service planning older people sometimes lose out again by virtue of their numbers. It is easier to achieve clearly thought through and implemented service plans at a local level for small, well-defined groups such as those with learning disability. As Means and Smith point out, older people are often poorly organised in terms of pressure group politics and do not achieve the purchase on local service development that parents' groups or disabled people can do (Means and Smith 1994).

Though there is some evidence of their inclusion in ideas of user empowerment, older people have largely been incorporated into the debate on community care through the discourse of rationalisation. This emerged under the impact of the New Managerialism in the 1980s and has become the predominant discourse of the 'new community care' that followed the NHS and Community Care Act 1990, notwithstanding earlier emphases in the guidance literature on more liberal conceptions like user-led services (Walker 1993; Lewis and Glennerster 1996). The rationalisation of services calls for greater targeting of resources, more effective use of support and the development of cost-effective interventions. Service banding, whereby cases are ranked into bands by severity, and the much stricter rationing of support, whereby low levels of need are excluded from publicly funded provision, are part of this, together with a significant rise in the use of charging (Baldwin 1997; Phelps 1997). These are the service realities within which most frail older people now live.

**Carers**

The last two decades have witnessed a remarkable rise in recognition of the importance of informal care within the policy agenda, exemplified in the popularisation of the term 'carer'. During the 1980s feminist writers took up the issue of informal care, linking it to a series of other debates concerning the unwaged work of women, the public/private divide and the gendered nature of the welfare state (Finch and Groves 1983; Dalley 1988; Ungerson 1987, 1990; Hooyman 1990). The perception of caring primarily as a women's issue has, however, declined somewhat, partly in the light of data showing that the gender bias was not as great as had been first assumed (Green 1988; Arber and Ginn 1991; Rowlands and Parker 1998). The feminist emphasis on carers has also been subject to criticism from the disability movement, who set it as diverting attention from the real issue – the needs of disabled people. Morris has criticised feminists for constituting their subject – women – in ways that excluded disabled women and their experiences, and she argues that the ideology of 'care' and 'carers' is itself a form of oppression (Morris 1993, 1997). Partly as a result of this critique, interest in carers in academic circles has waned (Twigg 1998).

Within the discourse of community care, however, carers still occupy a central place. The fact that most care that is provided for older and disabled people comes from their families has been increasingly recognised within policy discourse. Maximising the input of carers through the judicious use of formal support has been seen as a highly cost-effective strategy, and one in tune with New Managerialist thinking, with its emphasis on the rationalisation of inputs and outcomes. Though the predominant approach has been this instrumental one, there has also been increased recognition of the needs and interests of carers *per se*. A range of work during the 1980s and 90s exploring the impact of caring on people's lives, together with the work of pressure groups such as the Carer's National Association, resulted in a greater appreciation of the difficulties that carers can face (Lewis and Meredith 1988; Levin, Sinclair and Gorbach 1989; Glendinning 1992; Parker 1993). Moreover, because caring is a common experience, carers strike a chord with politicians and the public. As a result, carers have increasingly featured in policy initiatives in the 1990s. Carers have achieved a new prominence in policy and planning documents. The NHS and Community Care Act 1990 was the first statute to mention carers directly, and the associated guidance referred repeatedly to carers, constructing them as a quasi-client group, a process further developed in the Carers (Recognition and Services) Act 1996. This entitled carers to receive a separate assessment of their needs, though crucially it did not entitle them to resources. In 1999, the new Labour government published further proposals on a 'national carers strategy', covering the setting of new standards, additional money to fund respite care and a second pension for carers by the year 2050 (Department of Health 1999).

We now turn to the first of two specific forms of discourse that have been deployed to integrate users within the care system.

## User empowerment

At the heart of user empowerment lies the attempt to redress the unequal power relations of social care. A number of structural factors underlie this. The majority of users are poor, typically coming into the orbit of social care when experiencing severe difficulties in their lives. The dominant values of society are individualistic and market oriented: people are expected to care for themselves and only call on public help when their personal resources fail. People caught in the service system feel weak, devalued and in the power of forces they do not control. Traditions of gratitude and of low expectations make it difficult to express wishes or complain at poor service, while echoes of the Poor Law continue to depress expectations. People entering the service system enter an unfamiliar world where expectations are unclear; they are in the hands of experts, and passivity is a frequent response.

User empowerment is a conscious attempt to redress this situation of disadvantage and put the wishes of users at the heart of service. Empowerment is itself a contested term, and the suggested means to its achievement have been various (Servian 1996; Forbes and Sashidharan 1997; Ramcharan *et al.* 1997). It has proved to be attractive at the rhetorical level, but there are structural barriers to its achievement. We have already noted the weak position in which users find themselves both materially and in terms of the dominant values of society. User empowerment contains few concrete mechanisms for reversing this structural weakness. To a considerable degree it relies on goodwill and the reorientation of service providers to make greater space in their practice for the expressed wishes of users; to learn to work alongside users rather than to do things to and for them. These have long been part of the expressed aims of social work. Achieving them has been harder.

Second, the aims of the social care system are complex. Realising the wishes of users is a legitimate part of this, but it is not the whole. Social care has coercive aspects: not all users are so by choice (Forbes and Sashidharan 1997). This is clearest in relation to people with mental health problems or adults responsible for children at risk, but it applies also to other users where the management of risk is a central part of the task. Stevenson and Parsloe argue that while respect for expressed needs and wishes is at the heart of empowerment, it needs to be balanced by matters relating to risk and competence and responsibility to protect and sometimes control (Stevenson and Parsloe 1993).

Last, and perhaps of greatest significance, is the rationed nature of the care system and the dominance over the last two decades of a cost-cutting agenda. This is the greatest barrier to the wishes of users being heard and acted upon. The reality of social care is one of strictly limited resources in which there is little scope for the expression of preferences and where even basic needs are not always met.

### Users as consumers

The second of the two models is that of users as consumers. This offers the advantage – in theory at least – of a mechanism for achieving greater empowerment through the market. At the simplest level, purchase means power: who pays for a service controls and directs it. People are the best judges of their own interests, and can be assumed to make better choices than those imposed by professionals. Consumerism thus offers ways of undermining what the disability movement in particular has seen as the patronising paternalism and self-interest of professionals. The model works not just at the individual level, but that of the system, with the aggregation of individual preferences acting to create a pattern of service better tailored to people's responses. Monolithic, take-it-or-leave it services will be replaced by competitive, flexible and responsive ones.

What are the problems with the consumerist model? First, it assumes that purchasers have perfect knowledge both of their interests and of the market that will allow them to maximise their utility. But in relation to social care (and indeed more widely) this is not always the case. As already noted, most people come into the orbit of social care at a time of considerable personal difficulty and distress in which they are in no position to be active, assertive consumers. It is not patronising to recognise that, for example, people with dementia, in crisis or suffering from physical or mental difficulties may not be able to judge their own best interests. Many frail people have no energy or stomach to pursue different options. What they are seeking are trustworthy advisers and suppliers. As Baldock and Ungerson suggest, for many people, particularly of the generation who grew up under the post-war welfare settlement, public services represent just such a trustworthy source (Baldock and Ungerson 1994). The rhetoric of consumption had overemphasised the responsiveness of markets and underplayed the essentially adversarial character of market relations. Recent work within economics has reemphasised the significance of relations of trust. There is a considerable literature within the spheres of conventional market goods that seeks means to redress what is recognised as the consumer's lack of power in the face of the provider (Potter 1988).

Second, the consumerist approach implicitly assumes that social care is a simple good much like any other consumer purchase. But, as Baldock points out, social care is a highly complex form of social exchange. How it is provided is as important as what is provided. Social care is interactive – created and consumed in the same process (Baldock 1997). Furthermore it involves intimacies and closenesses that are normally excluded from the world of money purchase (Twigg 1997).

Last there is the question of money. Few older disabled people have the income or savings that enable them to purchase care, and the indications for the future suggest that this pattern will continue (Baldock 1998). Most will rely on state provision. It is possible to recast the nature of this to make it more like that of the market (and elements of this have been achieved through the institution of quasi-markets (Le Grand and Bartlett 1993; Hudson 1994), but it remains the case that provision is still largely in the hands of professionals who define and allocate levels of care.

The most pervasive influence of these ideas has been at the level of language. During the 1980s conscious attempts were made to change the culture of social services, to make it more responsive to users, and closer – in a key phrase deriving from Peters and Waterman's influential book (1982) – to the customer. This deployment of the language of consumerism has continued under the new Labour government, and the 1998 Green Paper on social security frequently refers to customers, promoting a relationship between users and agencies that draws on that of purchasers in a private market.

By and large the mechanisms that would turn social care into a real market have not been pursued (except of course within the logic of quasi-markets where the purchaser–provider split turns social care agencies into purchasers, though here the market is at the level of the agency not the individual). The single major exception to this is direct payments. As we have noted, take up is as yet limited, and has perhaps been artificially so by the reluctance of some social service departments to support its development locally and their unwillingness to give up control over resources.

## Conclusion

As we have seen, there are commonalties across the discourses that have constituted the main user groups of community care. Certain themes recur: the emphasis on disability as socially constructed, intimately linked to the operations of society itself so that its relief cannot be separated from its creation; a new assertiveness of the user's position within the system; suspicion of the dominance of experts. These have created radical challenges to the established service system. But there have also been powerful countervailing forces: the rationalisation of provision, the emphasis on cost effectiveness; traditions of containment rather than empowerment. Above all the fundamentally rationed nature of social care has acted to undermine more liberal or radical approaches, so that although conceptual gains have been made in the last two decades, their translation into gains in the lives of disabled, frail or troubled people has been more limited.

## References

Arber, S. and Ginn, J. (1991) *Gender and Later Life: A Sociological Analysis of Resources and Constraints.* London: Sage.

Arber, S. and Ginn, J. (1995) '"Only connect": Gender relations and ageing.' In S. Arber and J. Ginn (eds) *Connecting Gender and Ageing: A Sociological Approach.* Buckingham: Open University Press.

Audit Commission (1994) *Finding a Place.* London: Audit Commission.

Baldock, J. (1997) 'Social care in old age: More than a funding problem.' *Social Policy and Administration 31,* 1, 73–89.

Baldock, J. (1998) 'Old age, consumerism and the social care market.' In M. May, E. Brunsdon and G. Craig (eds) *Social Policy Review 10.* London: SPA.

Baldock, J. and Ungerson, C. (1994) *Becoming Consumers of Community Care: Household within the Mixed Economy of Welfare.* York: Joseph Rowntree Foundation.

Baldwin, S.(1997) 'Charging users for community care.' In M. May, E. Brunsdon and G. Craig (eds) *Social Policy Review 9,* London: SPA.

Bhui, K. and Christie, Y. (1996) *Purchasing Mental Health Services for Black Communities.* London: HMSO.

Brown, H. and Craft, A. (1989) *Thinking the Unthinkable: Papers on Sexual Abuse and People with Learning Difficulties.* London: FPA.

Brown, H. and Smith, H. (eds) (1992) *Normalisation: A Reader for the Nineties.* London: Routledge.

Bytheway, B. (1995) *Ageism.* Buckingham: Open University Press.

Campbell, J. and Oliver, M. (1996) *Disability Politics: Understanding Our Past, Changing Our Future.* London: Routledge.

Collins, J. (1995) 'Moving forwards or moving back? Institutional trends in services for people with learning difficulties.' In L. Ward and T. Philpot (eds) *Values and Visions: Changing Ideas in Services for People with Learning Difficulties.* Oxford: Butterworth-Heinemann.

Dalley, G. (1988) *Ideologies and Caring: Rethinking Community and Collectivism.* London: Macmillan.

Department of Health (1998) *Modernising Mental Health Services: Safe, Sound and Supportive.* London: The Stationery Office.

Department of Health (1999) *Caring About Carers.* London: The Stationery Office.

Emerson, E. (1992) 'What is normalisation?' In H. Brown and H. Smith (eds) *Normalisation: A Reader for the Nineties.* London: Routledge.

Ericsson, K. and Mansell, J. (1996) 'Introduction: Towards deinstitutionalisation.' In J. Mansell and K. Ericsson (eds) *Deinstitutionalisation and Community Living: Intellectual Disability Services in Britain, Scandinavia and the USA.* London: Chapman and Hall.

Finch, J. and Groves, D. (eds) (1983) *A Labour of Love: Women, Work and Caring.* London: Routledge.

Fitton, P. and Willson, J. (1995) 'A home of their own: Achieving supported housing.' In L. Ward and T. Philpot (eds) *Values and Visions: Changing Ideas in Services for People with Learning Difficulties.* Oxford: Butterworth-Heinemann.

Forbes, J. and Sashidharan, S.P. (1997) 'User involvement in services – incorporation or challenge?' *British Journal of Social Work 27,* 4.

Glendinning, C. (1992) *The Costs of Informal Care.* London: HMSO.

Green, H. (1988) *Informal Carers: A Study Carried Out on Behalf of the Department of Health and Social Security as Part of the 1985 General Household Survey.* London: HMSO.

Hooyman, N.R. (1990) 'Women as caregivers of the elderly.' In D.E. Biegel and A. Blum (eds) *Aging and Caregiving: Theory, Research and Policy.* London: Sage.

Hudson, B. (1994) *Making Sense of Markets in Health and Social Care.* Sunderland: Business Education Publishers.

Hughes, B. and Paterson, K. (1997) 'The social model of disability and the disappearing body: Towards a sociology of impairment.' *Disability and Society 12,* 3, 325–40.

Kestenbaum, A. (1996) *Independent Living: A Review.* York: Joseph Rowntree Foundation.

Le Grand, J. and Bartlett, W. (eds) (1993) *Quasi-markets and Social Policy.* Basingstoke: Macmillan.

Lewis, J. and Glennerster, H. (1996) *Implementing the New Community Care.* Buckingham: Open University Press.

Lewis, J. and Meredith, B. (1988) *Daughters who Care: Daughters Caring for Mothers at Home.* London: Routledge.

Levin, E., Sinclair, I. and Gorbach, P. (1989) *Families, Services and Confusion in Old Age.* Aldershot: Gower.

Lindow, V. and Morris, J. (1995) *Service User Involvement.* York: Joseph Rowntree Foundation.

Lonsdale, S. (1990) *Women and Disability: The Experience of Physical Disability.* Basingstoke: Macmillan.

McCarthy, M. and Thompson, D. (1995) 'No more double standards: Sexuality and people with learning difficulties.' In L. Ward and T. Philpot (eds) *Values and Visions: Changing Ideas in Services for People with Learning Difficulties.* Oxford: Butterworth-Heinemann.

McGill, P. and Emerson, E. (1992) 'Normalisation and applied behavioural analysis: values and technology in human services.' In H. Brown and H. Smith (eds) *Normalisation: A Reader for the Nineties.* London: Routledge.

Means, R. and Smith, R. (1994) *Community Care: Policy and Practice.* Basingstoke: Macmillan.

Morris, J. (1991) *Pride Against Prejudice: Transforming Attitudes Towards Disability.* London: The Women's Press.

Morris, J. (1993) *Independent Lives? Community Care and Disabled People.* Basingstoke: Macmillan.

Morris, J. (1997) 'Care or empowerment? A disability rights perspective.' *Social Policy and Administration 31,* 1, 54–60.

Oliver, M. (1990) *The Politics of Disablement.* Basingstoke: Macmillan.

Parker, G. (1993) *With This Body: Caring and Disability in Marriage.* Buckingham: Open University.

Peters, T.J. and Waterman, R.H. (1982) *In Search of Excellence: Lessons from America's Best Run Companies.* New York: Harper and Row.

Phelps, L. (1997) *Rationing Community Care: CAB Clients' Experiences of Home Care Services.* London: National Association of Citizens Advice Bureaux.

Potter, J. (1988) 'Consumerism and the public sector: How well does the coat fit?' *Public Administration 66,* Summer, 149–64.

Ramcharan, P., Roberts, G. Grant, G. and Borland, J. (1997) *Empowerment in Everyday Life.* London: Jessica Kingsley Publishers.

Rogers, A. and Pilgrim, D. (1996) *Mental Health Policy in Britain.* Basingstoke: Macmillan.

Rowlands, O. and Parker, G. (1998) *Informal Carers: An Independent Study Carried Out for the Office of National Statistics on Behalf of the Department of Health as Part of the 1995 GHS.* London: The Stationery Office.

Servian, R. (1996) *Theorising Empowerment.* Bristol: Policy Press.

Shakespere, T. (1994) 'Cultural representations of disabled people: Dustbins for disavowal.' *Disability and Society 9,* 3.

Stevenson, O. and Parsloe, P. (1993) *Community Care and Empowerment.* York: Joseph Rowntree Foundation.

Townsend, P. (1986) 'Ageism and social policy.' In C. Phillipson and A. Walker (eds) *Ageing and Social Policy: A Critical Assessment.* Aldershot: Gower.

Tuvesson, B. and Ericsson, K. (1996) 'Relatives' opinions on institutionalisation.' In J. Mansell and K. Ericsson (eds) *Deinstitutionalisation and Community Living: Intellectual Disability Services in Britain, Scandinavia and the USA.* London: Chapman and Hall.

Twigg, J. (1997) 'Deconstructing the social bath: Help with bathing at home for older and disabled people.' *Journal of Social Policy 26*, 2, 211–32.

Twigg, J. (1998) 'The rise and fall of "informal care": The natural history of a debate.' J.P. Sarola Memorial Lecture, given at the University of Joensuu, Finland.

Twigg, J. and Atkin, K. (1994) *Carers Perceived: Policy and Practice in Informal Care.* Buckingham: Open University.

Ungerson, C. (1987) *Policy is Personal: Sex, Gender and Informal Care.* London: Tavistock.

Ungerson, C. (ed) (1990) *Gender and Caring: Work and Welfare in Britain and Scandinavia.* Hemel Hempstead: Harvester.

Ungerson, C. (1997) 'Give them the money: Is cash a route to empowerment?' *Social Policy and Administration 31*, 1, 45–53.

Walker, A. (1993) 'Community care policy: From consensus to conflict.' In J. Bornat, C. Pereira, D. Pilgrim and F. Williams (eds) *Community Care: A Reader.* Basingstoke: Macmillan.

Walker, A. and Phillipson, C. (1986) 'Introduction.' In C. Phillipson and A. Walker (eds) *Aging and Social Policy.* Aldershot: Gower.

Ward, L. (1995) 'Equal citizens: Current issues for people with learning difficulties and their allies.' In L. Ward and T. Philpot (eds) *Values and Visions: Changing Ideas in Services for People with Learning Difficulties.* Oxford: Butterworth-Heinemann.

PART II

# Working Across Boundaries

# CHAPTER 8

# Social Care and Housing

*Murray Hawtin*

## Introduction

The Faith in the City Report defined housing as

> more than bricks and mortar, it is more than a roof over one's head. Decent
> housing is a place that is dry and warm and in reasonable repair. It also means
> security, privacy, sufficient space; a place where people can grow, make
> choices, become more whole people. It relates to the environment in which
> the house is located. (Archbishop of Canterbury 1985)

Other definitions include the principles that housing should be affordable and
should include support for those who need it. The close relationship between
inequalities in housing and health care has been recognised since at least the
1840s when Public Health legislation identified unhealthy city slums as a cause
of poor health:

> these evils, and the misery consequent on them, is much increased by peculiar
> faults in the form and construction of the humble dwellings of the poorer
> classes. (Select Committee 1840)

Views such as this eventually led to the development of socially rented housing
built and managed principally by local authorities. Public housing played a key
role in improving the housing conditions of those less well off, as well as in
redeveloping substandard urban areas, and became one of the main planks of
the Welfare State. However, more recently a new recognition of poverty has
undermined assumptions about the effectiveness of that Welfare State. The
Social Exclusion Unit has identified 'street living' as one of its priorities for
action, with an aim of reducing to as near zero as possible the numbers of people
sleeping rough. However, this is not the only manifestation of increasing

housing poverty. Structural forces in housing policy have resulted in the concentration of socially excluded groups, such as disabled people and the poor, in low-quality social and, increasingly, private sector housing. In addition, this has been exacerbated by care in the community policies. These policies rely on vulnerable people being able to live in adequate homes, but in reality social landlords are usually only able to provide accommodation on unpopular and deteriorating estates which are neither safe nor healthy.

Decent housing, in whatever tenure, is essential for a good-quality life, socially, emotionally and physically. The benefits of an adequate supply of good housing would reduce the reliance on residential care, can improve the employment prospects of its occupiers and help to alleviate poverty. Conversely, the poorest sections of society live in the worst housing with poor access to adequate health and social care (Boardman 1991; Curtis 1991). Of primary importance therefore is whether service provision is aimed principally at individuals in need or collectively as a general service.

Since the early 1980s, successive governments have focused their welfare policies on individual responsibility, perceiving the individual as a consumer and placing a philosophic as well as economic emphasis on the reduction of general need provision of state services in favour of a residualised approach supported by a more market-driven service. The White Paper *The Health of the Nation* (DoH 1992), which set out the Conservative government's policy on health care and prevention, emphasised a narrow range of key risk behaviours including smoking, alcohol consumption and exercise. It showed little concern with linking poor health with wider environmental factors such as poverty and housing. The current government, however, has recognised such important linkages in its White Paper *Our Healthier Nation* (DoH 1998), although it makes no commitment to action on housing through, for example, setting targets to improve the level of unfit housing. The White Paper *Modernising Social Services* (DoH 1998) also confirms the current government's commitment to the Conservative concept of community care, based largely on an individualised market approach to care.

Individualising service provision and targeting resources is based on a traditional view of disability which sees people's problems as arising from their individual physical and sensory impairment and is based on a philosophy of disablement as abnormal and pathological. This view has, however, been challenged and much of the current debate around disability has been transformed by the rise of the 'social model' of disability. Rather than seeing an individual's 'problems' in terms of their functional limitations, the social model focuses attention on the way in which people can be disabled by society and generally lose out compared with non-disabled people (for example, Barnes 1991). The reason for their material, social and political marginalisation is seen as less related to their individual impairment than to the *disabling environment* in which they live (Oliver 1990; Swain *et al.* 1993; Barton 1996). This may take place in a number of ways, whether by disability imposed through the design of buildings and transport, the impact of segregated education, through discrimination in spheres such as education, employment, income and housing, or through exclusionary practices in the domestic sphere arising from segregative accommodation. For example, only a small proportion of the housing stock available is accessible, the majority of which is provided by local authorities.

The relationship between housing and social care spheres is undeniable, and the linkages between those delivering such services have increasingly been stressed. However, the policy and implementational development of these services has been problematic, leading more recently to some to conclude that 'the relationship between social work and housing, far from becoming more closely integrated, is in decline' (Shaw *et al.* 1998, p.8).

This chapter starts by outlining the legislative as well as the broader policy context within which more recent developments have been made related to the housing dimension of social care. It then goes on to explore the arguments around the provision of 'special needs' housing within the context of developing ideas about 'normalisation', 'empowerment' and 'independent living'. Collaboration between social care and housing agencies has reflected the ambiguities between the two disciplines and their organisational development. The chapter therefore looks at some of the issues underpinning the gulf between housing and social care: such differences may stem from contrasting philosophical conceptions of welfare, from historic, professional and functional differences, and from more recent political priorities. Finally it outlines some specific intersections between housing and social care at policy and implementational levels, including provision of accommodation, joint planning, assessments, resources, housing management, networking, home-lessness and user involvement.

## The legislative context

Care in the community policies, shifting care from large institutions to community settings, began in the 1950s with the gradual closure of long-stay hospitals – especially psychiatric hospitals – and the resettling of people into the community. By the 1980s, with the intensification of the policy and the increase in the elderly population in need of care, there developed a huge increase in the provision of private residential care and a corresponding rise in cost to the social security budget. Perverse incentives were militating against the development of health and social care packages to support people in their own homes. The government therefore commissioned Sir Roy Griffiths to undertake a cost-benefit review of the way in which public funds are used to support community care policy (Griffiths 1988). The subsequent report laid down the backbone for the 1990 NHS and Community Care Act.

The housing world saw the attitude to housing in the Griffiths Report as one of tokenism at best, based on an assumption that there is a clear dividing line between funding and responsibility for 'bricks and mortar' and the provision of social support. Housing writers and practitioners argued strongly that in practice the two are inextricably bound together, that the strengths or weaknesses of one policy directly affect the other, and that housing should not be so easily marginalised (Oldman 1988; Clapham and Smith 1990). The Major City Councils Housing Group (1988), responding to Griffiths' 'Agenda for Action' (Griffiths 1988), expressed its concerns as:

- the lack of consistent data on vulnerable groups to define the scale of the problem to be faced
- the absence of national guidelines on good practice
- the complexities of coordinating the many agencies involved, exacerbated by different planning frameworks
- the remoteness of the present lead authorities in community care (the lead has changed from health (implicitly) to social services (explicitly))
- the need for adequate financial resources.

The housing proposals in the Griffiths Report were felt to be inadequate and not well thought through. Allen, however, argues that critics of the report, and subsequent legislation, fail to take into account that community care policy was (and still is) based not only on the economic principle to reduce the cost of residential care but also by the medical model of disability: 'by narrowly focusing on the "home space" rather than "social space" of disabled people, community care policy creates dependency on the former' (Allen 1997, p.96). Housing therefore becomes functionally important only as a means of achieving other policy objectives, i.e. integrating disabled people into a community. Housing policies are therefore not intended to have political implications in achieving goals such as independent living, normalisation or empowerment.

The importance of the role of housing in community care was, however, conceded in the White Paper *Caring for People* (1989): 'Housing is a vital component of community care and often the key to independent living' (p.25). Later on, in 1992, the Department of the Environment and the Department of Health produced a joint circular entitled *Housing and Community Care*. The circular stressed the importance of adequate housing in community care and the necessity for interagency collaboration. It also intended housing needs, arising from community care assessments, to be met by local housing strategies and submissions.

> Adequate housing has a major role to play in community care and is often the key to independent living. The government wants housing to play a full part, working together with social service departments and health authorities so that each effectively discharge their responsibilities. (DoE/DoH 1992, p.1)

In acknowledging the importance of housing to the success of community care subsequent guidance from central government (DoH/DETR 1997) gives examples of good practice and indications of possible approaches for housing, social services and health authorities. These, and many similar statements originating not only from central government but also from the NHS and local authorities, imply an expectation that housing should be positioned within the mainstream domains of community care policy and planning.

## The broader context

Despite the good intentions of joint government departmental exhortations for agencies to collaborate, many professionals are concerned that vulnerable people could suffer because of the inadequacies of housing policies. People who need support or care are usually the most vulnerable and often the most powerless in society. Collectively they tend to lack political representation and therefore have a very weak lobbying position. The impact of this lack of political leverage affects all aspects of their need, including their demands for housing and care resources. The great majority of social care users live in social housing and therefore have been significantly affected by the destructive impact of housing funding cuts over the last two decades, severely undermining the potential for housing to serve as a positive care intervention. It is often argued that there is a significant shortage of good-quality, suitable housing at affordable rents, a shortfall in new building to meet current and future needs, and that due to reductions in improvement grants and other spending on private housing improvements the stock in this sector is also deteriorating.

The government's determination to control public borrowing and capital expenditure has formed one of the most constant policies of the last 20 years. In 1979 the Conservatives regarded their housing policies, and in particular the 'right to buy', as key to their election success, and since then over 2 million dwellings have been sold. They set out not only to reduce public expenditure on housing but also to expand owner occupation. For some people owner occupation brought security, choice and better conditions, together with a capital asset which may appreciate over time. However, home ownership for others on low incomes who bought poorer quality properties was more problematic as costs, including those of repair and maintenance, increased. Housing suffered the severest of all public expenditure cuts; by comparison, spending on social security, education, health and social services increased in real terms over the same period. The better dwellings within local authorities have now largely been sold and councils are left with the less desirable properties; previous restrictions on spending on housing by local authorities meant that repair and maintenance has been cut back; badly designed and constructed buildings of the 1950s and 1960s are of varying standards and little appeal. The result is that council housing has developed an image of 'second best' or residual housing, used to only house those unable or unwilling to 'help themselves'.

In the UK, 1.6 million dwellings are below the fitness standard – or the 'tolerable standard' in Scotland – and are considered unfit for human habitation. In England, 1 in 5 homes need urgent repairs costing £1,000 or more, and in Northern Ireland a quarter of all homes need repairs valued at £3,000 or more. The highest proportion of run-down property is in the private rented sector, and people most likely to live in poor-quality housing are those on low incomes (Leather and Morrison 1997).

## Social needs and ordinary housing

From the 1960s onwards local authorities began to provide housing specifically for older people, encouraged, in 1969, by a government circular (82/92). Housing associations have traditionally provided for special needs, many being dedicated to providing only special needs housing. Since the early 1980s, however, new-build of sheltered housing has declined dramatically, particularly affecting disabled people. Most wheelchair housing, and the majority of mobility housing, is owned by local authorities. However, housing associations and the private sector have not been building wheelchair and mobility accommodation anywhere near the rate of local authorities before the cutbacks in housing expenditure in the 1980s.

Whilst for many the debate around accommodation for social care users has centred around the notion of 'special needs housing', this has increasingly come under question. Arnold *et al.* (1993) raised four important points about special needs housing:

- there is no useful consensus about what 'special needs housing' includes
- there is little reliable evidence on whether people with so-called 'special needs' either want or need 'special needs housing', or on the extent to which their expectations reflect traditional models of provision and levels of resources
- much 'special needs' accommodation is not used effectively, with some people getting more care than they need and others being unable to move on for lack of more appropriate housing

- the concept of 'special needs housing' carries with it the assumption that people with 'special needs' require on-site surveillance or care.

Means and Smith (1994) maintain that supported housing schemes have been used to compensate for the failures of mainstream housing including the availability of appropriate accommodation, affordability, repair (or more accurately, disrepair) and access. Their discussion starts by noting the criticism that 'special needs housing' deflects attention away from the need to provide affordable, appropriate and flexible housing within mainstream provision. Furthermore, inadequacies within mainstream housing provision may lead social care users to enter residential care or other supported housing schemes (Sinclair 1988; Oldman 1990), or to become homeless (Office for Public Management 1992).

Social care users have traditionally been often excluded from living a 'normal' life in an ordinary home; however, general housing can play a very important role in a process of 'normalisation'. Arguments for independent living, particularly from Britain's expanding disability movement, have reinforced demands for a political focus on 'ordinary' housing with support relocated to users' own homes. Although it can be argued that ordinary housing has limitations for some people, taking such housing as the starting point can potentially make a significant difference to the way in which social care is contextualised and developed.

Specialist housing, designed for people with health or social care needs, is often distinctive in character and although placed geographically 'within' a community may not necessarily be part of it. Residents of such accommodation may be viewed by others living or working in the area as 'different' or 'less-than-ordinary', although much of the rhetoric surrounding provision for them emphasises the benefits of an 'ordinary' or 'normal' lifestyle. It has been argued therefore that 'special needs' housing may add to the process of marginalisation and even stigmatisation. Clapham and Smith argue that conceptualising 'special needs' portrays housing problems as discrete and technical and provides criteria for labelling and discriminating between groups who are more or less deserving of public funds (Clapham and Smith 1990).

Although Cooper, Hawtin and Botchel (1994) found some evidence of a preference for shared living amongst the most isolated and vulnerable people, most studies have found that many people who receive care and support prefer to live in ordinary housing and use mainstream services (McCafferty 1994; Hudson, Watson and Allen 1996; Means and Smith 1996). The concern is not just about the fabric of housing (bricks and mortar, rents and mortgages, furniture and furnishings etc.), but is also about issues of lifestyle, well-being, social environment and independence. This means having control over decisions about one's own life and possibly reducing the emphasis on 'client'-type relationships.

Policy makers and professionals are increasingly accepting the importance of an 'ordinary' housing approach to the provision of accommodation and services. However, the bulk of 'special-needs' provision continues to reflect traditional outlooks and values. Such an 'ordinary' housing approach can only work with a reallocation of resources towards domiciliary support, adaptations, day care, home nursing, etc., and there is little evidence of government support for this policy. Unlike the provision of what might be termed 'small institutions' or communal environments which happen to be placed in 'the community', real acceptance of an 'ordinary' housing approach necessitates a change in services – in social care, housing and health.

## Issues of interagency collaboration

Since the 1990 NHS and Community Care Act there has been a plethora of recommendations, injunctions and good practice advice concerning interagency collaboration between social care and housing agencies. However, most research suggests that progress has at best been slow and in many respects disappointing. Arblaster *et al.* (1996) found that there was little evidence of three-way links between social care, housing and health agencies; links between social care and health were reasonably good but tended to leave out housing. They concluded that:

- there is a widespread lack of understanding of other agencies – their roles and responsibilities, boundaries between them and the constraints each other are working under
- organisations are often unsure of the services provided by, and personnel within, other agencies

- where collaboration at a strategic level exists it is often not implemented or mirrored at the service delivery level
- there are general difficulties in communications and sharing information at the level of service delivery between agency workers, including false expectations and mistrust of other professional groups.
- user involvement is unsuccessful at the strategic level and agencies rarely provide a coordinated interagency response to user demands.

The recent Audit Commission report on the role of housing in community care concluded that too many people fall through the net because of poor collaboration between housing, social services and health authorities (Audit Commission 1998, p.000). Arblaster *et al.* (1996) identified a wide range of local and national factors influencing such interagency working. In some instances these factors work to enable agencies to collaborate successfully towards meeting housing needs. In others, many of the preconditions for collaboration may be present; however one or two factors may inhibit collaboration. In other situations, nearly all the factors may tend to foster a narrow or limited approach so that the conditions are not conducive to effective collaboration between agencies. Four groups of interrelating factors determining the nature of the boundaries between housing and social care may be identified: the broad macro context; the means whereby policies are implemented; the structure of agencies; and organisational operation.

Local housing and social care agencies operate within a broad context which is largely given, and sets the broad parameters within which agencies determine their areas of responsibility and how they approach service provision. To some extent these factors affect both the need for interagency coordination and the scope for adopting effective joint ways of working. Factors include: *macro* factors (such as demographic trends, economic factors and political priorities); the *means* to service delivery (legislation, resources and links between government departments); the *structure* of agencies (the range of organisational types, the separation of purchasing and provision, geographic boundaries and local political priorities); and organisational *operation* of agencies (agency objectives, organisational structure and style and professional values and skills).

National and local government operate within political priorities which are partly determined by other contextual factors such as demographic trends and economic constraints, and partly by party policy. These priorities affect the work of local agencies both directly, by fixing the legal and financial framework, and indirectly, by creating the policy climate in which these agencies are able to operate.

Within the broad national context, local agencies use the legislation and available resources to provide services, influenced by how well the government itself coordinates its own activities. The legislative framework has a significant effect upon the way agencies operate, including their interest in collaboration with other agencies. This is determined not only by Acts of Parliament but also, and increasingly, by regulations, directives, circulars and case law. Resources affect the scope for implementing programmes locally. New arrangements in community care and other policies have led to confusion over funding arrangements and 'cost shunting'; issues within administering adaptations are illustrative of this problem which mitigates against collaboration (Heywood 1994, 1996; Pieda 1996). Also, with increasing pressure on resources there is almost inevitably an incentive for agencies to retreat to their 'core' responsibilities – whilst in times of plenty they might be able and willing to take on new tasks, this is less likely to happen in times of shortage. It is essential to recognise, when looking at factors affecting the relationship between housing and social care, the destructive impact of housing funding cuts over the last two decades (Arnold *et al.* 1993; DoH 1994; Arblaster *et al.* 1996). However, there may be resource benefits in working with another agency to achieve common goals. The degree of collaboration may also be affected by the extent to which agencies' resources are interdependent; the greater the resources involved the closer the working relationship is likely to be.

The ease of collaboration for local agencies is also affected by the extent to which central government programmes and policies are clearly coordinated. Where central government departments link their programmes or provide common guidance, local agencies can follow that lead. Where interagency programmes have been set up with finance, for example the single regeneration programme which brings together the resources and policies of a number of government departments, this encourages local agencies to work together to achieve specific ends. On the other hand, where the programmes of government departments have not been coordinated, or even work against each other, local agencies find it very difficult to establish effective links. For example, when the NHS and Community Care Act was first enacted there was no government model for coordination between the DSS and DoE until Circular 10/92 was issued. Indeed, at the national level until recently there has been no clear agenda nor coordination of government programmes within which local agencies could operate collectively (Arnold *et al.* 1993; House of Commons Health Committee 1994; Harker *et al.* 1996; Audit Commission 1998). To address this issue, Fletcher has called for a stronger national framework under the auspices of an interdepartmental cabinet committee chaired by a cabinet minister; 'such a committee should set a much stronger set of national outcome standards which local authorities have to comply with before resources are made available. The Rough Sleepers Initiative can provide a model here' (Fletcher 1998).

The third group of factors affecting interagency collaboration – the structure, nature and range of types of organisations – are directly and indirectly determined by central government. Historically, both local and central government departments have worked independently with little thought given to the effect of the development of their own policies on other departments. More recently, however, there have been a number of administrative developments which have impacted on departmental isolation. Changes have included: the review of single- and dual-tier local authorities and changes to government boundaries; changes in the boundaries in responsibilities of health authorities and other health agencies; a shift in responsibility from departments to quangos; the separation of purchasers from providers of housing, social care and health; and the increased role of the voluntary and independent sectors. In the process some agencies, including independent and voluntary agencies, have become more important, and greater significance has been ascribed to users' views, usually without their having power to control resources. Such changes in the structure of organisations have greatly influenced problems of interagency collaboration and new working relationships need to be established (Arblaster *et al.* 1996; Craig 1993; Craig and Manthorpe 1996).

Finally, effective interagency collaboration is undermined to some extent by differences in organisational operation related to professional structures, philosophies, culture, language and training as well as agency aims and objectives (Wagner 1988). Organisations develop their own structure, style and culture, and – as social care and housing professional groups and agencies developed their goals and priorities as separate areas of public policy over the years – the links between the professional groups have been weakened (Byrne *et al.* 1986). Housing groups, for example, are concerned with preparation for best value, stock transfer and managing deteriorating stock with reduced budgets, whereas social services' concerns includes child protection and the implementation of legislation such as the Children's Act and Community Care. Timescales also differ – unlike social care services which operate around the immediate needs of clients, housing is more capital based involving less flexible and lengthy 'lead in' times and coherent forward planning.

There is growing concern that housing management staff are increasingly becoming overextended by the increasing numbers of vulnerable people in social housing. Arnold and Page found that many housing departments feel that 'that they are left to pick up the pieces of previous "failed" community care policies, with lack of support from social services' (Arnold and Page 1992), and that many social workers are unaware of the practicalities of providing housing – they may have, for example, unrealistic expectations that housing departments should be able to make public sector lettings available on request for community care clients. Others (DoH 1994; Means and Smith 1994; Henwood 1995; Arblaster *et al.* 1996) have also highlighted differences, distrust and professional disputes: 'at the level of front-line working relationships between social workers and housing officers were often covertly, if not overtly hostile' (Clapham and Franklin 1994, p.59). Where social workers do understand the housing constraints, however, their advocacy role may conflict with a desire to collaborate. For example 'antisocial' measures such as probationary tenancies and speedy evictions for those involved in drug abuse may conflict with other care interests. Stewart argues that

> the holy grail of 'collaboration' can become a threat to good professional practice when clients' best interests, as jointly assessed with them, are compromised in order to protect harmonious inter-agency relations ... The presen-

tation of a 'seamless' united front can be experienced as an impenetrable barrier by someone who has been denied a service. (1998, p.57)

One agency is more likely to collaborate with another when it perceives there to be a benefit to itself or its users (Van de Ven 1976; Nocon 1994), not where there are seen to be negative effects.

Shaw, Lambert and Clapham see social work as being restricted to 'issues of special needs and acute problems of housing malaise such as over crowding or homelessness' (Shaw *et al.* 1998, p.7). Shaw argues that 'the relationship between social care and housing will continue to be fragmented and lacking in purpose if it is divorced from wider structural explanations' (Shaw 1998, p.7). He argues that this lack of engagement can be addressed through a greater understanding by those within social services of the political, economic, demographic and social context within which care and housing services operate, and that such an analysis needs to be based on social inclusion. Allen, however, argues that although focusing on individuals, social workers *do* recognise that they and their clients are products of social structures and that 'in contrast to the paternalistic housing officer, who considers his actions to be benevolent, the social workers' sociological understanding of the individual's location within an oppressive social structure might encourage her to adopt an anti-professional approach' (Allen 1998, p.30). Addressing issues related to understanding common professional theory and practice needs to start with the training process. Professional organisations which accredit training have, however, not given interagency collaboration and a deeper understanding of other welfare services a high priority, although organisations including the government's Community Care Steering Group support the further development of social work training to include a basic knowledge of housing issues, and for a social work element to be included in the professional housing training.

## Key intersections of interagency activity

Generally there has been a growing awareness of the interdependency of care, housing and other needs (as indicated in *Our Healthier Nation* and realised by the growing marginalisation of many tenants in the public rented sector). This awareness has made it almost inevitable that the relationship between housing and social care be reexamined. Despite a relatively low starting point and a poor commencement to the new community care programme there have been a number of positive examples of good practice and innovative provision, and a growing diversity of collaborative schemes. However, these have tended to be *ad hoc* and are the exception rather than the rule. Nevertheless, they show that there is a willingness to try to overcome the range of barriers (Arblaster *et al.* 1998; Means *et al.* 1997). This chapter concludes with a critical consideration of some key intersections between social care and housing.

*Provision of housing*

Housing provision, along with other activities including job creation, safety and community involvement, is in a key position to assist in preventative strategies in community care (Fletcher and Wistow 1997). Suitable housing with appropriate support may reduce or even remove care needs. Not only can well-designed ordinary housing, or housing that can be adapted, help people stay in their homes, but it can create more stable households which in turn lead to more stable communities. When applied simply to older people, more than half of the population aged over 65 are owner occupiers and for many their housing conditions are poor. Improving and adapting their homes can help them remain independent and may mean that care can be provided in their home rather than in an institution.

Housing needs to be suitable for both the person being cared for as well as the needs of any carer. The quality and quantity of new house building and renovation work has a direct impact on health. Adaptations and technical aids can make caring easier or less arduous. Good heating and safety measures can reduce anxiety and demands on the time of the formal or informal carer. Building regulations, fitness standards, improvement grants and the provision of aids and adaptations can all determine whether or not a resident remains independent or must move into residential care. The nature of new housing also affects the use of the stock by future generations. There are now no minimum standards for new housing other than the building regulations. With the Parker Morris standards abandoned in the late 1970s and increasing financial pressures, both local authority and housing association standards have declined, especially those of space. This had led to a concern that it is creating a legacy of inadequate, unpopular estates (Page 1993). Standards of private house building have also fallen, well over half of new private homes fall below the old Parker Morris space standards (Karn and Sheridan 1994). The government is proposing to extend the building regulations (Part M) to residential building from 1999. These require the provision of certain accessible features which currently apply to public buildings only. However, the concept of 'lifetime homes' has been developed to go beyond these basic requirements and cater for the changing needs of households. Such homes include an accessible entrance, downstairs WC suitable for a wheelchair, wider doors and circulation spaces and scope for adding a stairlift. Those supporting this concept argue that such standards should be adopted more widely and even be required for a proportion of all new private and public sector housing. The additional cost of building to such standards is small compared with the greater cost of adapting an existing house for a disabled person or providing residential care (Cobbold 1996).

Over the years, housing services have become involved in a range of care activities, although as discussed above the housing contribution has generally been considered to be principally through special schemes, rather than the development of 'ordinary' or general housing. However, whilst sheltered housing or hostels have become the familiar models of 'special needs' provision, the new range of accommodation types which have been developed for people with care needs, such as core and cluster schemes, do not fit easily into the category of 'home' or 'institution'. Housing authorities are becoming pro-gressively more involved in a spectrum of care activities, a role reinforced by the Housing Corporation which stated in June 1994 that associations should continue providing for a diverse range of special needs. Such provision includes group living schemes, central alarm systems and floating support.

*Joint planning*

A key factor determining the scale and nature of service provision is the need for that service, in terms of the size and type of population whose needs are to be met (Percy-Smith 1996). Local variations in demographic trends will determine the precise nature of needs for which local housing and social care agencies must cater. Local agencies may have good or poor knowledge and recognition of the needs of the local population, depending on the amount of local research and information. The new managerialism underpinning community care in the early 1990s espoused the view that individual needs are the responsibility of individuals. Planning services under a market welfare system is therefore based on an aggregation of individuals' assessed needs as cost effectively as possible. In reality, the main concern becomes rationing and the coordination of services, and little at all to do with developing a holistic and consensual vision, addressing a wide range of individual and collective needs.

> A service focused on individuals purchasing care will become a divisive one, needing considerable co-ordination for each person, and ignoring many associated issues which impinge on the lives of vulnerable people such as community safety and access to facilities. (Arblaster *et al.* 1996, p.46)

Since the Griffiths Report, housing services have felt marginalised in the planning process – both in formal joint planning and other forms of planning. This has been partly due to marginalisation by other agencies (particularly health and social services), partly due to an unwillingness of housing agencies to become involved, and partly due to the structural problems outlined above (Department of Health 1994; Arblaster *et al.* 1996; Lund and Foord 1997). However, more recently there has been some evidence of greater housing involvement in community care planning, particularly through mechanisms such as locality planning and special needs housing forums (Department of Health 1994; Lund and Foord 1997). Joint approaches to housing needs assessment are also becoming more common (Watson and Harker 1993; Arblaster *et al.* 1998). Lund and Foord (1997) analysed 120 housing strategies produced each year between 1993 and 1995 along with the related community care plans. Their conclusion was that the role of housing was enhanced within community care planning, although there was also little evidence of 'bottom-up' information being used to aggregate need for accommodation needs arising from community care. They also noted that there was often an assumption that needs did not exist where they had not been quantified. Watson and Conway (1996) detail the process of developing a joint strategy in their useful addition to the subject.

*Assessment*

It has been argued that interagency collaboration is as vital to meeting individual need at the local level as it is for the strategic planning process. In theory, the community care assessment process, with the emphasis on a needs-led approach and the wishes of users and carers, has the potential for providing good-quality information on individuals' informed needs and choices which could also be used at an aggregate level for planning and commissioning housing and care. Assessment for hospital discharge of frail and vulnerable people and discharge from other institutions including children's homes should also consider housing needs. A former social services director, Warner, confirms this view:

> An important element in the assessment of individual need is housing need – including adaptations, repairs or improvements. This will require Social Services and Housing Departments to establish close working relationships between care managers and identified people in housing departments ... Establishing these organisational linkages is crucial. (Warner 1993, p.85)

Southampton and The South West Hampshire Health Commission area, which undertakes joint assessments, sees them as:

> combining into one integrated process the contribution of, and information from, the individual, their carer and all relevant care agencies so that the needs of the individual are considered as a whole. (Tamblyn 1993, p.18)

Arnold *et al.* (1993) put forward a comprehensive seven-step model designed to focus on the interdependence of housing and care needs whilst also ensuring that the individual profile is retained.

*Housing management*

Griffiths (1988), and others, have been able to separate the housing task (bricks and mortar) from the social role, on either economic or ideological grounds. Allen (1998), in the context of exploring joint needs assessments, argues that housing management practices are

> preoccupied with the practical task of 'doing' and the technocratic training of knowing 'how to do it'. Unsurprisingly this system is insensitive to subjective expressions of housing need which is instead objectively identified and then stereotyped into pre-defined categories. (Allen 1998, p.94)

Allen suggests that the different approaches to their tasks implies that social workers and housing officers should not consider joint working at all other than when social workers wish to elicit housing resources. In practice, however, the situation is more complex. As noted above, local housing agencies are dealing increasingly with more vulnerable tenants as a result of care in the community, growing numbers of elderly people and the trend towards residualisation of public housing. In addition, many people with care support needs do not receive care, often because their needs are deemed insufficient to warrant scarce resources. At the estate level managers cannot easily ignore social problems and housing managers are often the first to be aware of a tenant in distress finding themselves providing support beyond basic housing management. The burden on housing workers is not only in assessing housing need, planning and contracting both in-house and external services, but also (the often unrecognised) tasks of monitoring, support and advice for people with community care needs. It is therefore doubtful that strict distinctions can be drawn in practice between housing's social role and its technocratic role. As Arnold and Page state, 'like other cost-inspired dividing lines, it is a line which is much more visible to budget holders and managers than to people who need their service' (Arnold and Page 1992, p.49).

A study by Clapham and Franklin found that 'It was apparent that the boundaries of housing management were drawn differently not only in different authorities, but also between different offices in the same authority' (Clapham and Franklin 1994). They also found that the service offered to tenants with community care needs varied both within and between housing departments. There is little agreement on a systematic classification of housing management tasks, although there are a number of roles that housing management can, and does, play that coincide with social care functions. These include:

- intensive housing management
- liaison with social services over community care, children at risk or the mentally ill
- helping to develop community projects such as 'good neighbour' schemes
- arranging adaptations for people with disabilities

- welfare aspects of wardens' work
- rehousing homeless people
- dealing with the effects of alcohol and drug abuse
- community support
- emotional support
- debt counselling/benefit advice
- preventing racial harassment.

Within such a complex relationship between health, welfare and housing, confusion about roles and responsibilities are inevitable.

### Networks and joint projects

Collaboration between housing and social care agencies often takes place in specific projects that may be set up by any of those agencies. Such projects may, for example, concern the plight of vulnerable groups with health or community care needs, such as people with alcohol and drug-related problems, people with HIV or Aids, or people who may present as homeless but have an underlying care need. A collaborative service is even more essential for these groups to ensure that they do not fall through the social care net; and a fast-track assessment is required so that a solution can be quickly identified and the purchasing responsibility agreed. There are also projects involving hospital discharges or admissions. However, research carried out by CHAR (CHAR housing campaign for single people) noted that 'for many providers of housing and support, the quality of consultation and notification for agencies working with people being discharged from institutions had actually deteriorated rather than improved' (Leigh 1994, p.55).

### Homelessness

The impact of homelessness epitomises the centrality of housing in meeting people's health and social care needs. Homelessness excludes people from mainstream services and from having a sense of belonging, privacy of space, or somewhere for personal possessions. There is no physical support, therefore no emotional support, and usually little social support either. As a result, homeless people characteristically have a range of social problems, and community care assessment systems do not work well with those with multiple needs. The National Health Service and Community Care Act 1990 assumed that people assessed for community care would already have some form of accommodation, and the increasing priority given to housing issues since 1990 has not much extended to homeless people. With a continued lack of resources it has not been possible to provide for individually assessed needs and provide the most appropriate accommodation and form of support. It has been argued that community care has in fact acted as a barrier to homeless single people getting appropriate services. Whereas homeless people with support needs were able previously to get a place in a registered care home paid for by the DSS, now, to access services that need funding they need a community care assessment and to be accepted as priority for funding. Consequently there has been a reduction in the number of registered care home places accessible to homeless people and this has not been compensated for by a rise in access to ordinary housing with domiciliary care packages.

There is an increasing body of evidence that many homeless people need care and support (in particular there are growing numbers of homeless people with mental health problems). Whilst no agency has had a clear statutory responsibility for such people there is a proliferation of agencies involved. One major example of cross-boundary work was the Homeless Mentally Ill Initiative which the Department of Health established in 1990 to address the needs of homeless people in central London with long-term mental health problems. A number of mental health teams were set up under the Initiative and outreach workers from these teams visited day centres and hostels, making referrals and collecting data. They were successful in reaching large numbers of homeless people with mental health problems; however, the lack of move-on accommodation meant that it was not always possible to maintain the contact. Consequently, people with high support needs remained homeless, reflecting the absence of a coordinated strategy on housing with care.

### User involvement and empowerment

It is increasingly recognised that service planning and delivery tends to be more effective with the active involvement of users. Government proposals such as those outlined in *Modernising Local Government* (DETR 1998) and *Best Value*

(DETR 1999), and funding-related incentives such as the single regeneration budget (SRB) are designed to enable service users to play a more important role in planning, delivering and monitoring services. However, research indicates that user involvement within joint housing and social service initiatives is restricted largely to choice between a limited range of existing options rather than the development of wider choices (Arblaster *et al.* 1996).

Participation, however, includes considerably more than purely consultation and should be seen as of intrinsic value not only to service providers but users themselves. The concept should embrace empowerment, which is central to the needs of disabled people marginalised by society. At the least such a process needs to enable those being empowered continually to understand their circumstances and use their potential to gain more control and power over their own lives; it needs to expose the processes of social exclusion and begin to counter these effects (Cooper and Hawtin 1997). As Braye and Preston-Shoot (1995) point out, therefore, empowerment may be valued as an end in itself as well as a means to achieving social change.

Community development approaches have been seen as one way of achieving empowerment and social change through the involvement of local people, representing the whole community, in the process (Hawtin and Cooper 1997; Botchel and Hawtin 1998). In the early 1970s social care agencies started to look more broadly at community development approaches to the provision of social care. However, after the closure of the influential Community Development Projects and the establishment of integrated social service and social work departments in the mid-1970s, training for community development and social work went separate ways (Shaw 1998). In the late 1990s, empowerment-based projects involving housing and social care in community development, or, more accurately, 'community action', is rare (Hawtin 1998).

There was, however, a short-lived revival in community social work following the Barclay Report in the early 1980s, and more recently there has been limited evidence that a 'community development' perspective is being taken within some agencies (Arblaster *et al.* 1998). Such initiatives are based on the view of the 'caring community'. The extent to which people with disabilities can live a 'normal' life is often seen as closely related to their integration with the community within which they wish to be identified. All members of the community are seen as potential users, carers or volunteers in some capacity or other. This approach takes a holistic view of residents' needs – being not just housing or social care needs in isolation – and brings together the relevant agencies and residents working and living in an area. In this way, the community has the capacity to become a 'caring community', in which many of its members recognise the need to help others and are willing, with some assistance if necessary, to do so. Such an approach seeks to include the wider community in developing solutions to care problems through devising their own agenda, developing their own initiatives and managing the delivery of services themselves in a way that meets their own specific needs.

## Summary

Since its origins in the mid-nineteenth century, the housing profession has adopted twin faces of a caring profession and one that is also concerned with 'bricks and mortar' (Conway 1995). The practices of one of the founding members of the profession in the last century, Octavia Hill, led the way for the social role (Whelan 1998). However, its more restricted functional or technocratic role has recently also been emphasised politically as well as practically through policies such as competitive tendering, an emphasis on quantitative performance indicators, the rules that housing authorities work under, the substantial investment in social housing provision and the lack of any care element in housing training. Housing policy in Britain has never been coherent or consistent, especially regarding social housing; however, the recent changes in policy within all sections of the public services represents a substantial shift of the state away from being a provider towards being an enabler, coordinator and commissioner of services in response to market forces. It represents a move to a needs-led approach, includes the involvement of service users as 'customers', and focuses on the development of a mixed economy of welfare.

Until the late 1980s the emphasis in community care was primarily on health and social services, but the last decade has seen widespread, although not complete, acceptance of the contention that housing is a key area of community care and can make a major contribution to good community care. The increased realisation of the importance of the housing dimension accompanied the run-down of long-stay hospitals and the lack of alternative 'institutional'-style provision in the community, together with the growth in the rate of homelessness, particularly amongst people with mental health problems. This has contributed to a demand not only for greater intersectoral collaboration, but also for a greater range of care and accommodation options to be provided, from full residential care through to various concepts of floating support to people in their own homes. There have been a range of ideas contributing to the growth in awareness of the housing dimension of social care and the development of policy and practice, including the following.

- Ideas about specific features of the living environment and the well-being of users of community care policy. For example, the emphasis of government declarations has, arguably, been more insistently on 'own home' rather than 'homely environments'. There has been more emphasis on staying in what has been termed 'own home' rather than having to move to a new 'own home', such as sheltered housing, whilst 'move-on' models of accommodation have been much criticised.

- The growth of consumerism and the emphasis on choice and preference, linked with the contention that most people prefer to live in a home of their own. The extent to which people have a realistic choice about the type, tenure and location they want has been disputed with current government policies favouring home ownership at the expense of other tenures.

- The perception that the basis of community care is the continuation, or the renewal, of the experience of ordinary living. The extent to which people with disabilities are able to live a 'normal' life is often viewed as closely related to their integration with the community within which they wish to be identified.

- The arguments for 'independent living' which reinforced demands for both ordinary housing, and for the location of care support to be switched to users' homes.

- The growing awareness of the interdependency of housing needs and other needs, particularly health and social care, has made it almost inevitable that the housing role be more carefully examined in community care.

- The targeting of subsidies to individuals rather than property, along with the growing marginalisation of many tenants in the public rented sector, has contributed to an awareness among housing, health and social care professionals that they share a similar client base with interdependent housing as well as care needs.

Although most researchers suggest that progress towards interagency working has at best been slow and in many respects disappointing, Fletcher and Wistow (1997), among others, have argued that the housing sector is in pole position to play a lead role in preventative strategies in community care. They note that housing is not an end in itself but links with other aspects of communities including job creation, safety and community involvement. Among the types of approach which they consider are Care and Repair, Staying Put and sheltered housing, linked with social care services as a community care service and housing alternative to residential care. In addition, not only can well-designed housing – such as 'lifetime homes' or forms of adaptable housing – help people stay in their homes, but this can create more stable households which in turn lead to more stable communities. Other positive examples of developments in this direction include some evidence of greater housing involvement in community care planning, particularly through mechanisms such as locality planning and special needs housing forums (DoH 1994; Lund and Foord 1997), examples of innovative provision and a growing diversity of schemes (although not necessarily choice for individuals; Arnold and Page 1992; DoH 1994; Watson and Conway 1996) and other examples of good practice (Means and Smith 1996).

### References

Allen, C. (1997) 'The policy and implementation of the housing role in community care: A constructionalist theoretical perspective.' *Housing Studies 12*, 1, 85–110.

Allen, C. (1998) 'Post-modernism and knowledgeable competence: Social work, housing management and community care needs.' In I. Shaw, S. Lambert and D. Clapham (eds) *Social Care and Housing.* London: Jessica Kingsley Publishers.

Arblaster, L., Conway, J., Foreman, A., Hawtin, M. (1996) *Asking the Impossible: Interagency Working to Address the Housing, Health and Social Care Needs of People in Ordinary Housing.* Bristol: Policy Press/Joseph Rowntree Foundation.

Arblaster, L., Conway, J., Foreman, A. and Hawtin, M. (1998) *Achieving the Impossible? Collaboration in Delivering Housing, and Community Care.* Bristol: Policy Press.

Archbishop of Canterbury Commission on Urban Poverty Areas (1985) *Faith in the City; Report by the Archbishop of Canterbury Commission on Urban Poverty Areas.* London: Church House Publishing.

Arnold, P. and Page, D. (1992) *Bricks and Mortar or Foundations for Action? Housing and Community Care.* Hull: The School of Social and Professional Studies, Humberside Polytechnic.

Arnold, P., Bochel, H. M., Brodhurst, S. and Page, D. (1993) *Community Care: The Housing Dimension.* York: Joseph Rowntree Foundation.

Audit Commission (1998) *Home Alone: The Role of Housing in Community Care.* London: Audit Commission.

Barnes, C. (1991) *Disabled People in Britain and Discrimination.* London: Hurst and Co.

Barton, L. (ed) (1996) *Disability and Society: Emerging issues and Insights.* Harlow: Longman.

Boardman, B. (1991) *Fuel Poverty: From Cold Homes to Affordable Warmth.* London: Bellhaven.

Braye, S. and Preston-Shoot, M. (1995) *Empowering Practice in Social Care.* Buckingham: Open University Press.

Byrne, D.S., Harrison, S.P., Keithley, J., McCarthy, P. (1986) *Health and Housing: The Relationship Between Housing Conditions and the Health of Council Tenants.* Aldershot: Gower.

Clapham, D. and Smith, S.J. (1990) 'Housing policy and special needs.' *Policy and Politics 18*, 193–206.

Clapham, D. and Franklin, B. (1994) *The Housing Management Contribution to Community Care.* Glasgow: Centre for Housing Research and Urban Studies.

Cobbold, C. (1996) *A Cost Benefit Analysis of Lifetime Homes.* York: York Publishing Services.

Conway (1995) 'Housing as an instrument of health care.' *Health and Social Care in the Community 3*, 141–150.

Cooper, C., Hawtin, M. and Botchel, H. (1997) *Housing Community and Conflict: Understanding Resident 'Involvement'.* Aldershot: Arena.

Cooper, C. and Hawtin, M. (1997) 'Community involvement housing and equal opportunities.' In C. Cooper, M. Hawtin and H. Botchel (eds) *Housing Community and Conflict: Understanding Resident 'Involvement'.* Aldershot: Ashgate Publishing.

Cooper, R., Watson, L. and Allen, G. (1994) *Shared Living: Social Relations in Supported Housing.* Sheffield: Joint Unit for Social Services Research.

Craig, G. and Manthorpe, J. (1996) *Wiped Off the Map? Local Government Reorganisation and Community Care.* Papers in Social Research No.5. Hull: Humberside University.

Craig, G. (1993) *The Community Care Reforms and Local Government Change.* Hull: University of Humberside, School of Social and Professional Studies.

Curtis (1991) 'Residential location as a gateway to health care.' In S. Smith, R. Knill-Jones and A. McGuckin *Housing for Health.* Harlow: Longman.

Department of the Environment/Department of Health (1992) *Housing and Community Care Circular 10/92.* London: DoE/DoH.

Department of the Environment, Transport and the Regions (1998) *Modernising Local Government.* London: HMSO.

Department of Health (1989) *Caring for People: Community Care in the Next Decade and Beyond.* Cm 849. London: HMSO.

Department of Health (1992) *The Health of the Nation.* London: HMSO.

Department of Health (1994) *Implementing Caring for People: Housing and Homelessness.* London: HMSO.

Department of Health (1998) *Modernising Social Services: Promoting Independence, Improving Protection, Raising Standards.* Cm 4169. London: The Stationery Office.

Department of Health (1998) *One Health Nation: A Contract for Health.* London: HMSO.

Department of Health/Department of the Environment, Transport and the Regions (1997) *Housing and Community Care: Establishing a Strategic Framework.* London: DOH/DETR.

DETR (1999) *Implementing Best Value: A Consultation Paper on Draft Guidance.* London: DETR.

Fletcher, P. (1998) 'Care comes into focus.' *Housing Today 85,* 28 May.

Fletcher, P. and Wistow, G. (1997) 'A question of respect.' *Agenda,* February, 12–15.

Griffiths, R. (1988) *Community Care: Agenda for Action.* London: HMSO.

Harker, M., Kilgallon, B., Palmer, J. and Tickell, C. (1996) *Making Connections: Policy and Governance for Community Care.* London: National Federation of Housing Associations.

Hawtin, M. (1998) 'User friendly.' *Community Care,* 25 June, 24–5.

Hawtin, M. and Bochel, H. (1998) 'Involvement and disablement.' In C. Cooper and M. Hawtin (eds) *Resident Involvement and Community Action.* Coventry: Chartered Institute of Housing.

Henwood, M. (1995) *Making a Difference? Implementation of the Community Care Reforms Two Years On.* London: Nuffield Institute for Health.

Heywood, F. (1994) *Adaptations: Finding Ways To Say Yes.* Bristol: School for Advanced Urban Studies.

Heywood, F. (1996) *Funding Adaptations: The Need to Co-operate.* Bristol: Policy Press.

House of Commons Health Committee (1994) *Better Off in the Community? The Care of People Who are Seriously Mentally Ill.* Report together with the proceedings of the Committee. Session 1993/4. London: HMSO.

Hudson, J., Watson, L. and Allen, G. (1996) *Moving Obstacles: Housing Choices and Community Care.* Bristol: Policy Press.

Karn, V. and Sheridan, L. (1994) *New Homes in the 1990s: A Study of Design Space and Amenity in Housing Association and Private Sector Production.* York: University of Manchester and Joseph Rowntree Foundation.

Leather, P. and Morrison, T. (1997) *The State of UK Housing: A Factfile on Dwelling Conditions.* Bristol: The Policy Press

Leigh, C. (1994) *Everybody's Baby: Implementing Community Care for Single Homeless People.* London: CHAR.

Lund, B. and Foord, M. (1997) *Toward Integrated Living: Housing Strategies and Community Care.* Bristol: Policy Press.

Major City Councils Housing Group (1988) *Housing and Community Care: A Challenge to Local Authorities.* London: MCCHG.

McCafferty, P. (1994) *Living Independently: A Study of the Housing Needs of Elderly and Disabled People.* London: HMSO.

Means, R. and Smith, R. (1994) *Community Care: Policy and Practice.* Basingstoke: Macmillan.

Means, R. and Smith, R. (1996) *Community Care: Housing and Homelessness: Issues, Obstacles and Innovative Practice.* Bristol: Policy Press.

Means, R., Brenton, M., Harrison, L. and Heywood, F. (1997) *Making Partnerships Work in Community Care: A Guide for Practitioners in Housing, Health and Social Services.* London: DETR/DoH.

Nocon, A. (1994) *Collaboration in Community Care in the 1990s.* Sunderland: Business Education Publishers.

Office for Public Management (1992) *Assessment of the Housing Requirements of People with Special Needs over the Next Decade.* London: Office for Public Management.

Oldman, C. (1988) 'More than bricks and mortar.' *Housing,* June/July, 13–14.

Oldman, C. (1990) *Moving in Old Age: New Directions in Housing Policies.* London: HMSO.

Oliver, M. (1990) *The Politics of Disablement.* London: Macmillan.

Page, D. (1993) *Building for Communities: A Study of New Housing Association Estates.* York: Joseph Rowntree Foundation.

Percy-Smith, J. *(ed)* (1996) *Needs Assessment in Public Policy.* Buckingham: Open University Press.

Pieda Consultancy (1996) *An Evaluation of the Disabled Facilities Grant System.* London: HMSO.

Shaw, I. (1998) 'Practice and research for housing the socially excluded.' In I. Shaw, S. Lambert and D. Clapham (eds) *Social Care and Housing.* London: Jessica Kingsley Publishers.

Shaw, I., Lambert, S. and Clapham, D. (eds) (1998) *Social Care and Housing.* London: Jessica Kingsley Publishers.

Sinclair, I. (1988) *Bridging Two Worlds: Social Work and the Elderly Living Alone.* Aldershot: Avebury.

Stewart, G. (1998) 'Housing, poverty and social exclusion.' In I. Shaw, S. Lambert and D. Clapham (eds) *Social Care and Housing.* London: Jessica Kingsley Publishers.

Swain, J., Finkelstein, V., French, S. and Oliver, M. (eds) (1993) *Disabling Barriers – Enabling Environments.* London: Sage.

Tamblyn, J. (1993) 'Home Environment and Care Assessment.' Paper presented to Care and Repair Cymru's Policy Conference.

Van de Ven, A.H. (1976) 'On the nature, formation and maintenance or relations among organisations.' *Academy of Management Review 1,* 4, 24–36.

Wagner, G. (1988) *Residential Care: A Positive Choice.* London: HMSO.

Warner, N. (1993) 'The role of housing in a successful community care programme.' *Housing Review 42,* 5, Sept/Oct.

Watson, L. and Conway, T. (1996) *Homes for Independent Living: Housing and Community Care Strategies.* Birmingham: Chartered Institute of Housing.

Watson, L. and Harker, M. (1993) *Community Care Planning: A Model for Housing Need Assessment.* London: National Federation of Housing Associations/Institute of Housing.

Whelan, R. (1998) *Octavia Hill and the Social Housing Debate.* London: The Institute of Economic Affairs.

# CHAPTER 9

# Social Care and Social Security

*Geoff Fimister*

The social security system interacts with the social care system at many points and in many ways. I should say at the outset that I shall use the term 'social care' to refer to community (including residential) care services provided in respect of people who are physically or mentally ill or disabled, or who have frailties due to old age. It should be borne in mind, however, that many of the same issues are to be found in one form or another in related areas, such as policy in respect of children and families, or of housing.

As for the term 'social security', I shall use this in the wide sense of the benefit system in general, rather than give it the more narrow meaning of *contributory* benefits. Indeed, the contributory benefit system is often irrelevant to the users of social care services, as their disadvantages will often have prevented them from acquiring a work history sufficient to see them through the various contribution tests. In the UK, the benefit system amounts to a complex set of interactions between contributory and means-tested provision and some benefits (especially in the context of disability) which are neither. Most people find it all very baffling – and – as noted above – this system itself interacts with social care provision. It does so through various entitlement rules and funding and charging arrangements, some of them quite labyrinthine. I do not have space to describe all of this in detail (for a full discussion, see Fimister 1995), but I propose in this chapter to draw out some of the key issues, place them in historical context and look for some pointers to the future[1].

---

1    This is a rapidly changing field. Even in the brief period since this chapter was written, there have been some changes which are not anticipated here.

## A brief recent history

In order to appreciate the way in which current issues manifest themselves, it is as well to have some impression of how we got to where we are. The history of these matters arguably can be traced back to the Elizabethan Poor Law and certainly to the Welfare State reforms of 1948. However, for our present purposes I shall pick up the tale in the early 1980s, when private sector residential care and nursing home provision began to expand rapidly. Partly, this was stimulated by changes in 1980 to the system of means-tested social assistance ('supplementary benefit' prior to April 1988, 'income support' thereafter) whereby a tightening of rules, designed to save money, had the inadvertent side effect of establishing entitlements more clearly in the private care home context. This situation was then allowed to persist because its effect in encouraging private provision suited the then government's ideological leanings. These technical changes, combined with demographic pressures, shrinking local authority provision and a reduction in long-stay hospital beds, served to create a lucrative environment for private sector care home proprietors.

From the government's perspective, though, the rosy glow of spreading privatisation gave way in a few short years to the clanging of alarm bells, as benefit costs soared. By the end of the 1980s, the government was able to complain that social assistance costs in private and voluntary sector residential care and nursing homes had risen '... in cash terms from £10m. in December 1979 to over £1,000m. by May 1989' (Department of Health 1989, para 8.5). (Note that, for convenience, I shall use the terms 'Department of Health' (DoH) and 'Department of Social Security' (DSS) throughout this chapter, although prior to a reorganisation in 1988 they were in fact two arms of a single 'Department of Health and Social Security').

As early as 1983, a system of local limits was imposed in order to try to hold back spending growth. A tight system of national limits followed in 1985. These measures, though, brought with them another problem – a geographically variable, but widespread, shortfall between benefit levels and care home fees. Many residents struggled financially and/or had to accept a reduced quality of accommodation, while relatives and charities came increasingly under pressure to make supplementary payments. A financial headache for the government had become also a significant political embarrassment, a combination which fuelled a growing ambition within the Treasury and the DSS to shift the problem elsewhere. What was needed was an effective way of cash-limiting spending while diverting political fallout (see Fimister and Hill 1993 for a discussion of this strategy in this and other contexts).

As it happened, in parallel to these financial and political pressures for a new system, there was also a genuine professional debate as to what was the appropriate response to the growing number of people in need of care services. The DoH, local government, health and social services professionals and various groups representing service users' perspectives all had an interest here. There was a broad consensus that the large amounts of social security money involved could doubtless be better spent, not least in shifting the focus of policy from residential to community-based options.

Between 1986 and 1988, several official reports appeared, the most influential of which was that by Sir Roy Griffiths, proposing a restructuring of community care services and a large-scale transfer of social security funds to local authority social services departments (SSDs) (Griffiths 1988) (note that I shall use the abbreviation 'SSD' to encompass also Scottish social work departments). The government was initially reluctant to see additional resources on this scale pass to local authorities, since the general strategy in relation to local government was to seek to weaken it relative to the centre. However, the Griffiths case was eventually largely accepted and a new system broadly along these lines was announced (DoH 1989). Local authority SSDs would act as the lead agencies in assessing need and developing community care plans. They were not expected to act primarily as providers, especially as regards residential care, where benefit entitlements would be structured so as to reduce charging revenue where a local authority home was used (see Fimister 1995, pp. 69ff.). The new system eventually began in 1993 (although existing care home residents largely remained under the old rules).

The transfer of social security funds to SSDs was a complex matter and was, of course, fraught with financial politics. How much would the DSS have spent in this area, had the old system continued? A joint central/local government working party with the fearsome title of the 'Algebra Group' was set up to estimate this, although the two sides predictably had to agree to differ. It is not the purpose of this chapter to delve into the general financial difficulties of the community care system, especially since the transfer of social security funds is only part of the picture, but the problems have been deemed sufficient to merit the establishment, by the new government, of a Royal Commission on the finance of long-term care (see below).

As the saga of the finance of residential care and nursing home places unwound, a parallel set of issues was bringing about change and controversy as regards the benefit régimes which applied to the more 'middle range' areas of supported accommodation, where a greater degree of independent living was envisaged than would normally be expected in a care home – 'adult placement' schemes, supported lodgings, hostels and the like. As in the case of care homes, means-tested social assistance included special rules for board and lodging accommodation and for hostels, which were similarly beset by financial and political difficulties – and, administratively, got in the way of computerisation. Various attempts to contain costs attracted both political controversy and legal challenge, so plans were laid here, also, to shift such special provision out of the benefit system.

Special rules for boarders, including those in supported lodgings and most similar types of accommodation, were abolished with effect from April 1989. Hostels followed suit in October. This followed a period of often heated debate between the DSS and other interested parties, such as local government and various voluntary organisations, accommodation providers and academics. In the abstract, there was indeed much to be said for incorporating benefits for marginalised groups into the mainstream system. However, the proposal that ordinary social assistance and housing benefit should be paid failed to take into account costs – notably for care – which were included in accommodation charges but excluded from the housing benefit scheme. The social security departmental agenda was dominated by the desire to scrap the special rules, whereas over at health, there was a reluctance to become involved in benefit matters. There was a clear danger that service users/benefit claimants would fall through the consequent policy gap.

In the event, the disappearance of resources from one part of the benefit system led to pressures in other parts. Social workers, welfare rights advisers, accommodation providers and others stepped up their efforts to help service users to claim benefits for the extra costs of disability; while the role of housing benefit in meeting the support element of accommodation charges was pushed often to the full extent of its legal limits (and sometimes beyond). The result was a complex pattern of gainers and losers from the changes of the late 1980s in this area of benefit and accommodation provision.

The story was, however, far from over in relation to supported lodgings and similar establishments. In 1993, the legislation requiring the registration of private sector care homes with social services or health authorities was extended to 'small homes' of fewer than four residents. This drew into the registration net many supported lodging-type arrangements (where board and personal care were both provided) which were, in ethos and organisation, not care homes at all – being much more geared to philosophies of independent living. However, the DSS saw in the advent of 'small homes' registration a ready means of distinguishing between different benefit regimes – essentially, whether housing benefit would be payable or not. No longer would the benefit authorities need to concern themselves with the exact nature of the accommodation and services provided. If the accommodation was registered, then HB would not be paid and the claimant would receive the much more limited entitlements applicable to a care home resident. If social services funding was drawn in as a result, benefits for the additional costs of disability would be withdrawn (under rules which seek to prevent overlap between the two) increasing still further the financial dependence of the accommodation on the SSD and usually leaving the service user to get by on the 'pocket money' rates applicable in a care home. So much for 'independent living'.

These ill-effects were fully explained to the DSS, during consultations, by local government and voluntary sector interests, but the administrative savings were too attractive to central government and so the changes went ahead anyway. (The DoH again seems to have stayed out of the argument.) As a consequence, a number of accommodation projects have been pulled into 'high dependency' benefit and SSD charging regimes – what we might call 'institutionalisation in the community'.

As the 1990s progressed, the role of housing benefit in helping to finance residents of unregistered, 'middle-range', supported accommodation continued to grow. Many saw this as a positive use of public money (see for example Griffiths 1995 and 1997). Moreover, benefits for the additional costs of disability continued to develop a higher profile (following their reorganisation in 1988 and 1992 these are essentially attendance allowance; disability living allowance; and the disability and severe disability premiums attached to various means-tested benefits) – again arguably to constructive effect as regards community care policy. However, the Treasury and the DSS saw it otherwise. Disability benefits are discussed further below. As for housing benefit, attempts by the Treasury and DSS to push for a restrictive 'fabric of the dwelling' interpretation of its role, combined with various court decisions, have clashed with community care objectives; led to widespread variation in practice; threatened the viability of a number of projects (indeed, caused some to close); and created overall 'planning blight'. The current government has inherited a difficult interdepartmental review of the finance of this sort of supported accommodation and has taken welcome (if not entirely comprehensive) steps to protect existing provision pending its outcome – now not expected before 1999. Ironically, part of the delay may be due to the fact that the DoH at last seems to be fighting the community care corner.

A marked feature of the above historical account is indeed the extent to which the different agendas of the various actors have led to policy conflict, not least between central government departments. It is, of course, in the nature of human affairs that different social, economic, bureaucratic and political interests will clash from time to time. To an extent, a degree of lack of 'fit' between the perspectives of different central government departments is, on this basis, to be expected (and such a thing is certainly not unheard of in local government also). However, it is arguable that the previous national administration allowed policy conflict to get out of hand in a number of areas, not least that of the interface between social security and community care, because the Treasury has been able to insist upon cuts with an excessive lack of regard for the knock-on effects. Whether the new regime is able to do any better in this respect remains to be seen. We turn now to the state of play in the wake of the 1997 general election.

### New government, new solutions?

The election of a Labour government in May 1997 placed a number of question marks over the whole benefit system – not just those aspects which interact directly with social care. Would the new government abandon the previous régime's general policy of eroding entitlements? In which case, would this herald an attempt to strengthen benefit provision? Or a period of stability, rather than constant change, on the benefit front? Or would the previous government's agenda be carried forward under new management? In the event, a period of stability was ruled out; but – confusingly – a heady mixture of all the other possibilities has emerged, leaving opinion divided as to whether the future for the benefit system is at least partially promising, or generally grim.

I would argue that, to make sense of the above, one has to divide the measures taken so far into three groups: 'pipeline' changes, which the previous government had announced and built into its spending plans and which the new regime has largely carried forward; unannounced options which the Conservatives were considering and which remained on the table as possibilities after the election; and manifestations of the Labour administration's longer term agenda.

Above all, though, the public spending environment is crucial: Labour had undertaken, prior to the general election, to remain within the Conservative government's spending plans for at least two years; and not to raise income tax, even at the top level, during the course of the next parliament. This meant that great pressure would be brought to bear on the largest area of public spending – social security – to generate savings which could be diverted into priority areas such as health and education. The result has been a number of reviews of different parts of the benefit system, coordinated to varying degrees. There are certain broad themes – notably the emphasis on getting as many claimants as possible into low-paid work – but little sign of any detailed master plan, be it sinister or benign.

It is not my purpose here fully to analyse the fascinating question of the current government's benefits agenda (see Fimister 1998 for a more comprehensive discussion). However, I would argue that the success of a true community care strategy will depend at least as much on the adequacy of the disposable incomes of its clients as it will on the provision of care services. The ability to afford an adequate diet and to keep warm and sufficiently well-clothed are obviously critical to the survival in the community of vulnerable people. The ability to afford transport, a social life and leisure activities are just as important in their own way. It would be appropriate, then, to consider now the state of play as regards the future of *retirement benefits and benefits paid in respect of sickness and disability.* I shall then move on to consider briefly the benefit issues around the position of carers; the future provision of long-term care; and the role of advice and advocacy.

### Retirement benefits

The new government's strategy on retirement benefits does not seek to reverse the cuts imposed by its predecessor. Perhaps the most disappointing aspect of this in anti-poverty terms is the decision not to restore the old uprating formula, which reflected rising earnings rather than merely price movements.

The Labour proposals which have so far been put forward, in varying degrees of detail, entail the following.

1. Continuation of the basic pension in its present form.

2. Changes to the means-tested top up (currently income support) to try to make payment as automatic as possible in order to address the take-up problem. In the meantime, income support rates for pensioners are to be improved by around £5 per week (around £7 for couples) from April 1999; and pensioners in general (and those on income support in particular) have received additional help with fuel bills. The government has also set up a number of pilot projects to experiment with ways of improving take up of income support amongst pensioners. Local authority and voluntary sector interests with experience in this field have been consulted and have made available their own findings and campaign reports.

3. The creation, in association with private sector providers (and possibly mutual organisations), of a new second-tier 'stakeholder' pension, alongside the state earnings-related pension scheme (which would continue as an option).

4. Exploration of a means to incorporate into the state earnings-related pension scheme a 'citizenship pension' for people who have limited contribution records. Caring responsibilities have most frequently been cited in this context – although the position of others, such as those excluded from the labour market by severe disability, will also be considered.

The above proposals have been fed into the government's overall review of pensions policy, which was announced at the 1996 Labour Party Conference as a consequence of the leadership's much-publicised clash with Barbara Castle over this issue. Following an initial period of consultation, which ended in October 1997, some preliminary proposals were distributed for further comment. A Green Paper on pensions is planned towards the end of 1988.

One issue concerning retirement pensions which was the subject of early action by the new government was the compensation programme for the victims of mis-selling of personal pensions during the late 1980s and early 1990s. Insult has been added to the injury of this major financial scandal by the extremely slow progress made by the pensions industry in compensating the victims (of whom there are possibly more than two million – *Guardian* 29 January 1998). The government has taken a tough line and demanded rapid improvement, backed by the threat (and in some cases, the reality) of sanctions. It has to be said, though, that this episode is hardly an auspicious advertisement for the projected key role of the private sector referred to above – which is no doubt why the March 1998 social security Green Paper (Secretary of State for Social Security *et al.*1998) laid such emphasis on the need for a more reliable regulatory process.

The government has also indicated that it intends at some stage to legislate for pension sharing upon divorce. Considerable consultation and exploration of the complex issues involved will be required, but the intention seems firm.

It can be seen from the above that the future incomes of pensioners living in the community – whether frail or not – are very much in the melting pot at present. When proposals finally emerge, how will we judge their adequacy? The new government has on the one hand extolled the virtues of success measures, but on the other has rejected calls to develop *minimum income standards* against which proposals can be assessed (see Veit-Wilson 1994). The absence of such standards is indeed a weakness of the overall process of benefit reform.

### Benefits for sickness and disability

A review of benefits for sickness and disability was inherited by the new government and is likely to report in one form or another by the end of 1998. It is wide ranging, encompassing benefits paid as a result of *interruption of earnings* and those which relate to the *additional costs* of disability. Considerable controversy has been created by various leaks and rumours suggesting that options for substantial cuts were under consideration. Disabled people's organisations have responded with a vehemence, including high-profile protests and demonstrations, which seems to have taken the government by surprise. The March 1998 social security Green Paper and associated ministerial comments went some way to provide reassurance, although doubts remain and stricter eligibility criteria for some key benefits are certainly under consideration.

Reports that the government has been considering cuts in, or restricted access to, disability benefits have been linked by some commentators to the inclusion of disabled people within the 'welfare to work' programme (although, if such a connection were indeed in ministers' minds, it would sit uneasily with reduced access to disability living allowance, which can play an important role in enabling a disabled person to take up employment).

Disability working allowance is to be replaced from October 1999 by a *disabled person's tax credit,* which will be more generous than the existing little-used scheme. Other measures announced in the March 1998 budget relating specifically to disabled people were: the immediate removal of sex discrimination in the award of the additional personal tax allowance where one member of a couple with children is incapacitated; lifting of the 16-hour limit on voluntary work undertaken by people on incapacity benefit; and a one-year linking rule (increased from eight weeks) from October 1998, to enable people with long-term incapacity benefits to return to their previous level of benefit if they take a job which they have to give up within that period.

The leaked information concerning possible cuts which was the subject of such controversy appears to have derived mainly from a civil service 'options' paper. Additional means testing and/or taxation, time limiting of incapacity benefit, abolition of the industrial injuries scheme and dissolving of attendance allowance and disability living allowance into local authority community care funds had all been floated as possibilities. As noted above, these seemed, following the March 1998 Green Paper, to have receded from the policy frame. Instead, emphasis was laid on the expectation of reduced spending as a consequence of more disabled people moving into work and possibly of tighter access criteria for benefits. However, at the time of writing (October 1998) a new round of leaks concerning options for cuts is again generating uncertainty.

The Green Paper proposed (p.54, para 10) 'a more effective test for future (incapacity benefit) claimants which assesses the scale of their employability'. On the face of it this seems welcome – but the fact that the existing rules would be retained for existing claimants implies that something *more* restrictive may be envisaged. The 'gateway' to attendance allowance and disability living allowance is also under review, in consultation with disability organisations. A pattern of gainers and losers may result, as the Green Paper (e.g. p.54, para 11) proposes to use savings from incapacity benefit to 'support severely disabled people with the greatest needs'.

The future of disability living allowance (DLA) and attendance allowance (AA) has been a particular area for concern. Take-up of these benefits has been rising sharply, with a consequent steep increase in their costs. This improved take up is probably mainly the result of more systematic and sustained efforts by local authorities, to a great extent linked to community care assessment procedures, and to greater numbers of severely disabled people living outside of institutions, because of the community care programme. Also, the advent of complex and extremely long self-assessment forms for AA and DLA has led far more disabled people to seek help with their claims, thus improving their chances of success. As DLA and AA encourage independent living and help to keep people out of institutional care, it may be concluded that the additional outlay is money well spent, facilitating community care and welfare to work objectives and keeping down public spending elsewhere in the system. The compartmentalised nature of central government policy making is, though, notoriously resistant to this sort of 'joined-up thinking'.

Ostensibly in response to a (now discredited) Benefits Agency study of fraud in this area of the benefit system, the 'Benefits Integrity Project' was launched by the previous government, involving large-scale reexamination of DLA cases. In theory, underpayments as well as overpayments could be identified by this exercise, but the emphasis has been very much on the latter. There is also some suggestion of indecent haste and questionable training of staff. Disabled people and their advisers have, of course, been concerned at possibly erroneous reduction or withdrawal of benefit and there are certainly many examples of this, reflected in a high claimant success rate where cuts are appealed against. The rate of erroneous awards appears to be much lower than predicted, with instances of fraud 'minimal'. On 9 February 1998, Harriet Harman announced that additional safeguards (an extra review stage) would be built into the decision-making process, while the March 1998 Green Paper (p.55, para 16) says that the project 'is not working well ... has a series of structural flaws ...' and will be reviewed in consultation with disability organisations.

In June 1998, a Disability Benefits Forum was set up by the government to facilitate communication with outside agencies. This is a welcome step, although it remains to be seen how effective – or harmonious – it ultimately will prove. Much will, of course, depend on the nature of the proposals eventually brought forward concerning the future of disability benefits.

### Carers

It is to be hoped that the position of those who care for sick, disabled and frail elderly people will also be adequately addressed by the benefit reviews. As their interests straddle the pensions and disability benefit reviews as well as the Royal Commission on the future of long-term care, one might hope that the issues will be comprehensively considered, or alternatively fear that they will fall between the various stools. Poverty amongst carers, many of whom are themselves frail or disabled, has been much discussed, but no comprehensive strategy has developed to tackle the problems. Inaction, though, cannot be sustained indefinitely, even from the perspective of public spending restraint: as female participation in the labour market becomes fully consolidated, the supply of informal carers may begin to falter, while the British Medical Association estimated in 1995 that such care was saving the government at least £33 billion per year (BMA 1995).

*The finance of long-term care*

This is an issue which extends far beyond the benefit context and it is not my purpose to explore it fully here. However, there is an intimate relationship between the finance of long-term care and the benefit system, both through the funding transfers described above and because of the way in which revenue from charges, for residential care and for day and home care services, is extracted from benefit incomes. A few brief observations would therefore be in order here.

The 1993 changes did not settle this issue and debate has continued throughout the 1990s. I have argued for a system free at the point of delivery, analogous to the National Health Service; or, as an alternative, a social insurance approach (Fimister 1995, Chapter 7). The Joseph Rowntree Foundation's enquiry (JRF 1997) also favoured provision based on these principles. It should be noted, though, that the merits of a social insurance-based system would depend very much on the detail of the particular scheme: partial benefits and/or restrictive contribution tests would to a great extent defeat the object. It is perfectly possible, on the other hand, to develop an adequate scheme which is financed through contributions but which does not deny access to the most vulnerable (see Fimister and Lister 1981 for the case against contribution tests).

The previous government produced proposals for limited changes to the current arrangements, but these went down with the ship at the general election. The current regime then set up a Royal Commission, chaired by Professor Sir Stewart Sutherland, which is expected to report early in 1999. A key problem politically has been the attempt to reconcile the much-lauded virtues of saving and inheritance with the desire of the Treasury to access the value of owner-occupied housing vacated by care home residents. The slogan of 'wealth cascading down the generations' sounds inspiring; the prospect of wealth cascading to the Treasury, as charges are used to reduce pressure for additional revenue support grant to local authorities, is thought not to be an electoral asset. This agenda is to a great extent driving current policy concerns and it will be very interesting to see what the Royal Commission makes of it.

*Advice and advocacy*

We know that it is one thing to be entitled to a benefit, but another to be sure of receiving it. Take up is a well-known problem affecting, in particular, means-tested and disability benefits (whether means tested or not). Moreover, claims can run into difficulties and advice and advocacy may be needed.

All citizens should have access to information, advice and advocacy, not least in relation to social security entitlements (National Consumer Council 1977). But in the social care context, there are particular opportunities to target take-up campaigns (for example, through day centres, community care assessments, social workers' caseloads) or to make available advice and advocacy services in strategic settings (for example hospitals, doctors' surgeries, service users' and carers' support groups). I have discussed these issues extensively elsewhere (e.g. Fimister 1986; 1995, Chapter 6) and there is indeed a substantial literature deriving from tried and tested welfare rights practice. Suffice it for our current purposes, then, to stress that all community care planning should explicitly address the question of the availability and accessibility of advice and advocacy services, both in relation to a person's care package itself and to the income needs which may well prove critical to its success.

There are more mercenary reasons, also, for local authorities to be interested in benefit maximisation, concerning affordability of rents, council tax and a variety of service charges; and the effects on revenue support grant of the numbers of local claimants of certain benefits.

## Conclusions

I have argued that benefit income is a crucial aspect of community care in a number of different respects. I have sketched the historical background of the current debate and have sought to set out the state of play in late 1998.

I would like to close by observing that the future of the benefit system is simultaneously a practical question of day-to-day survival for millions of people, and one of the most technically complex areas of public policy. This latter characteristic has the effect of helping to disempower not only the majority of people who depend on benefits, but also many of those professionals to whom social care service users would normally turn for advice. Obviously, this is wrong. The answer must lie in a combination of constructive benefit reform and the provision of effective and comprehensive information, advice and advocacy services. However, these are as much matters of financial politics as they are of rational problem solving.

## References

British Medical Association (1995) *Who Cares for the Carers?* London: BMA.

Department of Health (1989) *Caring for People: Community Care in the Next Decade and Beyond.* Cm 849. London: HMSO.

Fimister, G. (1986) *Welfare Rights Work in Social Services.* London: Macmillan.

Fimister, G. (1995) *Social Security and Community Care in the 1990s.* Sunderland: Business Education Publishers.

Fimister, G. (1998) *The Benefits Agenda: An Analysis of the Government's Reviews and Proposals.* Newcastle upon Tyne: City Council Welfare Rights Service.

Fimister, G. and Hill, M. (1993) 'Delegating implementation problems: Social security, housing and community care in Britain.' In M. Hill (ed) *New Agendas in the Study of the Policy Process.* Hemel Hempstead: Harvester Wheatsheaf.

Fimister, G. and Lister, R. (1981) *Social Security: The Case Against Contribution Tests.* London: Child Poverty Action Group.

Griffiths, R. (1988) *Community Care: Agenda for Action.* London: HMSO.

Griffiths, S. (1995) *Supporting Community Care: The Contribution of Housing Benefit.* London: National Institute for Social Work.

Griffiths, S. (1997) *Housing Benefit and Supported Housing: The Impact of Recent Changes.* York: Joseph Rowntree Foundation.

Joseph Rowntree Foundation (1997) *Inquiry into Meeting the Costs of Continuing Care.* York: JRF.

National Consumer Council (1977) *The Fourth Right of Citizenship: A Review of Local Advice Services.* London: NCC.

Secretary of State for Social Security/Minister for Welfare Reform (1998) *New Ambitions for Our Country: A New Contract for Welfare.* Cm 3805. London: The Stationery Office.

Veit-Wilson, J. (1994) *Dignity Not Poverty: A Minimum Income Standard for the UK.* London: Commission on Social Justice/Institute for Public Policy Research.

# CHAPTER 10

# Central–Local Relations
## The Changing Balance of Direction versus Discretion in Social Care

*Melanie Henwood*[1]

### Introduction

The publication in 1989 of the White Paper on community care (Department of Health 1989), can, in retrospect, be seen to have marked a significant turning point in the management of relations between central government and local authority social services departments (SSDs). It was, indeed, one of the main objectives set out in the White Paper that there should be a clarification of the responsibilities of agencies, and increased accountability for performance (ibid., para 1.11). A major difficulty with achieving effective community care over the preceding 15 years had been identified as the limited success of measures designed to secure effective collaboration between health and local authorities, both of whom had a role to play. The White Paper sought to replace past approaches with a new model 'based on strengthened incentives and clearer responsibilities' (para 6.1).

*Caring for People* acknowledged that the record of joint planning had been a mixed one: 'a modest success can be claimed if judged against realistic criteria but it nevertheless falls short of the aspirations of the mid-1970s' (para 6.9). Further efforts were argued to be needed to improve coordination, and the then

---

1     This chapter draws upon a programme of work on interagency collaboration carried out at the Nuffield Institute for Health, University of Leeds, in conjunction with Bob Hudson, Brian Hardy and Gerald Wistow, and also on work conducted with Gerald Wistow for the Royal Commission on Long Term Care.

Secretary of State for Health suggested that the new arrangements for organising and delivering community care constituted a framework which would make interservice coordination easier to achieve (Clarke 1989). A 'fresh approach to collaboration and joint planning' was envisaged by the White Paper (para 6.4), based on four elements: first, clarification of 'who does what' through the more explicit recognition of the distinction between health and social care as the basis for funding health and social services respectively; second, allocation of responsibility to SSDs for ensuring that assessment and care management processes take place within a multidisciplinary context where appropriate; third, a redefinition of joint planning through an emphasis on outcomes rather than the mechanics of joint planning and joint finance; and, finally, strengthened financial incentives for joint working through the transfer of social security funds to social services departments and the creation of new specific grants (Wistow 1994).

On the basis of a major empirical study of interagency collaboration, we have argued that whether the White Paper's framework of strengthened incentives and clearer responsibilities really constituted a significantly different environment for collaboration, was open to question (Hudson *et al.* 1997). In particular, it remained the case that some purchasing responsibilities were still ambiguous, and the distinction between health and social care had not been clearly defined. In particular, the ringfencing of the special transitional grant (STG), and the linking of this to joint hospital discharge agreements, provided a new mechanism for relating agency responsibilities to resource allocation processes. Griffiths himself had sought to make receipt of such a grant conditional upon submission of a satisfactory community care plan.

We have reviewed elsewhere the research literature on collaboration and central–local relations in health and social services (Hudson *et al.* 1997). Conclusions from a range of studies have generated broad principles for facilitating interagency collaboration, and four broad principles appear to be at the heart of most recommendations for strengthening strategic approaches to collaboration. These are as follows.

- *Shared vision:* specifying what is to be achieved in terms of user-centred goals; clarifying the purpose of collaboration as a mechanism for achieving such goals, and mobilising commitment around goals, outcomes and mechanisms.

- *Clarity of roles and responsibilities: specifying and agreeing* 'who does what', and designing organisational arrangements by which such roles and responsibilities are to be fulfilled.

- *Appropriate incentives and rewards:* promoting organisational behaviour consistent with agreed goals and responsibilities, and harnessing organisational self-interest to collective goals.

- *Accountability for joint working:* monitoring achievements in relation to the stated vision; holding individuals and agencies to account for the fulfilment of predetermined roles and responsibilities, and providing feedback and review of vision, responsibilities, incentives and their interrelationship (Hudson *et al.* 1997).

These four principles provide a framework against which the new arrangements for collaboration contained in *Caring for People,* and elaborated in subsequent guidance, can be analysed. Box 10.1 presents this analysis, and indicates that all four principles were reflected to a lesser or greater extent. However, more detailed investigation of the framework against specific areas of joint working in community care, paints a more variable picture. Table 10.1 examines the framework for collaboration against four key areas of joint working: community care planning; joint commissioning; hospital discharge and continuing care; and the interface between primary care and social care.

While the framework for collaboration has been developed to varying degrees across each of the four policy areas, it is only in the area of hospital discharge and continuing care that all four principles could be seen to be relatively well developed and coherently expressed.

*Box 10.1 The new framework for collaboration*

**Principles: elements of arrangements to promote collaboration**
*Shared vision*

- White Paper principles emphasising needs and outcomes
- ministerial speeches emphasising seamless care
- user/carer-focused services and interagency working as the key to successful implementation
- Joint letters

*Roles and lead roles for planning, assessment and*

*care management*

- Responsibilities
- Policy and practice guidance
- Joint letters; key tasks and no unilateral withdrawals
- Purchaser–provider split including shared responsibilities for purchasing on behalf of individuals/populations within the same territory
- Distinction between health and social care

*Incentives and rewards*

- STG pre-conditions as incentives and rewards for SSDs to reach strategic agreements with health
- STG as incentives and reward for health to collaborate with
- SSD in hospital discharge and continuing care at the individual level
- Joint finance, dowries and other specific grants

*Accountability*

- Joint working mandatory not optional
- NHS monitoring and review mechanisms
- Joint SSI/RHA monitoring
- Arbitration and disputes procedures (local and regional)

| | | **Table 10.1 Structuring the collaborative environment** | | |
|---|---|---|---|---|
| *Policy area* | *Shared vision* | *Clarity of roles and responsibilities* | *Incentives and rewards* | *Accountability* |
| Community care planning | Uncertainty about purpose of community care plans until publication of practice guidance in 1995 which provided some clarification | 1990 NHS and Community Care Act introduced the statutory requirement for local authorities to produce and publish plans | Underdeveloped mechanisms. The government rejected the Griffiths proposal that a specific grant should be conditional on the submission and approval of community care plans | Absence of any arrangements to hold authorities to account for the production of plans, or to monitor local performance against plans |
| Joint commissioning | Joint commissioning was not referred to in *Caring for People*. Practical guidance issued in 1995 provided a very broad definition | Continuing lack of clarity. Guidance can be seen as permissive rather than directive, and left many issues (including legality unresolved) | No structured incentives in evidence | No formal accountability process developed |
| Hospital discharge and continuing care | Neither hospital discharge or continuing care were strongly emphasised in the White Paper. However, both were given a pivotal importance in the subsequent 'key tasks' letters | Clarification of roles and responsibilities demanded by requirements to reach local agreements for discharge, and subsequently following the 1995 guidance on continuing health care | Special transitional grant was made conditional on evidence of discharge agreements. Other incentives included the motivation to avoid opprobrium in failing to reach local agreement | National programme of monitoring and review accompanied both discharge and continuing care requirements |

| | | Table 10.1 continued | | |
|---|---|---|---|---|
| *Policy area* | *Shared vision* | *Clarity of roles and responsibilities* | *Incentives and rewards* | *Accountability* |
| Primary health care/ social services | Primary health care/social services interface was not a prominent aspect of the White Paper. Its importance was subsequently emphasised in the 'key tasks' letter, and in specific guidance to GPs | Permissive guidance encouraging, but not requiring, joint working at the interface | Few, if any, in evidence, beyond the general incentive for GPs to work with social services if they want to be able to agree assessments and access for residential/ nursing home places | No formal accountability process |

## Hospital discharge and continuing care: a case study in mandate and accountability

The area of hospital discharge and continuing care is distinctive for the level of central mandate which has characterised the development of policy. The key stages of that policy from the time of the 1989 White Paper *Caring for People* are worth examining.

### Hospital discharge

The significance of good hospital discharge procedures and practices assumed a new importance following the 1990 NHS and Community Care Act. However, this would not have been anticipated simply from a reading of *Caring for People*. Indeed, the White Paper made only passing mention of discharge arrangements in noting that it would continue

> to be the responsibility of the Health Authority to ensure that discharge procedures are in place and agreed with the local authority so that people can return home with the support they need or move to appropriate care. (para 4.6)

Full implementation of the NHS and Community Care Act was delayed from the original target of April 1991 until April 1993 (Henwood, Jowell and Wistow 1991). During 1991/92, considerable central attention was focused on supporting and directing localities in their preparations for implementation. In addition to specific help targeted at individual authorities through the 'Community Care Support Force', much of this broader support was focused through a series of joint letters issued by the Social Services Inspectorate and the NHS Executive. The first of these identified eight 'key tasks' on which local authorities, working closely with other agencies, including health authorities, would need to concentrate (Department of Health 1992a).

Authorities were reminded that they would need jointly to review their arrangements for discharging patients from hospital, and to ensure that these satisfied the new requirements around assessment of individual need. Key Task 3 reiterated this requirement by underlining the need to ensure the 'robustness and mutual acceptability of discharge arrangements'. Further DoH letters in 1992 restated the centrality of the eight key tasks, and indicated a concern that further progress needed to be made. A new requirement was that all authorities should reach agreements by 31 December 1992 on strategies covering health and local authority responsibilities for nursing home placements, and estimates of the numbers likely to be involved in the first year of implementation, together with agreement on how hospital discharge procedures would be integrated with community care assessment arrangements (DoH 1992b). The incentive to reach such agreement was strengthened by the subsequent requirement that payment of the community care special transitional grant (STG) would be contingent on evidence of written agreements being in place.

The increasingly clear requirements attached to discharge agreements between the time of the White Paper in 1989 and the implementation of the new legislation in 1993 might be seen with hindsight to reflect two conclusions. First was the realisation that hospital discharge was central to the business of both health and local authorities, and that there was potential for major destabilisation to develop. Without workable agreements in place, the NHS would be unable to achieve discharges which were conditional on the local authority having completed assessment, care planning and purchasing, and local authorities might rapidly be seen to have failed to meet the new requirements around community care. Second, the development of local agreements could not (on the basis of past experience, and on the strength of evidence emerging from DoH monitoring of local preparation) be left simply to local goodwill and cooperation.

Between 1993 and 1995 no further guidance or requirements were introduced around hospital discharge. However, the DoH did issue *The Hospital Discharge Workbook* in 1994. While the document emphasised that policy remained 'as set out in earlier Circulars', its publication might be seen as a further indicator of ongoing concern about the patchy quality of hospital discharges, and the need to secure improvements in routine practice.

## Continuing health care

The development of policy on continuing health care has also become increasingly explicit. Similarly, the relationship between policy in this area and on hospital discharge has been addressed more directly. In preparing for April 1993, and developing the '31 December' agreements, the DoH expected health and local authorities to observe a principle of 'no unilateral withdrawal'. Thus, there should be

> a clear joint understanding of the current pattern of provision, the flows of clients and of the resources committed to continuing care. We would not expect a health or local authority to change the current (March 1992) pattern of provision or the commitment which each is making. (DoH 1992a, Annex B)

Guidance on continuing health care was issued in 1995 mainly in response to 'a number of concerns' raised in a report by the Health Service Commissioner. This had investigated the failure of Leeds Health Authority to make available long-term care for a seriously incapacitated patient no longer requiring acute health care (Report of the Health Service Commissioner 1994). While the report related to the specific circumstances of an individual case, its publication also reflected a more widespread concern that the boundary between health and social care had shifted such that many patients who would previously have been cared for in NHS long-stay wards were now to be found in nursing homes, and were often the responsibility of the local authority. Such matters had also been highlighted by the Health Select Committee (Health Committee 1995a).

The guidance required health authorities (and GP fundholders) to review their current arrangements for, and funding of, continuing health care, and to make any necessary adjustments to their contracts to ensure they were funding the full range of continuing health care services. The interface between continuing health and social care was underlined in the guidance by its attention to discharge arrangements in the context of multidisciplinary assessment. Following a similar approach to the one which has been described in the requirements to produce the 31 December agreements of 1992, the guidance also required health authorities to produce draft documents setting out local policies and eligibility criteria by the end of September 1995. These would be subject to local consultation (and to monitoring and review by region), with final policies and criteria to be ready for implementation the following April (DoH 1995a). The guidance was explicit in highlighting key areas in which collaboration would be needed between agencies 'in agreeing or changing their respective responsibilities for continuing care' (para 1).

The guidance set out to confirm and clarify the responsibilities of the NHS. Thus, it was stated that 'the arrangement and funding of services to meet continuing physical and mental health care needs are an integral part of the responsibilities of the NHS' (DoH 1995a, para 1). The restatement of these responsibilities can be seen as a recognition that some health authorities may have gone too far in moving out of long-term care provision. The then Secretary of State for Health told the Health Select Committee that 'it makes sure that the health service does not come across the boundary when it should not' (Health Committee 1995b, para 10).

The guidance on continuing health care was followed during 1995 and 1996 by further executive letters reporting on progress with implementation, and identifying further priorities for development (DoH 1995b–e, 1996a, 1996b). This sequence of guidance, further advice, and executive letters can be viewed as a clear indication of the priority which the DoH was attaching to the successful implementation of policy on continuing health care.

This overview of the policy context surrounding hospital discharge and continuing health care has highlighted the strong central mandate which increasingly characterised developments since 1989. The preparations for community care in general, and discharge arrangements in particular, were accompanied during 1992 by highly specific and directive executive letters from the DoH, and were parallelled by ongoing monitoring of compliance with this central agenda. A very similar approach was followed during 1995/96 in respect of arrangements for continuing health care.

The essence of the collaborative agenda in the area of hospital discharge and continuing care has been the provision of clearer definitions of health and social services responsibilities. Such clarification was reinforced by the national requirement to secure local discharge agreements (with funding conditional on evidence of such agreements); an implementation support programme including practical guidance and workshops; and structured accountability processes through a national programme of monitoring and review carried out across service boundaries by NHS regional offices, and the Social Services Inspectorate.

In the area of hospital discharge there appears to be evidence of tangible achievements at both strategic and operational levels. Good practice is still not universal (DoH 1998c), and implementation of continuing care guidelines is a developing process. However, both hospital discharge and continuing care provide an example of relative success for collaboration since the early 1990s, characterised by the translation of agreements on broad policies and principles into practical and routine joint working arrangements.

It is also evident that the policy vision for collaborative working was not fully developed in the 1989 White Paper, nor in the NHS and Community Care Act, passed the following year. Guidance issued in subsequent years has continued to refine the model, and to introduce new dimensions. This is perhaps to be expected; policies evolve and develop over time. However, each iteration of the policy has not always been accompanied by a clarity of purpose over *why* specific developments have taken shape. There is a distinction to be made between clarifying what are the policy objectives, and specifying *how* they are to be achieved. In the area of hospital discharge and continuing care, the objectives were mandated in some detail, but this approach did not extend to specifying the *content* of local policies or procedures.

Clearly there is a difficult balance to be achieved between central government providing direction or facilitation. However, the greater the degree of latitude in guidance on roles and responsibilities, the more likely it is that new ways of working will be adopted only by enthusiasts. Incentives and rewards have not, until recently, been a major feature of the management of collaboration, other than in relation to some financial levers where it seems likely that the grafting of specific grants to policy requirements can be particularly effective.

For there to be accountability for performance against requirements, there need to be mechanisms to monitor compliance. The area of hospital discharge and continuing care is, once again, distinctive for the high level of monitoring which has accompanied implementation. This is in stark contrast to the lack of specific monitoring of other aspects of community care, and also contrasts with the tight monitoring and review which accompanied preparations for community care between 1992 and 1993, and which was reinstated, albeit only in part, in 1995 in relation to the implementation of continuing care arrangements.

## Recent policy developments

The policy context has continued to evolve. A number of benchmarks can be identified which indicate not only the ongoing importance of both hospital discharge and continuing care to the NHS and community care agenda, but also the increasing recognition of the connections between health and social care at these key interfaces (DoH 1996c, 1997a–c). In November 1996 the DoH issued the executive letter *Funding for Priority Services* (1996c) which set out arrangements for targeting resources at a number of key objectives including 'tackling delayed discharge as part of the commitment to continuing care' (para 2). Health authorities were encouraged to develop a strategic and coherent approach on a 'Whole system basis' to tackle key local problems and development needs. In particular, the Continuing Care Challenge Fund was introduced to support initiatives to avoid inappropriate admissions, facilitate safe discharges and avoid readmissions. The funding arrangements allowed for allocations to health authorities and for the transfer of such monies to local authorities to support joint schemes.

Letters from the new Secretary of State for Health (Frank Dobson) in August and October 1997 addressed the subject of *Managing Winter* (DoH 1997a), in anticipation of problems of winter pressures on health and social services, and the need for integrated planning and action. The letters signalled that the new government was 'determined to help all concerned to improve their work across the boundary between community care and continuing health care' (para 2). Additional resources were announced to ease pressures over the winter period, but also in the expectation that 'improvements in the NHS processes – including joint working with social services – brought about by this extra investment should lead to lasting changes in the pattern of care' (DoH 1997b).

*Better Services for Vulnerable People* (DoH 1997c) introduced the requirement for the development of Joint Investment Plans for services to meet the continuing and community care needs of the local population; improve arrangements for multidisciplinary assessment; and to develop health and social care settings for older people focusing on optimising independence through timely recuperation and rehabilitation opportunities. These requirements were a direct response to the findings from monitoring of progress with continuing care implementation that there were ongoing problems with identification of responsibilities, and inadequate collaboration: 'some health and local authorities are still not able to effectively plan their respective and joint investment in continuing and community care. They are not delivering the coordinated care that is necessary' (p.1).

In December 1997 the White Paper on the NHS was published (Secretary of State for Health 1997). A major theme of the document was partnership, and the need 'to integrate health and social care resources so that patients genuinely get access to seamless services' (para 9.10). The White Paper did not contain specific proposals to address health and social care collaboration, although it signalled that further work was taking place on ways of breaking down the traditional barriers between health and social services. However, the White Paper did announce the introduction of a general *statutory duty* for NHS trusts to work in partnership with other NHS organisations, and with local authorities 'to work together for the common good' (para 4.8).

On its own, it is questionable whether such a duty would be any more effective than the duty to collaborate under which the 1973 NHS Act places health and local authorities. However, the duty of partnership was further underlined by the September 1998 discussion document on dismantling the so-called 'Berlin Wall' between health and social services (DoH 1998a). The proposals are intended to 'remove barriers to joint working' by introducing new powers to enable the development of pooled budgets, lead commissioners, and integrated provision. The document addresses both the *incentives* to improve joint working, but also – and importantly – new measures to *monitor, review* and *hold to account.*

The document recognises that 'shared objectives and a shared sense of responsibility are essential to delivering improved outcomes across boundaries' (para 4.53). To underpin this, the government also issued national priorities guidance addressing both health and social services (Department of Health 1998b). Arrangements for monitoring, reviewing and holding to account in delivering objectives across the boundaries will be incorporated into the performance frameworks for the NHS and social services. Building on the experience with continuing care (and in mental health services), joint monitoring and review by the NHS and social care regional offices is to be a feature, and will include performance indicators for services requiring input from health and social care. Table 10.2 presents an analysis of the proposals contained in *Partnership in Action* (1998a) against the collaborative framework addressed earlier in this chapter.

## Conclusions

This chapter has explored the shift in central–local relations which has occurred between the DoH on the one hand, and health and local authorities on the other, since the 1989 community care White Paper. It has been argued that the framework for collaboration contained in *Caring for People* offered only limited progress in clarifying responsibilities and increasing accountability. However, the policy environment has continued to evolve and develop since 1989. The series of further executive letters, guidance, and other policy advice issued since that time can be seen to have refined the specification of responsibility and accountability, *at least in some respects.*

The area of hospital discharge and continuing care can be identified as one in which the framework for collaboration was increasingly specified. As Table 10.1 highlighted, it was only in this area of policy that the collaborative environment was fully developed. That this should be the case is of interest because this policy area can be identified as one in which the boundary between

## Table 10.2 Evaluating new opportunities for Joint working between health and social services

| Policy area | Shared vision | Clarity of roles and responsibilities | Incentives and rewards | Accountability |
|---|---|---|---|---|
| Partnership in action. Proposals must: Improve the actual services users and carers receive | Clear statements that for the right services to be delivered to local people at the time they need them, health, social services and other parts of local government must work together in partnership (p.000) | Major structural change rejected: new statutory health and social services authorities viewed as too expensive and disruptive to introduce. | Extension of Section 28A monies with indicative transfer level instead of joint finance. | New measures to monitor and review joint working to be introduced through joint priorities guidance, performance frameworks for social services alongside health. Performance indicators to be developed for services requiring input from health and social care. Possibly leading to comparative indicators within a national framework. |
| Ensure wasteful duplication and gaps in services are avoided | | Proposals do not change health care being available free at the point of delivery. Authorities applying for flexibilities will be required 'to align their continuing care and social care eligibility criteria and to make clear the charging position locally' (p.000) | Objective to remove the constraints in the system which stop better cooperation, while also providing 'incentives to make things better without creating unwanted distortions elsewhere' (p.000) | National services frameworks to take account of social care a swell as health service inputs. |
| Ensure public funds are used more efficiently and effectively. | | Certain barriers to joint working to be removed to enable partnership developments. | New powers to be given make use of new flexibilities, but 'such powers will not be mandatory' (p.000) | |
| | | Opportunities for pooling of budgets, lead commissioning and integrated provision. | | |
| | | Removal of statutory requirement of Joint Consultative | Further support to health and social | Joint reviews by NHS and Social Care Regional |

health and social care, and the need for clarity of respective responsibilities, is especially stark. However, this is not to conclude that the experience with hospital discharge and continuing care has been without difficulty, nor that all of the questions of boundary clarification have been resolved satisfactorily. Examples of 'cost shunting' and of otherwise stumbling across the 'Berlin wall' between the two agencies are still legion in this area.

We have argued elsewhere (Hudson *et al.* 1997) that structuring the collaborative environment through clarification of responsibilities and strengthened processes of accountability can introduce more favourable conditions for successful interagency collaboration, but does not guarantee success. In practice, the collaborative environment can be significantly enhanced or substantially undermined by the behaviour of people operating within it. Ideally, therefore, a strategy for collaboration is more likely to succeed if it addresses both structure *and* behaviour (Hudson *et al.* 1997).

The publication of the discussion document on new opportunities for joint working between health and social services (DoH 1998a) can be seen as the latest stage in the evolution of policy since 1989. It is an attempt to square the circle by addressing head on the issues which can impede joint working between health and local authorities. The mechanisms of pooled budgets, lead commissioner arrangements and integrated provision are offered as new flexibilities for overcoming traditional barriers. Moreover, the discussion document can be seen as an attempt to draw together a strategic coherence which links 'health action zones'; 'better government for older people'; 'health improvement programmes'; 'joint investment plans' and 'joint commissioning' within an overall agenda for health and social care.

Since 1989 the management of community care in general, and of health and social care collaboration in this area in particular, can be seen to have become increasingly centralised. Some of the core policy objectives have been the focus of increasingly tight specification. Compliance with the centralist agenda has been encouraged by the twin mechanisms of financial incentives on the one hand and monitoring of performance on the other. Experience with this model has clearly influenced the proposals for improved joint working between health and social services. However, whether implementation of the partnership proposals is assured remains unclear. While comprising the most comprehensive package of proposals for improving collaboration, some of its major components remain optional rather than mandatory. The underlying issue, therefore, is whether its combination of incentives and performance management arrangements will be sufficiently strong to ensure that progress takes place across the board, and is not confined to the enthusiasts who are actively seeking new legislative flexibilities. The analysis presented in Table 10.2 suggests that the document may be heavier on the accountability and performance management mechanisms than on providing sufficient incentives and rewards.

## References

Clarke, K. (1989) *Secretary of State's Statement to Parliament on the Future Arrangements for Community Care.* Press Release 82/298, Department of Health.

Department of Health (1989) *Caring for People: Community Care in the Next Decade and Beyond.* Cm 849. London: DoH.

Department of Health (1992a) *Implementing Caring for People.* EL(92)13, CI(92)10. London: DoH.

Department of Health (1992b) *Implementing Caring for People.* EL(92)65, CI(92)30. London: DoH.

Department of Health (1994) *The Hospital Discharge Workbook: A Manual on Hospital Discharge Practice.* London: DoH.

Department of Health (1995a) *NHS Responsibilities for Meeting Continuing Health Care Needs.* HSG(95)8, LAC(95)5. London: DoH.

Department of Health (1995b) *Discharge from NHS Inpatient Care of People with Continuing Health or Social Care Needs: Arrangements for Reviewing Decisions on Eligibility for NHS Inpatient Care.* HSG(95)39, LAC(95)17. London: DoH.

Department of Health (1995c) *Developing Continuing Health Care Policies: A Checklist for Purchasers.* London: DoH.

Department of Health (1995d) *Developing and Implementing Eligibility Criteria for Continuing Health Care: A Checklist for Purchasers.* London: DoH.

Department of Health (1995e) *NHS Responsibilities for Meeting Continuing Health Care Needs – NHS Executive/SSI Monitoring.* EL(95)88, CI(95)37. London: DoH.

Department of Health (1996a) *NHS Responsibilities for Meeting Continuing Health Care Needs – Current Progress and Future Priorities.* EL(96)8, CI(96)5. London: DoH.

Department of Health (1996b) *Progress in Practice: Initial Evaluation of the Impact of the Continuing Care Guidance.* EL(96)89, CI(96)35. London: DoH.

Department of Health (1996c) *Funding for Priority Services 1996/97 and 1997/98.* EL(98)109. London: DoH.

Department of Health (1997a) *Managing Winter 1997/98.* London: DoH.

Department of Health (1997b) *NHS Finance – Additional Money for Patient Care. EL(97)61.* London: DoH.

Department of Health (1997c) *Better Services for Vulnerable People.* EL(97)62, CI(97)24. London: DoH.

Department of Health (1998a) *Partnership in Action (New Opportunities for Joint Working between Health and Social Services).* A Discussion Document. London: DoH.

Department of Health (1998b) *Modernising Health and Social Services: National Priority Guidance* 1999/00 – 2001/02. London: DoH.

Department of Health (1998c) *Getting Better? Inspection of Hospital Discharge (Care Management) Arrangements for Older People.* London: Social Care Group/Social Services Inspectorate. London: DoH.

Griffiths, Sir R. (1988) *Community Care: Agenda for Action.* London: HMSO.

Health Committee (1995a) Session 1995–96, *First Report, Long Term Care: NHS Responsibilities for Meeting Continuing Health Care Needs,* Volume I. London: House of Commons.

Health Committee (1995b) Session 1995–96, *First Report, Long Term Care: NHS Responsibilities for Meeting Continuing Health Care Needs, Minutes of Evidence,* Volume II. London: House of Commons.

Henwood, M., Jowell, T. and Wistow, G. (1991) *All Things Come (To Those Who Wait?): Causes and Consequences of the Community Care Delays.* London: King's Fund.

Hudson, B., Hardy, B., Henwood, M. and Wistow, G. (1997) *Inter-Agency Collaboration: Final Report.* London: Nuffield Institute for Health, Community Care Division.

Report of the Health Service Commissioner (1994) Failure to Provide Long Term NHS Care for a Brain Damaged Patient, Second Report for Session 1993–94. London: HMSO.

Secretary of State for Health (1997) *The New NHS: Modern. Dependable.* Cm 3807. London: The Stationery Office.

Wistow, G. (1994) 'Community care future: Inter-agency relationships – stability or continuing change?' In M. Titterton (ed) *Caring for People in the Community: The New Welfare.* London: Jessica Kingsley Publishers.

# PART III

# Comparative Perspectives

# CHAPTER II

# The Changing Role of Social Care: UK Variations

## Social care across Great Britain: consolidation or fragmentation?

*Alison Petch*

Equity, the extent to which individuals within different localities have the same access to social care opportunities, becomes increasingly key as discretionary authority on decision making and implementation is devolved, the number of local agencies multiplies, and the scope for variation, for example though the introduction of charging policies, escalates. Variation needs to be explored at a broader level, however – the extent to which it exists within Great Britain in the policy and practice of social care. This chapter will explore the similarities and differences amongst England, Scotland and Wales and, in particular, will update a flurry of writing which appeared in the late 1980s (Hunter and Wistow 1987, 1988; Titterton 1989, 1991). Northern Ireland, with its different organisational structures and legislative base (Department of Health and Social Services (Northern Ireland) 1990), will not be discussed in any detail.

There are a number of historical or continuing factors which contribute to demonstrable policy and practice differences on the 'Celtic fringe'. These include a number of features relating to the 'balance of care', the allocation of resources and the manner of implementation:

- differential rates of *per capita* expenditure on health and social services: higher for both health and social care in Scotland, with more of this going on institutional provision; higher on health in Wales, but lower on social care

- differential rates of hospital bed provision: higher in both Wales and most particularly Scotland

- differential rates of long-stay hospital residents: higher rates in Scotland and lower in Wales than in England

- variable participation of the mixed economy in social care provision

- greater (Wales) or lesser (Scotland) adoption of an interventionist style by the national government office

- competing professional interests: in Scotland, for example, historical allegiance to models of institutional provision; in Wales political commitment targeted in large measure on learning disability

- divergences in interagency collaboration and specifically joint planning: Wales, as England, had a requirement since the mid-1970s for health authorities and social services authorities to establish a joint consultative committee, while in Scotland joint working has been characterised as 'stop, start, stutter' (Kohls 1989).

Perhaps most significant, however, as devolution prepares to impact, is the awareness of a different value and attitude base. Analysis of the annual British Social Attitudes Surveys (Jowell *et al.* 1996) has repeatedly demonstrated a willingness to support enhanced spending on health, education and social care, increasing taxation if necessary. But in Scotland, the support for public spending in support of social justice is more marked: for example 60 per cent in Scotland believe that income should be redistributed from the better off to the less well off, while only 43 per cent in southern England endorse such a view. Moreover, in its vote for devolution, the Scottish populace accepted the possibility of a 3 per cent variation in tax-raising powers.

The White Paper *Caring for People* (Department of Health 1989), setting the strategy for much of social care in the 1990s and beyond, offered separate chapters for both Scotland and Wales. The chapter on Scotland endorsed the priorities of SHAPE (Scottish Health Authorities Priorities for the Eighties) and SHARPEN (Scottish Health Authorities Review of Priorities for the Eighties and Nineties), but highlighted in particular the need to redefine and clarify the responsibilities of the agencies concerned with care, to develop a range of options for those in need of care, and to ensure appropriate use of residential care. For Wales, a particular emphasis was laid on the need to improve the balance and distribution of provision, both geographically and across care groups, with the Welsh Office having already set in train a framework for agencies across the sectors to work together to develop new, more decentralised services. The requirement for each social services authority to produce a social care plan, 'concise and action-orientated', drawing together the views of users and the contributions of each agency, was laid. A number of developments in specific grant aid for each of the care groups were outlined, replacing joint finance arrangements via the health authorities for social care.

The NHS and Community Care Act 1990, which followed *Caring for People*, was the first major piece of social care legislation to embrace Scotland, Wales and England, specifying for Scotland amendments to the Social Work (Scotland) Act 1968. Many of the preceding documents (the 1986 Audit Commission Report, the 1988 Griffiths Report, the 1988 Wagner Report) had not officially applied to Scotland.

*Learning disability*

Both chapters of the White Paper reviewed the issues considered important in progressing developments for each care group. In Wales there has been particular pride in the All Wales Strategy (Welsh Office 1983, 1992), a commitment of £26 million over ten years to the development of an integrated pattern of comprehensive services for individuals with learning disabilities based on principles of normalisation. The central commitment of resources was a key feature, removing the need for local political allocation. The focus of the strategy has been twofold, designed to reduce the numbers in long-stay hospitals and to increase the capacity of families to care through enhanced levels of day and domiciliary support. Initial progress was deemed slow (Beyer, Todd *et al.* 1991; McGrath 1991), but more recently there have been significant developments in domiciliary support and short-term care. Todd *et al.* (1993), as part of a larger longitudinal evaluation focusing on the lifestyles and service usage of 404 individuals conducted by the Welsh Centre for Learning

Disabilities, reported on the responses of users (primarily carers) to the strategy. The development of family support services was widely appreciated; there remained concerns, however, around the nature of day activity and the lack of opportunities approximating employment.

In Scotland, also, developments in the field of learning disability tend to be brought to the fore. Early strategy reports were produced by the Scottish Office Home and Health Department in 1972 (*Services for the Mentally Handicapped*) and in 1979 (*A Better Life: Report on Services for the Mentally Handicapped in Scotland*). These marked a divergence from the policy adopted in both England and Wales following the 1971 White Paper, *Better Services for the Mentally Handicapped* (Department of Health and Social Security 1971). Hunter and Wistow (1987) highlight the more institution-based focus of the Scottish directives, with a 20 per cent higher proportion to be accommodated in some form of institutional setting and more of this provision to be hospital based rather than residential. The revised strategy of 1979 raised the institutional focus even further, increasing the target for hospital and residential places from 160 places per 100,000 to 180 (England and Wales, 138).

| Table 11.1 Long-stay beds in Scotland | | | | |
|---|---|---|---|---|
| *NHS hospital beds* | *1980* | *1990* | *1993* | *1996* |
| People with mental health problems | 14468 | 8351 | 5790 | 4678 |
| Learning disability | 6644 | 5021 | 3943 | 3231 |
| Geriatric long stay | | 8880 | 7853 | 6139 |
| Psychogeriatric | | 5914 | 6509 | 5282 |

*Source: Scottish Office Community Care Bulletin 1996.*

A critical appraisal of the balance of care in this field was undertaken between 1983 and 1985 by Baker and Urquhart (1987). This revealed the high potential for movement from hospital- to community-based settings, with an estimate at that time of over 90 per cent of hospital residents 'capable of being accommodated in other circumstances'. Table 11.1 reveals the progress that has been made since that date. Stalker and Hunter (1997), on the basis of interviews with key stakeholders, found that of 14 hospitals, only one had declared its intention to close (although in the early 1990s that had been the intention for an additional five), several lacked targets, and others were behind schedule. As with other groups, there could be tensions at the boundaries of health and social care, both in terms of practice and organisational responsibility. Indeed, a number of health trusts are already providing or seeking to provide social care, notwithstanding legal uncertainties. Particular issues associated with bridging finance and resource transfer are addressed below. Those interviewed were particularly critical of what they perceived as the failure of the Scottish Office to 'take a clear policy lead in relation to resettlement, to set and monitor targets and to provide sticks and carrots' (p.5). It is perhaps significant that the Scottish Office is currently working on the preparation of a 'strategy for learning disability'.

### Mental health

Mental health epitomises the need to recognise the necessity of multiagency working to respond to the range of social care needs, discussed further below. The trigger for recent strategy for people with mental health problems in Scotland was an inquiry into the closure of psychiatric hospitals in Scotland (House of Commons 1995a; 1995b). For a long time there had been concerns that policy had been contradictory, promoting care in community settings on one hand whilst allocating large sums to hospital rebuilding. Indeed, a commentary on the 1985 Scottish Office policy statement *Mental Health in Focus* (Scottish Home and Health Department 1985), used the vivid epithet 'lost in the haar' (Drucker 1986). The committee reported: 'It is vital that the Scottish Office takes a stronger lead in ensuring progress towards the implementation of coherent mental health strategies, including the appropriate bed and hospital closures throughout Scotland' (p.xii). The Scottish Office response to the inquiry report was to commit itself to the production of a strategic statement to assist 'staff in health, social work and housing agencies, including Scottish Homes, to develop a joint approach to the planning, commissioning and provision of integrated mental health services'. In September 1997, it launched a framework for mental health services in Scotland (Scottish Office 1997).

The framework focuses on the needs of people with severe and/or enduring mental health problems, including dementia, and seeks to deliver comprehensive mental health services to the population of an area, based on the development of a local mental health strategy. It provides a template to assist in local agreement of priorities for action 'that are related to outcomes and to clinical and cost-effectiveness', and establishes a yardstick against which the Scottish Office can monitor progress. The intention was that by April 1998, each area should have drafted a six-year implementation plan specifying the steps to be taken following the service review. Prior to local government reorganisation in April 1996, local authority and health board boundaries were coterminous. The destruction of this coterminosity has led to more complex planning procedures and the requirement that boards and authorities agree the level and scale at which they wish to develop their mental health strategies. Within each strategy there is a requirement to clarify the resources to be contributed by each agency, and the establishment of a local joint commissioning team, with membership from all relevant agencies including users and carers and a lead individual responsible for operational implementation clearly identified. Moreover, explicit links are to be made with other planning mechanisms, the community care plan and the local authority housing plans and children's service plans. To assist in the implementation of the framework, a Mental Health Development Fund has been created, to run for the three years 1998–2001 and to seed new ways of joint working between agencies. It is too early to assess the effectiveness of this local initiative, although there is concern that the relative weakness of Scottish Office monitoring and enforcement evident in the past could lead to widening disparity in the quality of response in different localities. With the DoH currently preparing to launch a framework for the development of mental health services south of the border, this is an area where Scotland can be regarded as having taken the lead.

In Wales, a consultative document on mental health services, *Mental Illness Services: A Strategy for Wales*, was published by the Welsh Office in 1989. This laid out the key principles leading a strategy for the development of services over two decades, building on a policy and priority document produced for health services in Wales in 1985. The focus is on district health authorities, in full cooperation with social services, housing authorities and the voluntary sector, developing local provision which will obviate the need for admission and for long-term hospital care. Targets have been attached to this strategy in the Mental Illness Protocol for Health Gain issued by the Welsh Health Planning Forum in 1993. A Welsh case study of psychiatric resettlement is offered by Crosby and Barry (1995), well-resourced local social care initiatives having considerably enhanced the process over the 1970s and 1980s when the in-patient numbers in the nine psychiatric hospitals in Wales had fallen from over 6000 to under 4000 in 1987.

Throughout Great Britain, social care provision for individuals with mental health problems has benefited considerably from the mental illness specific grant, the only source of ringfenced monies associated with the implementation of *Caring for People* and provided in recognition of the very low level of social services expenditure (estimated at 3 per cent) on this group at that time. The local authority contribution to costs is 30 per cent, and the remainder provided centrally, albeit from top-sliced funds. Evaluation of the effectiveness of the grant in England (Social Services Inspectorate 1995) and in Scotland (Laffey and Petch 1997) has highlighted some interesting variations in the way which the grant has been utilised. In particular, a high proportion of the projects developed in Scotland have been managed by the voluntary sector (two-thirds in the first three years), whereas in England the local authority has been the leading sector.

The final element that should be considered when focusing on social care provision for mental health is the implementation of the care programme approach (Shepherd *et al.* 1995; Scottish Office 1996). Very different approaches have been adopted north and south of the border. In Scotland the focus has been on building on initial pilot projects in Glasgow and Stirling and on targeting, with the focus on those with severe and enduring mental health problems. In England, however, the approach has been more inclusive, with guidance referring to all those in contact with specialist mental health services. The absence of comprehensive evaluation precludes a definitive judgement; experience, however, for example of mental health case management in the US, would favour the Scottish approach.

*Assessment and care management*

A core feature of *Caring for People* and the subsequent legislation is the process of care management, detailed as seven stages, including that of assessment. The exploration of the implementation of care management in England by Lewis and Glennerster (1996) has been replicated for Wales in the programme of work at the Centre for Social Policy, Research and Development at Bangor (McGrath *et al.* 1996, 1997; Parry-Jones 1998; Parry-Jones *et al.* 1998) and for Scotland at the Social Work Research Centre at Stirling (Stalker 1994; Stalker, Taylor and Petch 1994; Petch *et al.* 1996). Diversity of interpretation unites the three countries. A postal survey of frontline practitioners in Wales in 1995, supplemented by interviews with health and social care managers in the eight Welsh counties, highlighted uncertainties in the definition of care management, broad overlap between the roles of care managers and social workers but associated tensions, and little evidence of devolved budgets. There is variation within Wales: five counties, for example, had created specific care manager posts, although in one county the posts combined the roles of care manager and social worker. In the other three counties the role was combined with that of social worker, extending the responsibilities of that function. Primarily this provision for care management in Wales relates to older people and individuals with physical impairment; the national strategies for mental health and learning disability outlined above have generally been pursued in the context of multidisciplinary and multiagency teams. Frontline practitioners reported considerable administrative burden following the introduction of the new community care arrangements, dissatisfaction enhanced by an absence of training for the range of new responsibilities, for example financial assessment and contracting. Of particular significance was the task area reported as most ineffective, the recording of unmet need (29 per cent responding 'no' to effectiveness compared with per cent for all but three of 19 other tasks).

The work in Scotland replicates much of the above. Prior to local government reorganisation, two main models of care management were in evidence: care management as a separate role with workers recruited to specific posts, evident in two regions, and care management as a task carried out alongside other tasks, predominantly by social workers. The latter was the majority model, accompanied in several areas by an assertion that the essential features of care management already existed and a resistance to change practice (MacDonald and Myers 1995). Key features such as budgets devolved to the frontline were in the main absent, a dimension which has been further promoted in recent guidance relating to frail older people (Scottish Office 1998a). Local government reorganisation, creating 32 unitary authorities, has inevitably disrupted emerging patterns and there has not yet been any definitive account of the responses of the new authorities to care management. The impression remains, however, that similar features prevail: duplication of assessment, not only between agencies but within the local authority, insufficient distinction of different complexities of care management, inadequate recording and aggregation of unmet need, and an inability, in the main, to create imaginative responses to need based on local purchasing by individual care managers.

## Mixed economy of care

In one of the key areas addressed by *Caring for People*, the role of the mixed economy, there is a statutory variation between Scotland and the other countries. Whereas in England there was a requirement that 85 per cent of the transfer monies from the Department of Social Security to the local authority were spent on services from the independent sector, in Scotland this requirement was not laid down. Some argue that this was because the relative underdevelopment of the independent sector, most particularly in relation to domiciliary care, would have rendered this unworkable. Others cite more mundane drafting procedures which did not allow the ready introduction of the rule.

Curtice, Fraser and Leca (1997) report on the first phase of a study designed to explore the role of the different sectors in the domiciliary care market in Scotland. To some extent this dispelled the myth of monopoly providers: 59 per cent of 590 identified providers were private and voluntary sector agencies. None the less, the market share of the independent sector was relatively small, 76 per cent of total domiciliary care hours being provided by social work agencies. In terms of contracting by local authorities, there remained a certain wariness of the independent and most specifically private sector, although the majority of authorities were making use of the independent sector to some extent. This is, of course, a volatile area and following local government reorganisation a greater diversity of practice is emerging.

It should be noted that, as with other DoH initiatives, Scotland and Wales did not benefit from the Caring for People who Live at Home initiative which funded 15 local authorities to stimulate day and domiciliary provision within the independent sector (Perkins *et al.* 1997). The second phase of the Scottish domiciliary care study is focusing on frail older people at the margins of institutional care, exploring in some detail the contribution of the different sectors to intensive home care arrangements and seeking to identify the triggers, including policies on care package limits, which currently lead to residential or nursing home admission.

Delineation of the voluntary sector by Kendall and Knapp (1996) demonstrates an interesting variation in the proportion of local authority expenditure directed towards the sector. Whereas in England this was 1.5 per cent (1991/92), in Scotland it was higher, 1.8 per cent, and in Wales lower, 1 per cent. Moreover, the work of McGrath *et al.* in Wales (1996) suggests considerable variation between the counties in the promotion of voluntary sector providers, an adherence to a state provider ideology. In Scotland, voluntary sector providers have been of particular significance in mental health, including dementia. The major voluntary providers in Scotland have recently formed Community Care Providers Scotland (CCPS), one of whose first activities has been a briefing paper on 'best value' for voluntary sector service providers.

Private providers in Scotland, as elsewhere, tend to be primarily in the residential and nursing home sector. In the residential care sector they provide 22 per cent by volume, while voluntary providers offer 32 per cent and local authorities 46 per cent (Accounts Commission 1997b). Tables 11.2 and 11.3 demonstrate, however, that the sector mix shows major variation across the different groups, the major shift to the voluntary sector for mental health and development by the private for older people. For older people, Bland *et al.* (1992) have undertaken a detailed analysis of the quality of care and costs across the different sectors. In both Scotland and Wales, rurality is a factor which impinges on the diversity of providers and in consequence on choice and on the level of support which can be offered to informal care.

## Table 11.2 The mixed economy in residential and nursing home care in Scotland

| Residential and nursing home care | 1987 | % share | 1993 | % share | 1996 | % share |
|---|---|---|---|---|---|---|
| Local authority | 9993 | 45.9 | 9147 | 27.5 | 8116 | 20.8 |
| Voluntary | 4463 | 20.5 | 4245 | 12.8 | 4213 | 10.8 |
| Private | 2267 | 10.4 | 3822 | 11.5 | 4583 | 11.8 |
| Nursing home | 5063 | 23.2 | 6065 | 48.3 | 22068 | 56.6 |

Source: ADSW submission to Scottish Affairs Committee 1996.

## Table 11.3 Changes in the mixed economy of residential care, Scotland

| Mixed economy: residential care | Year | Local authority | Voluntary | Private |
|---|---|---|---|---|
| People with mental health problems | 1980 | 80 | 20 | 0 |
|  | 1996 | 5 | 86 | 9 |
| Learning disabilities | 1980 | 51 | 49 | 0 |
|  | 1996 | 21 | 66 | 14 |
| Physical disability | 1980 | 0 | 100 | 0 |
|  | 1996 | 6 | 93 | 2 |
| Frail older people | 1980 | 65 | 34 | 1 |
|  | 1996 | 48 | 25 | 26 |

Source: Scottish Office Community Care Bulletin 1996.

The commissioning process for social care in Scotland has been the focus of scrutiny by the Accounts Commission (1997b). This provides data for 1996/97 on the distribution of the budgeted spend: 37 per cent residential care, 18 per cent nursing home care, 27 per cent home care, 16 per cent day care, and 2 per cent respite care. There is wide variation between authorities, however: from 10 per cent to 60 per cent on residential care, from 6 per cent to 47 per cent on home care and from 3 per cent to 27 per cent on day care. Aggregated to compare community-based provision with institution-based care, the council investing most heavily in community provision was spending more than two and a half times as much of its budget as the council investing least (78%:30%).

## Scottish Affairs Committee

An important recent benchmark of current social care practice in Scotland is a second inquiry by the Parliamentary Scottish Affairs Committee (House of Commons 1997a, 1997b) reviewing the implementation of community care in Scotland. The memoranda submitted by over a hundred different bodies (House of Commons 1997c) provide a substantial body of evidence, while the recommendations of the committee highlight a number of key areas. Major questions are raised about the overall level of resourcing, inadequate to meet the aims of the 1990 Act, with particular concerns about the transparency and timing of resource transfer from health to social care (echoed by the Accounts Commission 1997a), and the national allocation of bridging finance for bed closure programmes. In 1996/97, two-thirds of the £18 million total was allocated to Glasgow, an inequitable distribution of which the committee was highly critical, recommending a weighted capitation.

Other significant recommendations from the inquiry preface a number of current concerns in social care. A fundamental need to address the role of housing has been taken up by Scottish Homes who reviewed their existing care in the community policy of 1993 and issued a revised policy statement (Scottish Homes 1998). At the same time the Scottish Office guidance stressing the key role of housing (Scottish Office 1994) is to be supplemented. A recommendation on the development of domiciliary support that integrates both health and social care is echoed in several of the emerging holistic augmented care schemes. The committee urges all local authorities to adopt the discretionary direct payments scheme, a recent survey suggesting that Scotland in the main is responding with some caution to the option (Hasler, Zarb and Campbell 1998). Mechanisms for pooled budgets and for joint commissioning find echoes in the Scottish Office's latest policy statement in this field, an action plan.

This action plan, *Modernising Community Care*, launched by the Scottish Office in October 1998, seeks accelerated activity in a number of key areas. Past attempts to jump-start interagency working (Scottish Home and Health Department 1980b; Scottish Office, 1985) had generated limited activity. Improved and more rapid decision making is sought through the delegation of decision making and budgets, the streamlining of management and the transfer of resources to the frontline and the improvement of cross-agency partnerships. There are to be renewed efforts to shift the balance of care through the development of more flexible domiciliary care services and housing, and through health and social care cooperation. In addition, services are to be better targeted to the needs of each locality, with the emphasis again on local partnerships.

At the same time, the Department of Health has released a discussion document, *Partnership in Action* (DoH 1998), committed to addressing the 'no man's land between health and social services' and 'sterile arguments about boundaries' (p.3). In particular, consultation is sought prior to the framing of legislation designed to facilitate pooled budgets, lead commissioning and integrated provision. The action plan, however, can only seek preliminary views on such key initiatives, conscious that there will be a new legislative framework whose intentions it cannot pre-empt: 'any changes would depend on decisions by the Scottish Parliament' (p.3). As this chapter was being written, the individuals to stand as the first candidates for the new parliaments in Scotland and Wales were being elected and draft manifestos were starting to circulate. The priorities for social care are yet to be determined.

## References

Accounts Commission (1997a) *Shifting the Balance: Resource Transfer for Community Care.* Edinburgh: Accounts Commission for Scotland.

Accounts Commission (1997b) *The Commissioning Maze: Commissioning Community Care Services.* Edinburgh: Accounts Commission for Scotland.

Baker, N. and Urquhart, J. (1987) *The Balance of Care for Adults with a Mental Handicap in Scotland.* Edinburgh: ISD Publications.

Beyer, S., Todd, S. and Felce, D. (1991) 'The implementation of the All-Wales mental handicap strategy.' *Mental Handicap Research 4,* 115–40.

Bland, R., Bland, R., Cheetham, J., Lapsley, I. and Llewellyn, S. (1992) *Residential Homes for Elderly People: Their Costs and Quality*. Edinburgh: HMSO.

Crosby, C. and Barry, M. (eds) (1995) *Community Care: Evaluation of the Provision of Mental Health Services*. Aldershot: Avebury.

Curtice, L., Fraser, F. and Leca, T. (1997) *The Range and Availability of Domiciliary Care Services in Scotland*. Edinburgh: The Stationery Office.

Department of Health (1989) *Caring for People: Community Care in the Next Decade and Beyond*. Cm 849. London: HMSO.

Department of Health (1998) *Partnership in Action: New Opportunities for Joint Working between Health and Social Services*. A Discussion Document. London: DoH.

Department of Health and Social Security and Welsh Office (1971) *Better Services for the Mentally Handicapped*. London: HMSO.

Department of Health and Social Services (Northern Ireland) (1990) *People First: Community Care in Northern Ireland for the 1990s*. Belfast: HMSO.

Drucker, N. (1986) 'Lost in the haar: A critique of Mental Health in Focus.' In D. McCrone (ed) *The Scottish Government Yearbook 1986*. Edinburgh: Institute for the Study of Government in Scotland.

Hasler, F., Zarb, G. and Campbell, J. (1998) *Key Issues for Local Authority Implementation of Direct Payments*. London: Policy Studies Institute.

House of Commons (1995a) *Closure of Psychiatric Hospitals in Scotland: Vol. I*. Scottish Affairs Committee Session 1994–95, Third Report. London: HMSO.

House of Commons (1995b) *Closure of Psychiatric Hospitals in Scotland: Vol. II, Minutes of Evidence and Appendices*. Scottish Affairs Committee Session 1994–95, Third Report. London: HMSO.

House of Commons (1997a) *The Implementation of Community Care in Scotland: Vol. I*. Scottish Affairs Committee Session 1996–97, Second Report. London: HMSO.

House of Commons (1997b) *The Implementation of Community Care in Scotland: Vol. II, Minutes of Evidence with Appendices*. Scottish Affairs Committee Session 1996–97, Second Report. London: HMSO.

House of Commons (1997c) *The Implementation of Community Care in Scotland: Vol. III, Memoranda of Evidence*. Scottish Affairs Committee Session 1996–97, Second Report. London: HMSO.

Hunter, D.J. and Wistow, G. (1987) *Community Care in Britain: Variations on a Theme*. London: King Edward's Fund for Hospital.

Hunter, D.J. and Wistow, G. (1988) 'The Scottish difference: Policy and practice in community care.' In *Scottish Government Yearbook 1988*. Edinburgh: Unit for the Study of Government in Scotland.

Jowell, R., Curtice, J. Park, A. Brook, L. and Thomson, K. (1996) *British Social Attitudes: The 13th Report.* Aldershot: Dartmouth.

Kendall, J. and Knapp, M. (1996) *The Voluntary Sector in the UK.* Manchester: Manchester University Press.

Kohls, M. (1989) *Stop, Start, Stutter: A Report on Joint Planning.* Care in the Community Scottish Working Group. Edinburgh.

Laffey, B. and Petch, A. (1997) *Dedicated Resources: Dedicated Responses – Evaluation of the Mental Illness Specific Grant.* Edinburgh: The Scottish Office.

Lewis, J. and Glennerster, H. (1996) *Implementing the New Community Care.* Buckingham: Open University Press.

MacDonald, C. and Myers, F. (1995) *Assessment and Care Management: The Practitioner Speaks.* Community Care in Scotland Discussion Paper No 5. Stirling: Social Work Research Centre, University of Stirling.

McGrath, M. (1991) *Multi-disciplinary Teamwork: Community Mental Handicap Teams.* Aldershot: Avebury.

McGrath, M., Ramcharan, P., Grant, G., Parry-Jones, B., Caldock, K. and Robinson, C. (1996) 'The roles and tasks of care managers in Wales.' *Community Care Management and Planning 4,* 185–94.

McGrath, M., Ramcharan, P., Grant, G., Parry-Jones, B., Caldock, K. and Robinson, C. (1997) 'Care management in Wales: Perceptions of front-line workers.' *Community Care Management and Planning Review 5,* 5–13.

Parry-Jones, B. (1998) *Assessment and Care Management of Older People in North Wales: The Experience of Health and Social Care Practitioners Adapting to the Community Care Reforms.* Bangor: Centre for Social Policy Research and Development, University of Wales.

Parry-Jones, B., Robinson, C., Ramcharan, P, and Grant, G. (1998) *Assessment and Care Management in Wales: Summary Report.* Bangor: Centre for Social Policy Research and Development, University of Wales.

Perkins, E. and Allen, I., with Bourke Dowling, S., and Leat, D. (1997) *Creating Partnerships in Social Care: An Evaluation of the Caring for People who Live at Home Initiative.* London: Policy Studies Institute.

Petch, A., Cheetham, J., Fuller, R., MacDonald, C. and Myers, F. with Hallam, A. and Knapp. M. (1996) *Delivering Community Care: Initial Implementation of Care Management in Scotland.* Edinburgh: The Stationery Office.

Scottish Home and Health Department/Scottish Education Department (1972) *Services for the Mentally Handicapped.* Edinburgh: HMSO.

Scottish Home and Health Department/Scottish Education Department (1979) *A Better Life: Report on Services for the Mentally Handicapped in Scotland.* Edinburgh: HMSO.

Scottish Home and Health Department (1980a) *Scottish Health Authorities' Priorities for the Eighties (SHAPE).* Edinburgh: HMSO.

Scottish Home and Health Department (1980b) *Joint Planning and Support Financing Arrangements.* NHS Circular No 1980(GEN)5.

Scottish Home and Health Department/Scottish Education Department (1985) *Mental Health in Focus: Report on the Mental Health Services for Adults in Scotland.* Edinburgh: HMSO.

Scottish Home and Health Department/Scottish Health Service Planning Council (1988) *Scottish Health Authorities' Review of Priorities for the Eighties and Nineties (SHARPEN).* Edinburgh: HMSO.

Scottish Homes (1998) *Care in the Community Policy Statement.* Edinburgh: Scottish Homes.

Scottish Office (1985) *Community Care: Joint Planning and Support Finance.* NHS 1985(GEN)18, SW5/1985, SDD15/1985, SED1127/1985.

Scottish Office (1994) *Community Care – The Housing Dimension.* Circular ENV 27/1994.

Scottish Office (1996) *Community Care: Care Programme Approach for People with Severe and Enduring Mental Illness Including Dementia.* Circular No SWSG16/96, DD38/96.

Scottish Office (1997) *A Framework for Mental Health Services in Scotland.* Edinburgh: Scottish Office.

Scottish Office (1998a) *Community Care Needs of Frail Older People: Integrating Professional Assessments and Care Arrangements.* Circular No SWSG10/1998.

Scottish Office (1998b) *Modernising Community Care: An Action Plan.* Edinburgh: Scottish Office.

Shepherd, G., King, C., Tilbury, J. and Fowler, D. (1995) 'Implementing the Care Programme Approach.' *Journal of Mental Health 4,* 261–74.

Social Services Inspectorate (1995) *Building Community Services, the Mental Illness Specific Grant: A Review of the First Four Years 1991–1994.* London: HMSO.

Stalker, K. (1994) 'Implementing care management in Scotland: An overview of initial progress.' *Care in Place 1,* 104–19.

Stalker, K. and Hunter, S. (1997) *The Resettlement of People with Learning Difficulties from Scottish Hospitals: Interim Report.* Stirling: Social Work Research Centre, University of Stirling.

Stalker, K., Taylor, J. and Petch, A. (1994) *Implementing Community Care in Scotland: Early Snapshots.* Community Care in Scotland Discussion Paper No 4. Stirling: Social Work Research Centre, University of Stirling.

Titterton, M. (1989) 'The missing Scottish dimension in social care policy: A commentary on the Griffiths Report on Community Care and the Wagner Report on Residential Care.' In *Scottish Government Yearbook 1989*. Edinburgh: Unit for the Study of Government in Scotland.

Titterton, M. (1991) 'Caring for mentally disabled people in Scotland.' *Social Policy and Administration 25*, 136–48.

Todd, S., Shearn, J., Beyer, S. and Felce, D. (1993) 'Reflecting on change: Consumers' views of the impact of the All-Wales strategy.' *Mental Handicap 21*, 128–36.

Welsh Office (1983) *All-Wales Strategy for the Development of Services for Mentally Handicapped People*. Cardiff: The Welsh Office.

Welsh Office (1989) *Mental Illness Services: A Strategy for Wales*. Cardiff: The Welsh Office.

Welsh Office (1992) *The All-Wales Mental Handicap Strategy: Framework for Development From April 1993*. Cardiff: The Welsh Office.

# CHAPTER 12

# Who Pays? Who Provides?

## Towards a Comparative Approach to the Study of Social Care

*Michael Hill*

## Introduction

Comparative work on specific issues in social policy (as opposed to efforts to survey the whole field) tends to start with surveys of developments in a number of countries set out side-by-side, leaving the reader to make comparisons. Examples of this in the field of social care include Brian Munday's edited collection *European Social Services* (1993) and the survey by Kraan *et al.* of innovation in care for the older people in three European countries (1991). More sophisticated comparative studies involve quantitative work which seeks to assemble in comparable forms key input or output indicators from different countries and qualitative work which aims to bring analysis under control through the use of the 'regime' theories influenced by Esping-Andersen's seminal work (1990). The York study of social assistance is one of the best recent examples of the latter genre (Eardley *et al.* 1996). There is a lack of such work on social care, with the partial exception of work on policies for children (Bradshaw *et al.* 1993), and even this deals much more effectively with general services and benefits than with specific services orientated to social problems. The one area in which there has been significant progress in comparative work on social care is in relation to the topic of payments for care (Evers, Pijl and Ungerson 1994; Ungerson 1995, 1998). The relative absence of systematic comparative work on social care, and the fact that the most progress seems to have been made in relation to payments for care, is perhaps not surprising. It is not easy to generalise about care systems and comparisons between different countries need to involve the very careful specification of institutional and cultural contexts.

This examination of 'international perspectives' will not attempt to offer another, inevitably very abbreviated, paper which says in country 'x' they do this and in country 'y' they do that – isn't that interesting! It will also not respond to the even more suspect temptation to say in country 'x' they have this interesting, and by implication borrowable, idea and so on. What it will do is to explore some of the issues that need to be taken into account if effective comparative models for the study of social care policy are to be developed. In doing this it will not entirely shrink from the risky business of referring to relevant developments in some countries, but will do so in a context in which the implication is that before getting into the business of policy borrowing there is a need to look very carefully at policy context.

*Elements for a comparative model – who pays and who provides?*

As indicated above, the work of Clare Ungerson on payments for care offers the most fruitful route into the comparative analysis of care. Ungerson suggests, in a recent paper, that a typology can be developed to analyse payments for care which owes little to 'welfare regime' theory, and in an earlier article she suggests that Esping-Andersen's concept of decommodification offers little help with the analysis of this topic (Ungerson, 1995, p.38). In reaching the latter conclusion she draws upon Lewis's argument (1992) 'that Esping-Andersen's dichotomous formulation of commodification/ decommodification is ... too rigid to take account of the unpaid work in the household' (ibid.). But it seems a pity to reject regime analysis because of shortcomings in the work of the founding 'father' when there have been some excellent feminist modifications of regime theory, which share Ungerson's concerns. O'Connor thus has argued that the use of the concept of decommodification 'must be supplemented by the concept of personal autonomy or insulation from dependence, both personal dependence on family members and/or public dependence on the state agencies' (O'Connor 1993, p.515). In the field of care this consideration is applicable both to the cared-for and the carer. As far as the latter is concerned, various contributors to the edited collection by Sainsbury

(1994) have sought to add considerations about the extent to which regimes are 'women-friendly' to comparative theory.

The extent to which caring relationships involve dependency, or expectations of dependency, is very central to Ungerson's work. In a recent paper which gives particular attention to such issues, she offers the following typology of payments for care:

1. 'carer allowances' through social security payments of tax relief

2. wages paid by state agencies

3. 'routed wages' via payments to care users

4. 'symbolic payments' from care users to family, neighbours and friends

5. organised 'paid volunteering'. (Ungerson 1998, p.4)

For the purpose of completeness it is necessary to add to this list – care provided without any explicit payment at all. But, equally, there may be important differences between the various public providers of either care or cash. Accordingly, the following alternative typology is suggested for comparative analysis:

1. no payment

2. token payment

3. payment by 'cared for'

4. payment by 'cared for' assisted by a targeted benefit

5. payment by means of benefit or tax relief for the carer

6. payment for service as direct claim on an insurance system

7. payment for service as direct claim on social care system

8. payment for service as a direct claim on the health care system.

In addition there are important complications to types 4–8 – depending (a) upon whether the full cost is met or whether a co-payment is required and (b) upon whether or not there is a means test involved. On top of all this actual care 'packages' may be mixtures of types. With eight types, two crucial additional considerations and the likelihood of mixtures it is probably not appropriate to try to create an elaborate typology. Rather, the aim above has been to specify the range of possible relationships that may be involved.

But then, of course, no contemporary discussion of social care can disregard the issues about the ways in which payment and provision may be split. Accordingly we need a list of potential providers along the following lines:

1. family

2. friends

3. volunteers

4. non-profit organisations

5. private (for-profit) organisations

6. public health service organisations

7. public social care organisations

8. other public organisations (education, housing, etc.).

Having tried to set out lists which identify a wide range of possible payers and providers, an exercise which presumes to offer a modified 'regime' model for comparative analysis has got to try to identify some ways in which actual systems are likely to embody underlying tendencies or to cluster in some respects. The regime analysis approach offered by Esping-Andersen with its focus on the extent of decommodification offers one dimension for such modelling based upon the alternatives of (1) conditional means-tests support, (2) insurance based entitlements and (3) universalistic entitlements. The feminist concern with dependencies suggests alternatives of (1) individualist assumptions, (2) family responsibility assumptions and (3) the acceptance of collectivist obligations. These are set out in two dimensional terms in Table 12.1 with the last of these taken out, since universal entitlement schemes use individualist assumptions.

| Table 12.1 Dimensions of regime types | | | |
|---|---|---|---|
| | *Means tested* | *Insurance based* | *Universalistic* |
| Individual | 1 | 2 | 3 |
| Family based | 4 | 5 | 6 |

The next section explores the extent to which it may be possible to replace the numbers in Table 12.1 with real examples. It will suggest that this is likely to be much more difficult than in the original regime analysis work, given the extent to which there are mixed and changing systems everywhere, but the very exercise of exploring this throws up some important analytical issues.

## Can we give substance to the regime model?

Perhaps the greatest difficulty in trying to develop comparative generalisations about social care arises from the way in which social care is difficult to analyse separately from health care. Clearly, health care systems can be placed in general terms by means of the main regime analysis dimension associated with Esping-Andersen, with Britain along with the allegedly 'decommodified' Scandinavian in the universalist cell, most other countries in the more commodified insurance-based category and the United States standing out (at least for non-pensioners) as a system where means-tests keep many out of the public system. We are then faced with an interesting issue about the extent to which the state systems (both insurance based and tax based) were designed with an assumption that health care systems could offer virtually comprehensive social care systems. The subsequent shift away from the institutional approach to the care of disabled and mentally ill people, which can be treated as a near universal trend, and the reduction in the extent to which hospitals are prepared to offer extended in-patient care for largely 'social care' reasons is then shifting the actual social care systems of all countries with extensive public health care systems out of Box 3 in Table 12.1.

Of course, the generalisation above about the original expectations of universalistic or insurance-based social care system is essentially oversimplified.

However heroic, for example, were the political assumptions attending the creation of the National Health Service, the British government also had to engage in legislation to deal with the last vestiges of the social care elements in the Poor Law (in the 1946 Children Act and the 1948 National Assistance Act in particular). Furthermore – as, for example, any parent of children born in the years immediately after the founding of the NHS can testify – public services operated with many, largely taken for granted, assumptions about the role the family would play in care.

It may be suggested that in many countries the social care issue which was dominant in the first 20 to 30 years after 1945 was the care of children within the nuclear family. In this field the divergence between the Scandinavians (and particularly Sweden) and the rest of the OECD member countries which figure in comparative analyses was the willingness to countenance state support for child care, both in the form of institutional provisions and in benefits to support parents taking time off work to care for children. In this respect Sweden, for example, enacted legislation which still places it largely in Box 3 of the table whilst Britain remained in Box 1.

The evolution of situation with regard to care for adults has been rather different. Here, two universal tendencies have put issues high on the contemporary social care policy agenda that were of low salience 30 years ago. Reference has already been made to one of these, the shift in the willingness of health care systems to accept what we now see as 'social care' responsibilities. The other is the growth in the size of the older population (particularly the very old) likely to be in need of care. These two trends are, of course, interrelated in some respects. The impact of these developments has been then very different in different societies. In the British case the shift has been from Box 3 to Box 1, arising both from the very conditional availability of social care services (with means testing a dominant rationing principle) and from the failure to develop adequate social security benefits enabling tax or insurance-based subsidies for care costs. Indeed, in some respects the British shift has been from Box 3 to Box 4, inasmuch as there are various ways in which assumptions about family roles are still made and the only benefit for carers is set below subsistence level. This theme will be picked up again below.

The interesting comparative question, which is a topic for research and cannot therefore be answered by this essentially speculative essay, is the extent to which systems which have been regarded as much more robustly 'universal' than Britain's are being driven, by the size of the emergent problem relative to the fiscal response, in the same direction. Clearly one difference here lies in something else, outside the main social care policy arena, in the adequacy of public pension policies. The levels of income replacement offered, for example, by even the basic Swedish pension offers more scope than is available to pensioners without private means in Britain. But the high costs of care make this a difference of degree rather than an ultimate difference in kind.

Perhaps the important distinction here is between tax-based and insurance-based health care systems. Whilst insurance benefits may be less 'decommodified', there has been a tendency in many countries to try to ensure that health care provision is nevertheless more or less universally available. Some health insurance schemes (for example that of Australia (Palmer and Short 1994) or equally the very recently established Taiwanese system (Hwang and Hill 1997)) are more appropriately earmarked health tax systems than health insurance ones. But another advantage of the insurance principle in relation to health policy is that it may more effectively establish 'rights'. Such rights may make it more difficult for governments to erode the social care activities of health services. The author has been very impressed by the range of social care services provided through a health insurance to a chronically sick relative in Switzerland.

This point may be very relevant to the issues about 'care insurance'. The establishment of care insurance in Germany will tend to limit the shift from insurance-based health care to means-tested social care. The case of Japan is particularly interesting in this respect. This is a society where family care has been particularly important and health insurance has been slow to become comprehensive, and which has recently introduced a compulsory 'chronic care insurance' scheme (Peng 1998). Japan has faced particular difficulties in reducing lengths of hospital in-patient stays. Has that had any influence upon the rapidity with which it has moved into care insurance?

These rather speculative comments on insurance have been influenced by the possibility that the Royal Commission on long-term care may stimulate a wider

British debate about care insurance. The suggestion is that care insurance has so far developed within strongly insurance-based health care systems. The introduction of this idea to Britain, where social insurance is so seriously decayed, would be more likely to assume either the form of an earmarked, and perhaps regressive, tax or a less than universal semi-private insurance (as embodied in ideas put forward by the last Conservative government).

## Adding the family side of the equation

A brief comment on Britain above suggested that it might be in Box 4 rather than Box 1 of Table 12.1. This part of the paper will explore the issues about the distinction between individualistic and family assumptions in social care policy. Table 12.1 offers three possible boxes for the family-based options. The idea of universalistic policies based upon family assumptions (Box 6) may seem something of a contradiction in terms. Nevertheless, there may be grounds for suggesting that the founding assumptions for state health services were based upon high expectations of family-based social care. The corresponding low scale of provision of social care services, when societies still had low numbers of very old people, seems to have involved little consideration of rationing principles on the grounds that there would be few vulnerable people without family care. Students from Chinese societies have regularly to be told that their stereotype that Western societies have welfare states offering cradle to the grave care needs to be corrected. But doing that involves getting them to understand the importance of implicit rather than explicit assumptions in Western societies.

The crucial point here is that 'universality' in relation to services does not preclude the need for rationing decisions (see Rothstein 1998 for a discussion of this issue with reference to Swedish social policy). Issues about the availability of family support may be used for those rationing decisions. It may be argued that early discharge from hospital to free a bed for others in need is a kind of rationing decision here. The availability of family care is often crucial for these decisions (a Swedish informant has indicated that this applies there, as in the United Kingdom). It seems reasonable to suggest that issues of this kind will arise everywhere. More subtle comparative observations are difficult, it would require an elaborate study to try to identify differences between societies in the assumptions that are made in relation to decisions of this kind.

It was suggested above that insurance rights may limit the use of discretion to ration services. However family assumptions may be embedded in insurance-based policies (Box 5) in both explicit and implicit ways. These relate to the ways in which the respective obligations of husbands and wives are constructed and the extent to which specific benefits need in practice to be topped up by contributions (in cash or services) from relatives. On the basis of a reading of, for example, the German long-term care insurance provisions it is very difficult for the outsiders to make a judgement about adequacy. The rules all seem to relate to the needs of individuals regardless of family circumstances. But the following passage in a description of the scheme suggests some underlying limitations along these lines, particularly in its last sentence with its use of the word 'relieve':

> The largest long-term care 'service' in the country has always been the family. People who live at home and need help with day-to-day activities are usually taken care of by their relatives. This is a good arrangement ... Therefore, home care must be given priority over institutional care. For this reason, the law focuses on providing benefits that improve conditions for home care and relieve the burdens on care providers. (Bundesministerium für Arbeit und Sozialordnung 1998)

This discussion has so far identified the following ways in which family assumptions may be made in relation to care policies.

1. The extent to which assumptions about what families do affect the overall supply of services.

2. The use of assumptions about what families may do in situations in which rationing is needed.

3. The crafting of benefit rights in ways that assume family inputs.

All of these points may apply to care services that are also rationed through means tests. The embedding of family assumptions into means tests may be very explicit indeed. This is the case in a number of Chinese societies – Hong Kong, Singapore and Taiwan – where governments have been prepared to use notions of 'filial obligation' to propagate the idea that social care should only be available where no family support services are possible. Means tests are applied to extended families, even where co-residence is absent, to enforce family obligations. Debates are developing in these societies about the extent to which these family obligations can be sustained in the context of social and economic change. Some scholars go further to suggest that 'filial obligation' is rather more a handy justification for government inaction than a sacred unifying principle for the Chinese family (Marcus Chiu, personal communication).

The survey of social assistance rules in OECD member countries carried out by Eardley *et al.* (1996) did not identify any rules that extended means testing outside the household. But while the majority of the nations surveyed only means tested within the family, the use of the whole household as the unit of assessment was found in Austria, Japan, Switzerland and Turkey. It is recognised that eligibility rules for social care measures will not be the same as those for social assistance, whilst many countries operate these two policy areas together there may be specifically more draconian rules in relation to specific services. For example, in France

> If the individual old person lacks the means to pay the charges made to users of services, then their children, children's spouses and grandchildren are obliged to contribute up to a certain ceiling, under the general legal principle of the *'obligation alimentaire'*, the duty to support one's close family. (Ely and Saunders in Munday 1993, p.133)

However, even if means testing is confined to the nuclear family, rationing policies are still likely to be applied which either assume duties of care on the part of spouses or that the resources of spouses should be taken into account in determining charges. Unfortunately the study of OECD countries quoted above did not go into issues about services.

A related issue here is that of support for a carer (other than a spouse) when that carer is a relative. This, of course, has been one of the explicit concerns of the research by Ungerson and her associates. Ungerson reports:

> The income provided through such allowances is very variable – from the Danish wage equivalent allowances through the British and Irish barely sub-sistence allowances to the USA tax breaks ... In addition, there are individual programmes on a state by state basis which act as supplements to Federal arrangements [some of which] come close to 'proper wages'. (Ungerson 1998, p.6)

A full consideration of these options needs to be related to all the other possibilities – the willingness of the state to pay a relative as a carer or to pay an allowance to those in need of care that can be used to pay a relative. On top of these there is the more obscure issue of the extent to which the presence of a relative in the household is used as a justification for the refusal of a care service. While the British approach on all these issues has tended to involve a reluctance to accept the individualist approach, the evidence from some other countries is sufficiently ambiguous to inhibit the allegation that we stand alone in that respect.

## Conclusions

This paper has tried to establish the foundations for comparative work on social care rather than either to offer a range of generalisations or to report a series of mini-case studies. Its stance is that whilst, in the study of social security in particular and in the study of health services to some extent, there are now various ways in which the policies of various countries may be meaningfully compared, this is not the case in respect of social care. But it is suggested that by developing the regime analysis work pioneered by Esping-Andersen and by drawing on the work of the various writers who have examined the feasibility of the application of his model to family policy and to 'women's welfare states' it may be possible to start to build an approach to the comparative study of social care. What then is needed is some careful and subtle comparative work which aims to tease out exactly who gets what under what circumstances in various countries.

In the meantime, throwing caution to the wind, it may be suggested that the Chinese societies of Taiwan, Hong Kong and Singapore offer very clear examples of services very limited by linked family assumptions and means tests (Box 4 in Table 12.1), while Britain and France (and probably other southern European countries) come in a somewhat more limited sense into the same category. The Scandinavian countries may be able to maintain positions in Box 3 with universal entitlements for most and little service discrimination on a family basis, but there are some issues that need careful examination about the extent to which family considerations may influence rationing policies. But the really interesting countries to watch at the moment are Germany and Japan that are aiming to extend individualistic insurance-based entitlements (Box 2), which stand out from other societies like Switzerland where more limited health and social security insurance policies are underscored by strong assumptions about family obligations.

## References

Bradshaw, J., Ditch, J., Holmes, H. and Whiteford, P. (1993) *Support for Children: A Comparison of Arrangements in 15 Counties.* London: HMSO.

Bundesministerium für Arbeit und Sozialordnung (1998) *Social Security in Germany.* http://www.bma.de.

Eardley, T., Bradshaw, J., Ditch, J., Goush, I. and Whiteford, P. (1996) *Social Assistance in OECD Countries: Synthesis Report.* London: HMSO.

Esping-Andersen, G. (1990) *The Three Worlds of Welfare Capitalism.* Cambridge: Policy Press.

Evers, A., Pijl, M. and Ungerson, C. (eds) (1994) *Payments for Care.* Aldershot: Avebury.

Hwang Y-S. and Hill, M. (1997) 'The 1995 health reforms in Taiwan.' *Hong Kong Public Administration 6,* 2, 79–96.

Kraan, R.J. *et al.* (1991) *Care for the Elderly: Significant Innovations in Three European Countries.* Boulder, CO: Westview Press.

Lewis, J. (1992) 'Gender and the development of welfare regimes.' *Journal of European Social Policy 2,* 3, 159–73.

Munday, B. (ed) (1993) *European Social Services.* Canterbury: University of Kent.

O'Connor, J.S. (1993) 'Gender, class and citizenship in the comparative analysis of welfare state regimes: Theoretical and methodological issues.' *British Journal of Sociology 44,* 3, 501–18.

Palmer, G.R. and Short, S.D. (1994) *Health Care and Public Policy.* Melbourne: Macmillan.

Peng, I. (1998) 'The Japanese Welfare State: Perspectives and Patterns of Change.' Paper given at an international conference on social welfare policy, Chi Nan University, Taiwan.

Rothstein, B. (1998) *Just Institutions Matter.* Cambridge: Cambridge University Press.

Sainsbury, D. *(ed)* (1994) *Gendering Welfare States.* London: Sage.

Ungerson, C. (1995) 'Gender, cash and informal care: European perspectives and dilemmas.' *Journal of Social Policy 24,* 1, 31–52.

Ungerson, C. (1998) 'Cash in Care.' Paper given at the 1998 Social Policy Association Conference.

# CHAPTER 13

# Conclusion

## 'Modernising Social Services' –
## A Blueprint for the New Millennium?

## Bob Hudson

### Introduction: looking back and looking forward

In November 1998, after considerable delay, the government published its long-awaited White Paper on the future of the personal social services – *Modernising Social Services* (Department of Health 1998). The title implies the existence of an outmoded system needing the smack of a new 'third way' to drag it into the new millennium – a clean break not only with the traditional 'Old Labour' approach reflected in the Seebohm Report (1968) but also with the quasi-market model favoured by the last Conservative government (DoH 1989), which is dismissed as concentrating too much on structure and process at the expense of outcomes. To what extent does the White Paper deliver on the promise implied in its title?

The introduction to the White Paper acknowledges the existence of 'some excellent services in many places and a generally high appreciation of services by users' (para 1.4), but nevertheless states that 'social services are often failing to provide the support that people should expect' (ibid.). A number of difficulties are identified, each of which could just as easily have been found in the Seebohm Report or the 1989 White Paper, *Caring for People* (DoH 1989) – an indication that it is not *diagnosis* which is politically at issue in the personal social services, but *prescription*. The six areas are as follows.

*Protection*

The White Paper observes that

> All too often children and vulnerable adults have been exposed to neglect and
> abuse. Any decent society owes to every child a safe and secure upbringing,
> and to every elderly or disabled man or woman, the right to live in dignity,
> free from fear of abuse. (para 1.4)

The Registered Homes Act 1984 placed upon local authorities the duty to
register and inspect homes provided by the independent sector, the Children
Act 1989 covered the registration and inspection of children's homes, while the
NHS and Community Care Act 1990 also required local authorities to inspect
their own homes through arms-length inspectorates which have normally been
based within social services departments (SSDs). The White Paper sees these
arrangements as giving rise to three types of problem: lack of independence
(local inspectorates have a conflict of interests), lack of coherence (responsibilities are split between different authorities and professions), and lack of
consistency (in England there are 250 registering authorities with standards
varying from one area to another).

*Coordination*

Fragmentation within and between services has been identified as a major
shortcoming for many years, and previous attempts to deal with the problem
have been widely seen as ineffective (Nocon 1994). As the White Paper puts it:

> Sometimes agencies put more effort into arguing with one another than into
> looking after people in need ... Everyone deserves to be treated as an individ-
> ual, and to have the system geared to their needs, not vice-versa. (para 1.4)

*Inflexibility*

In terms very similar to the White Paper of a decade earlier (DoH 1989),
*Modernising Social Services* complains that 'social services sometimes provide
what suits the service rather than what suits the person needing care' (para 1.4).
Although it is acknowledged that the introduction of care management has
resulted in more responsive services than in the past, a range of fundamental
continuing problems is identified: the lack of a planned, information-based
approach to commissioning; budgetary arrangements that make it difficult for

care managers to put together a tailored care service for individuals; the need for better relationships with both independent providers and in-house providers; and crude systems for setting contract prices.

## Clarity of role

In part, concerns about role clarity are related to those of fragmentation – the boundary between health and social care still remains unclear and confusing. However, the White Paper is more concerned here with the uncertainty about what social services actually *do* or should be *expected* to do. It is noted that:

> Up to now, neither users, carers, the public, nor social services staff and managers have had a clear idea which services are, or should be provided, or what standards can reasonably be expected. The lack of clarity of objectives and standards means that on the one hand social services cannot easily be held to account, and on the other hand they can get blamed for anything that goes wrong. (para 1.4)

## Consistency

Social services function as a local service and vary from one part of the country to another in response to differing local needs and circumstances – something which might also be expected to arise from a system of local democracy in which different political priorities emerge. On the other hand, there has long been evidence of ostensibly unwarranted variations in provision and charging regimes, which has led some to argue for minimum national standards.

## Inefficiency

An important finding of the joint review process has been that there is scope for many authorities to get more for what they spend on social services (DoH/Audit Commission 1997). The White Paper suggests that by running services more efficiently, some councils could save as much as £10 million, which could be used for better services.

## A 'third way' for social services?

Having engaged in this fairly negative assessment of social services' performance, the White Paper briefly turns from nasty to less nasty, stating that:

> The Government has no wish to add further to the criticism of those who work in social services. We recognise that the law and the central framework within which social services operate is also at fault. They need to be changed so that they help those working in the services, rather than hindering them. (para 1.5)

The broad approach to the future – depicted predictably as constituting a 'third way' – is said to be one which 'moves the focus away from who provides the care, and places it firmly on the quality of services experienced by, and outcomes achieved for, individuals and their carers and families' (para 1.7). Seven 'key principles' are said to underlie the approach, and these overlap considerably with the six key objectives outlined in the 1989 White Paper on community care. Table 13.1 contrasts the two documents.

A comparison of the two sets of aims does not suggest starkly different approaches. Both have a commitment to keeping people in their own homes with maximum independence, both wish to see better assessments of individual need, and both are concerned with clarity of responsibilities. One important difference is that the Conservative White Paper was more concerned about *who* should provide the service (the 'flourishing independent sector') than with the nature of that service, although it is noticeable that Labour's White Paper has no specific proposals for dismantling the mixed economy of care which has been built up under successive Conservative governments. However, the most significant difference relates to the *degree of centralisation*. Although the Conservative White Paper was seen at the time as having potentially centralising elements, in practice this was confined to the requirement to spend the bulk of the special transitional grant (STG) in the independent sector. Other key features of the 1989 White Paper, such as introducing assessment and care management arrangements, producing annual community care plans and making support for carers a high priority, were very much the product of local commitment – or the lack of it.

| Table 13.1 The 1989 and 1998 White Papers: comparison of aims/principles | |
|---|---|
| *1989 White Paper* | *1998 White Paper* |
| Promote the development of domiciliary, day and respite services to enable people to live in their own homes wherever feasible and sensible. | Care should be provided to people in a way that supports their independence and respects their dignity. |
| Ensure that service providers make practical support for carers a high priority. | Services should meet each individual's specific needs, pulling together social services, health, housing, education or any others needed. And people should have a say in what services they get and how they are delivered. |
| Make proper assessment of need and good care management the cornerstone of high quality care. | Care services should be organised, accessed, provided and financed in a fair, open and consistent way in every part of the country. |
| Promote the development of a flourishing independent sector alongside good quality public services. | Children looked after by local authorities should get a decent start in life ... Every person should be safeguarded against abuse, neglect or poor treatment whilst receiving care. |
| Clarify responsibilities of agencies and so make it easier to hold them to account for their performance. | Staff should be sufficiently trained and skilled for the work they are doing. |
| Secure better value for taxpayers' money by introducing a new funding structure for social care. | People should have confidence in their local social services, knowing that they work to clean and acceptable standards. |

Such local discretion will not be permitted under the new regime. The stick is brandished immediately in the secretary of state's Foreword, when he states:

One big trouble social services have suffered from is that up to now no Government has spelled out exactly what people can expect or what the staff are expected to do. Nor have any clear standards of performance been laid down. This Government is to change all that.

The Secretary of State is as good as his word in this respect, with the White Paper containing six main centralising features.

1. The 'nationalisation' of local authority social services

2. The circumscription of local discretion

3. The expectation of greater efficiency

4. The enhancement of protection

5. The pursuit of professionalism

6. The promotion of partnership.

## The 'nationalisation' of local authority social services

The accepted wisdom of recent years has been that the different patterns of accountability in the NHS and personal social services respectively have necessarily involved different types of central–local relationship. Specifically, the NHS is directly accountable to the Secretary of State for Health and hence to parliament, whereas social services are purchased and organised by social services departments which are accountable to locally elected councils. Accordingly, whilst it has been common practice for some time for the DoH to set out national targets and other arrangements to be met by the NHS locally, this has not been felt to be appropriate for social services. This is no longer the position. The Labour government has had little hesitation in setting out a range of national requirements which apply to *both* services, and in doing so has moved towards a 'nationalisation' of local authority social services. There have been three important developments: the setting of national *objectives*; the publication of national priorities *guidance*; and the development of national *frameworks*.

### National objectives

The development of new national objectives for social services is described in *Modernising Social Services* as 'the foundation of the proposals in this White Paper' (para 2.32), and by feeding directly into the National Priorities Guidance they constitute 'a single statement of priorities for both health and social services which all authorities around the country should follow' (ibid.).

## Box 13.1. National objectives for social services

*Adult services*

- To promote the independence of adults assessed as needing social care support arranged by the local authority, respecting their dignity and furthering their social and economic participation.

- To enable adults assessed as needing social care support to live as safe, full and normal a life as possible, in their own home wherever feasible.

- To ensure that people of working age who have been assessed as requiring community care services are provided with these services in ways which take account of and, as far as possible, maximise their and their carers' capacity to take up, remain in or return to employment.

- To work with the NHS, users, carers and other agencies to avoid unnecessary admission to hospital, and inappropriate placement on leaving hospital; and to maximise the health status and thus independence of those they support.

- To enable informal carers to care or continue to care for as long as they and the service user wish.

- To plan, commission, purchase and monitor an adequate supply of appropriate, cost-effective and safe social care provision for those eligible for local authority support.

*Common objectives*

- To actively involve users and carers in planning services and in tailoring individual packages of care; and to ensure effective mechanisms are in place to handle complaints.

- To ensure through regulatory powers and duties that adults and children in regulated services are protected from harm and poor care standards.

- To ensure that social care workers are appropriately skilled, trained and qualified, and to promote the uptake of training at all levels.

- To maximise the benefit to service users for the resources available, and to demonstrate the effectiveness and value for money of the care and support provided, and allow for choice and different responses for different needs and circumstances.

Objectives are articulated for children's services and adult services, along with a number of common objectives. The adult and common objectives are set out in Box 13.1.

Perhaps inevitably, such objectives have a 'motherhood and apple pie' aura about them, and in many respects they bear a close similarity to the objectives contained in *Caring for People*. What counts for more is the way in which they are interpreted locally, and in particular whether such interpretation is a matter of local discretion. It is at this point that the other two elements of 'nationalisation' become significant.

*National Priorities Guidance*

The publication of *National Priorities Guidance* (NPG) for health and social services (DoH 1998a) preceded the social services White Paper by a couple of months. The accompanying press release described the guidance as 'a radical departure for how health and social care services will work together' (98/404), while the guidance itself observes that 'This document ... treats the health and social care system as one. The Government expects to see quantifiable year-by-year improvements in services as part of a ten year modernisation programme' (para 19). The NPG covers the three-year period from 1999/00 through to 2001/02 and allocates responsibilities in three ways – those with a social services lead, those with an NHS lead and those with a shared lead. Table 13.2 shows these allocations.

| Table 13.2 National priorities guidance: allocation of lead responsibilities | | |
|---|---|---|
| *Social services lead* | *Shared lead* | *NHS lead* |
| Children's welfare | Cutting health inequalities | Waiting lists/times |
| Interagency working | Mental health | Primary care |
| Regulation | Promoting independence | Coronary heart disease |
| | | Cancer |

Each of these areas of responsibility has related targets which vary in specificity. Examples of high specificity are:

- reduce by 10 per cent, by 2002, the proportion of children who are reregistered on the child protection register from a baseline for the year ending March 1997
- reduce nationally the emergency psychiatric re-admission rate by 2 percentage points from the 1997/8 baseline by 2002
- reduce the per capita rate of growth in emergency admissions of people aged over 75 to an annual average of 3 per cent over the five years up to 2002/3.

Most objectives are less precise. Examples include:

- put in place effective working arrangements for cooperation and information-sharing in regulatory functions
- improve provision of appropriate, high quality care and treatment for children and young people by building up locally based child and adolescent mental health services
- provide carers with the support and services to maintain their health, and with the information they need on the health status and medication of the person they are caring for.

The vehicle for responding to these objectives is the Health Improvement Programme (HImP), which the White Paper says will 'offer local authorities greater insight and a stronger voice in the formative stages of NHS service plans' (para. 56). At the same time, social services authorities will be expected to reflect HImP objectives in their own local plans such as community care plans and children's services plans. There are arguments about the *appropriateness* of many of these objectives, but there is no doubting the degree of central control which the DoH now wishes to exercise over local social services activity.

### National frameworks

National frameworks represent an even greater level of specificity than national objectives and much of the National Priorities Guidance. There are two different sorts of proposals for such frameworks – those for *services*, and those for *performance assessment*. The idea of national service frameworks (NSFs) was announced in the NHS White Paper of December 1997 (DoH 1997) with further arrangements outlined in a Health Service Circular of April 1998 (NHS Executive 1998). The intention is that NSFs will set national standards and define service models for a defined service or care group; put in place strategies to support implementation; and establish performance measures against which progress within an agreed timescale will be measured. The aim is 'to reduce unacceptable variations in care and standards of treatment based on research evidence on standards, outcomes and cost-effectiveness' (DoH 1998, para 2.34). Work on developing the first two NSFs (on mental health and coronary heart disease) is already underway, and will be followed by a framework on services for older people. Further frameworks will follow at the rate of one per year.

Plans for extending frameworks for performance assessment reflect the determination of the government to measure and assess performance against identified outcomes. For the NHS, a framework has already been developed which covers six dimensions of performance – health improvement, fair access, effective delivery of appropriate health care efficiency, patient/user experience and health outcomes of NHS care. A similar framework is now being developed for assessing the performance of social services authorities in a way which is consistent with the 'best value regime', which requires public services to measure themselves against the best. This will involve an enhanced role for the social care regional offices of the Social Services Inspectorate, which will be given the power to invoke penalties for failure and offer rewards for success.

Overall, these various measures do amount to an unprecedented degree of centralisation – the determination of national objectives sets out the requisite vision; National Priorities Guidance lays down the desired service outcomes; national service frameworks set the standards to be met; and performance assessment frameworks ensure that all of these are duly implemented. It indeed amounts to a veritable 'nationalisation of local authority social services'.

## The circumscription of local discretion

The most significant circumscription of local discretion has already been covered in the previous section, but this still leaves behind some discretion in the *way* things are done. Some of this is probably inevitable and arguably desirable – it is, for example, not possible for a central body to dictate the precise nature of interaction between professionals and service users. Nevertheless, there are two important new ways in which residual areas of local discretion will be reduced. The most obvious of these relates to the widespread variations in discretionary charging practices. Although ostensibly committed to dealing with this variation, the social services White Paper was able to await the verdict of the Royal Commission on Long-Term Care which was due to report later in 1999.

Less apparent have been concerns about inconsistency within and between the local systems for deciding who qualifies for services – the various eligibility and assessment criteria which have grown since *Caring for People*. Here the government is developing guidance on what it calls 'fair access to care', which will set out the principles authorities should follow when devising and applying eligibility criteria, including the need for compatibility with NHS continuing care criteria. Authorities will be expected to demonstrate: consistency in the way that every person's needs are assessed; clear objectives, based on the overriding need to promote independence; a common understanding of risk assessment; and the existence of regular reviews. Detailed guidance on these are promised and the White Paper states that by April 2001, every local authority will be working within the fair access guidance.

## The expectation of greater efficiency

The White Paper takes the view that local authority social services are generally inefficient, citing both the findings of a number of the joint reviews of the last few years, as well as some research by the Personal Social Services Research Unit at the University of Kent (para 7.16). The answer is felt to lie in a combination of sticks and carrots, with the former carrying far more weight than the latter. Gentle encouragement to do better comes in two main forms. First, authorities are urged to improve the standard of their commissioning with the aid of two centrally provided tools – further guidance on the kind of information needed to improve the impact of commissioning, and a self-audit tool to help authorities to review their care management arrangements. Second, the government proposes to recognise and reward good practice by inviting the 'best' authorities to apply for 'beacon status' – recognised centres of excellence and expertise which receive (as yet unspecified) 'rewards'.

Of more significance to most councils will be the sanctions which are implicit in two further measures – 'efficiency savings' and the best value regime. The White Paper has little to say about the anticipated efficiency savings, but is brutally efficient in expressing the requirements:

> The Government has decided to set targets for improvements in the efficiency with which social services are delivered. In 1999/00 the target will be a 2 per cent improvement in efficiency. In 2001/01, by which time it is expected that the duty of Best Value will apply, a further 2 per cent improvement will be required, followed by a further 3 per cent improvement in 2001/02. (para 7.16)

---

### Box 13.2. Best value arrangements for social services

- Creation of local objectives which reflect national objectives.
- Meeting of government-prescribed national standards.
- Fundamental performance reviews of all authority services over a five-year cycle.
- Local performance plans which provide a clear and practical expression of an authority's performance.
- Annual external reviews of the social services aspects of the local performance plan.
- Linking of SSI inspections to the performance assessment framework.
- Expansion of the joint review programme so that each local authority is reviewed every five years, consistent with the best value regime cycle.

These measures amount to a stringent scrutiny of social services activity. What used to be called 'new public sector managerialism' may well have passed social services by for much of the 1990s, but in the future there will be little difference in the ways in which the NHS and local authority social services are treated by central government.

---

In two short sentences, then, local authority social services find themselves exposed to the sorts of financial regimes to which health authorities have been exposed for several years. Alongside this will be the Best Value arrangements set out in the local government White Paper (Department of the Environment, Transport and the Regions 1998) which will apply to all local government functions, and constitute a duty to deliver services to clear standards by the most efficient, economic and efficient means available. The main elements to be introduced for social services are outlined in Box 13.2.

## The enhancement of protection

Protection is identified in the White Paper as the first of several 'failings' on the part of social services, therefore it is unsurprising to find proposals to enhance protection to be prominent – indeed most of these proposals had been widely trailed for some time. The main change is the proposed regionalisation of the inspection and regulation role with the creation of eight regional commissions for care standards (CCSs) in England based upon the boundaries of the NHS and social care regions to replace the current 250 registering authorities. Unlike the existing 'arms-length' arrangements, these will be independent statutory bodies with the chairs appointed by the Secretary of State, and they will have a remit which both combines and extends the current responsibilities of local authorities and health authorities. Regulatory responsibilities will cover: residential care homes for adults; nursing homes; children's homes; domiciliary care providers; independent fostering agencies; residential family centres; and boarding schools. Alongside these changes of structure and function, the White Paper seeks to minimise inconsistency of standards by the proposed development of national regulatory standards to be applied consistently by all eight CCSs.

Although generally welcomed, these proposals have not entirely escaped criticism. On the one hand, local government interests resent the removal of responsibilities from local authority control and the accompanying loss of local accountability. On the other hand, representatives of the independent sector – which has long lobbied for some such reform – feel aggrieved that in some respects the changes do not go far enough. There are three main issues of contention. First, that some areas of service activity, notably day care for adults and field social work, remain outside the CCS remit. Second, that the new organisations will be insufficiently independent. The National Care Homes Association and the Registered Nursing Home Association, for example, claim that many of the benefits of the new arrangements will be lost if the staff currently employed by local authority inspection units are simply moved sideways into the new commissions. And finally, there has been early conflict over the proposed national standards. The first move by the government has been to commission the Centre for Policy on Ageing to advise on proposed national standards for residential and nursing home care for older people, but a difference of view over appropriate standards has already led to the chair of the National Care Homes Association resigning from the advisory group.

The goal of enhanced protection is also seen in two other aspects of the White Paper – local surveys of users and carers, and the Long-Term Care Charter. The requirement to find out what local citizens needs are, and what they think of how the council is doing, arises from the Best Value regime. Every council will be obliged to carry out local surveys of user and carer experience of, and satisfaction with, social services. It is noted in the White Paper that the government will not be prescriptive about the detail of these surveys, but will introduce a small set of questions that will be used by all authorities. These satisfaction surveys will commence in April 2000. An earlier start has been made on developing a 'long-term care charter' which is expected to be introduced by autumn 1999. The aim is to set out more clearly at national level what users and carers can expect if they need support from health, housing and social services.

## The pursuit of professionalism

Implicit in the shift towards greater centralisation and allegations of inefficiency is the suggestion that those who work in and run local authority social services are in some way not performing their task as well as they might. This is the context to proposals in the White Paper for enhancing professional standards for staff and changing the local government policy-making context. In the case of the one million staff employed in social services, the White Paper acknowledges their difficult position ('there are few public accolades for getting it right and virulent criticism for getting it wrong' (para 5.2) and states that the government 'has no wish to undermine or attack those who work in the social care sector' (para 5.3).

The government nevertheless judges that 'institutional change is essential to improve standards and public confidence' (para 5.6). The main proposal – and one which was widely trailed and anticipated – is the introduction (when parliamentary time allows) of a new statutory body, the General Social Care Council (GSCC) to regulate the training of social workers, set conduct and practice standards for all social services staff and register those in the most sensitive areas. Although the creation of such a body may seem to put social care on a parallel footing with the ways in which doctors and nurses exercise self-regulation, the reality is that the proposal is yet another example of centralised control and monitoring. The first task of the council – which does not even have a majority of social services professionals on the governing body – will be to set enforceable standards of conduct and practice for the whole workforce which will be published in codes. Individual practitioners will be required to sign up to the codes as a condition of their employment.

A second main task of the council will be professional registration, but – in recognition of the fact that 80 per cent of the social services workforce has no recognised qualification or training – this will be confined to those who are already professionally qualified and those working in residential child care who have qualified at NVQ Level 3. Unlike some other professional groupings, however, there will be no restriction on entry to social services jobs to those who are registered, or are eligible for registration. The White Paper sees such a restriction as undesirable given the moves towards multidisciplinary work with medical, nursing and other professions, although the argument is not evenly applied to the registration arrangements for these collaborating professions. Although generally welcomed then, the proposed GSSC could be argued to be a somewhat half-hearted step towards enhanced professional status for social services staff.

Alongside these changes to arrangements for staff there is the less-noticed proposal for changing the ways in which elected members exercise their responsibilities for social services. As with other local government activities, social services will be affected by the proposal to change the long-standing committee system (DETR 1998). Authorities will be required to draw up proposals for new structures based on a clear distinction between executive responsibilities and the other roles of elected members, with some sort of a shift expected to take place towards the introduction of executive cabinets and executive mayors. Under such arrangements there will be a scrutiny role for backbench councillors – a role which the White Paper implies has not been effectively undertaken through the committee system. In a nice aside, it is stated that 'it is not generally acceptable for elected members to claim that they are shocked when evidence emerges of serious service failure' (para 7.29). In effect, the Social Services Committee, the most enduring outcome of the 1968 Seebohm Report, will go, although the government will retain the legal requirement for every social services authority to appoint a director of social services who will be directly accountable to the chief executive. It remains unclear whether these proposals will breathe effective political direction into local social services, especially when the shift towards closer working relationships with the NHS is creating a new range of decision-making bodies, such as primary care groups, upon which elected members have no direct voice.

### Enhanced partnership

The idea of 'partnership' infuses all aspects of New Labour policy making, and local authority social services is no exception. Many of the proposals in the White Paper stem from the discussion document, *Partnership in Action* (DoH 1998b) which was published slightly earlier.

This specifically addresses the interface between the NHS and social services – both the nature of the problems and the ways in which they might be overcome – and constitutes the strongest political warning to the two agencies which has ever been issued in an official publication. Three levels where joint working is needed are identified.

- *Strategic planning.* At this level, agencies will need to plan jointly for the medium term, and share information about how they intend to use their resources towards the achievement of common goals. The means for doing this are identified as health action zones, health improvement programmes and joint investment plans. The latter (the framework for which was in place by April 1999) are based upon a joint assessment of need and shared objectives, initially for older people.

- *Service commissioning.* Here it is expected that, when securing services for their local populations, agencies will have a common understanding of the needs they are jointly meeting, and the kind of provision likely to be most effective. The move to primary care groups (in England) is seen as providing 'a unique opportunity for the key partners to test new approaches to joint commissioning' (p.14), and yet more guidance on good practice from local joint commissioning initiatives will be issued.

- *Service provision.* Regardless of how services are purchased or funded, the key objective is that the user receives a coherent integrated package of care, and this is the third identified level of joint working. The discussion document sees several fresh opportunities at this level: the emerging primary care trusts, the Primary Care Act pilot schemes, and the experiences gained from special initiatives such as the 'winter pressures' money. In the particular case of older people, the government further required that by 1999 a framework was in place for multidisciplinary assessment in community health and acute care settings, with local authorities required to spend part of their funding in support of rehabilitation and recuperation facilities. Much of this seems similar to many previous attempts at collaboration through exhortation, even if the exhortation is more systematic and the tone more strident. However, there is a recognition in *Partnership in Action* that more needs to be done.

Three proposals for allowing more flexibility between agencies are made. First, the legalisation of *pooled budgets* to allow health and social services to bring resources together to commission and provide services in a way that would be accessible to both partners in the joint arrangements – the sort of arrangement which was ruled illegal in Lewisham in the early 1990s. Unlike the current position, the pooled resource would lose its health or social services identity and be available for either type of support. Of course, where there is mistrust between agencies, and a fear of 'cost-shunting', then there would also be an unwillingness to commit budgets to the pool. Greater legal flexibility is no panacea for a basic lack of trust! The second flexibility is that of *lead commissioning*, where one authority is permitted to take the lead in commissioning the range of services for a particular group on behalf of both agencies. Learning disability and mental health are cited as examples where this could be usefully applied. Again, such an arrangement could only flourish in a collaborative relationship already characterised by a high degree of mutual respect and trust. And finally, there is the suggestion of permitting more *integrated provision* by allowing health and social services agencies to take on at least some of each other's functions.

The social services White Paper adds to this agenda in a number of ways. In arguing for a more accessible service, it espouses the 'one-stop-shop' model (perhaps better termed the 'first-stop-shop') to ensure that an approach to one agency will automatically trigger contributions from partner agencies as required. Also, in recognition that *Partnership in Action* is primarily concerned with the social services–NHS boundary, the White Paper emphasises the importance of relationships with other agencies such as housing, the probation service, the police, the employment service, education and other children's services and the voluntary sector.

A more significant measure than these exhortations, however, is the fact that the White Paper firmly grasps the importance of making partnership working conditional upon access to resources. The main vehicle for this is the £1.3 billion of new money contained in the social services modernisation fund, and in particular two 'promoting independence' grants – the partnership grant and prevention grant – which between them total almost £750 million over a three-year period up to 2001/02. The largest of the two, the partnership grant, is intended to foster partnership between health and social services in promoting independence as an objective of adult social services, with a particular emphasis upon improving rehabilitation services, whilst the prevention grant focuses more upon developing preventive strategies to target people most at risk of losing their independence. In both cases, conditions will be attached which require local authorities to draw up plans jointly with NHS agencies, and experience with such measures as 'winter beds' monies suggests that this can be an effective way to promote joint working.

## Conclusion: new vision or incremental change?

Reaction to the publication of the White Paper was noticeably muted – a general welcome mixed with some reservation. The Association of Directors of Social Services, for example, felt wronged by the removal of inspection from local authorities, as did the Local Government Association. Others saw the whole thing as a damp squib. Philpot describes it as 'for the most part rather mild fare ... continuing down the Blairite Third Way, it offers mostly more of the same' (Philpot 1998). In similar fashion, the editorial of the weekly, *Community Care*, complains of a White Paper in which 'appearance mostly predominates over substance' (*Community Care* 1998).

It is easy to understand why the incremental argument predominates. Many of the changes proposed in *Modernising Social Services* do build upon earlier policies and proposals. The changes to inspection and regulation, for example, arise from the much earlier Burgner Report (1996), the idea of a GSSC has a long history and was a specific Labour Party election pledge, whilst even the social services White Paper which emerged from the dying Conservative government (DoH 1997a) contained comparable proposals for changing and extending inspection and regulation, and for creating approved social workers for families and children. However, what this view overlooks is that the real change is not so much in *what is done*, so much as the *way in which* it is done. As this chapter has demonstrated, social services will in future be subject to an unprecedented degree of central command and surveillance with far-reaching consequences for their future existence, let alone direction. The only certainty about local authority social services in the new millennium is uncertainty.

## References

Burgner Report (1996) *The Regulation and Inspection of Social Services.* London: Department of Health.

Community Care (1998) 'Uncertain path.' *Editorial*, 3/9 December.

Department of the Environment, Transport and the Regions (1998) *Modern Local Government: In Touch with the People.* London: The Stationery Office.

Department of Health (1989) *Caring for People: Community Care in the Next Decade and Beyond.* Cm 849. London: HMSO.

Department of Health (1997) *The New NHS: Modern, Dependable.* London: The Stationery Office.

Department of Health (1997a) *Social Services: Achievement and Challenge.* London: The Stationery Office.

Department of Health (1998) *Modernising Social Services: Promoting Independence, Improving Protection, Raising Standards.* London: The Stationery Office.

Department of Health (1998a) *Modernising Health and Social Services: National Priorities Guidance 1999/00-2001/02.* London: DoH.

Department of Health (1998b) *Partnership in Action: A Discussion Document.* London: DoH.

Department of Health/Audit Commission (1997) *Joint Reviews of Local Authorities' Social Services: Annual Report 1997.* London: DoH.

National Health Service Executive (1998) *National Service Frameworks. Health Service Circular 1998/074.* London: DoH.

Nocon, A. (1994) *Collaboration in Community Care in the 1990s.* Sunderland: Business Education Publishers.

Philpot, T. (1998) 'Let history judge.' *Community Care, 3/9* December, 18–20.

Seebohm Report (1968) *Report of the Committee on Local Authority and Allied Personal Services.* London: HMSO.

# The Contributors

**Sue Balloch** is Reader in Health and Social Care at the University of Brighton. She was previously Director of Policy at the National Institute for Social Work. As Senior Researcher in NISW's Research Unit she was responsible for the management of the workforce studies. She has lectured in social policy at Goldsmith's College and worked to develop anti-poverty strategies at the Association of Metropolitan Authorities. Publications include studies of the effects of unemployment on social services, anti-poverty strategy, credit unions, refugees, local government charging policies and the social services workforce.

**Geoff Fimister** Having undertaken social policy research in various capacities at Loughborough and Glasgow Universities, Geoff Fimister moved to Newcastle-upon-Tyne in 1974 to set up Newcastle City Council's Welfare Rights Service, where he is currently a principal welfare rights officer. He has for many years been a welfare rights adviser to the Association of Metropolitan Authorities (now absorbed into the Local Government Association) working on housing, social services, financial and anti-poverty issues. He is a member of the LGA teams involved in consultations with central government over housing benefit and community care matters.

**Brian Hardy** is a principal research fellow in the Community Care Division, Nuffield Institute, University of Leeds. He has, for the last nine years, been part of the joint Nuffield Institute/PSSRU research team investigating the development of social care markets within the Department of Health-commissioned mixed economy of care programme. He is the author and co-author of a number of books and articles in this area.

**Murray Hawtin** is a senior policy analyst with the Policy Research Institute, Leeds Metropolitan University. He has a long background as a social worker, community development officer and housing officer. He has undertaken a number of research projects related to housing and social care, and has also written widely on housing and health and tenant participation.

**Melanie Henwood** has been since 1991 an independent health and social care analyst, and also a visiting fellow with the Community Care Division of the Nuffield Institute for Health, University of Leeds. Previously she has held posts at the King's Fund, the Family Policy Studies Centre and the University of Bath. Her main research interests are in long-term care for older people, the role of family or informal care, and the interface between health and social care in both policy and practice.

**Michael Hill** is Visiting Professor in the Department of Social Policy and Politics at Goldsmith's College, University of London. He is also Emeritus Professor of Social Policy at the University of Newcastle-upon Tyne. He is joint editor of the *Journal of Social Policy* and author of several books on social policy and the policy process, including *Understanding Social Policy* (1999, sixth edition), *Social Policy: A Comparative Analysis* (1996) and *The Policy Process in the Modern Capitalist State* (1997).

**Bob Hudson** is a principal research fellow at the Nuffield Institute for Health, University of Leeds. Prior to that he was a visiting fellow in community care in the Institute of Health Studies, University of Durham, and a senior lecturer in social policy at New College, Durham. For many years he has written widely in the academic and weekly press on social policy issues, and he is currently engaged on a range of research projects associated with the reform of the National Health Service.

**Jeremy Kendall** is Research Fellow at the PSSRU, based at the London School of Economics. His research interests include the voluntary sector in comparative perspective in the UK and abroad, and the mixed economy of social care. Recent publications include *The Voluntary Sector in the UK* (with Martin Knapp) and *The Contract Culture in Public Services* (with Perri 6). He is editor of *Voluntas*, the international journal of voluntary and non-profit organisations.

**John McLean** is a researcher at the National Institute for Social Work. He has previously worked in residential and field social work with older people, children and adolescents, users with severe learning difficulties and users with mental health problems. Publications include studies of responses to health education on HIV, and the work experience of social services staff in relation to gender, job stress, commitment, violence and anti-discriminatory practice.

**Alison Petch** has been Director of the Nuffield Centre for Community Care Studies at Glasgow University since 1993, concerned with the evaluation of community care policy and practice. Prior to that she undertook a range of health and social policy research, including seven years at the Social Work Research Centre at the University of Stirling.

**Nirmala Rao** is Senior Lecturer in Politics and Head of the Department of Social Policy and Politics at Goldsmith's College, University of London. She formerly held posts at the Policy Studies Institute and the Runnymede Trust. She is author of numerous publications in the field of local politics including *The Making and Unmaking of Local Self-Government* (1994), *Welfare Pluralism* (1996) and, with others, *Local Government Since 1995* (1997).

**John Stewart** is Professor of Local Government in the Institute of Local Government Studies at the University of Birmingham. He was appointed to the institute in 1966 to launch management courses for local government officers, and was Director from 1976 to 1983. From 1990 to 1992 he was Head of the School of Public Policy, which includes the institute and other departments concerned with the public sector at home and overseas. He has written extensively on the case for local government, and on public management more generally.

**Julia Twigg** is Reader in Social Policy at the University of Kent. She has written extensively on informal carers and in particular the role of services in support of them. More recently her work has addressed the management of the body in community care, exploring through a study of bathing in the community, the experiences of both recipients and providers.

**Gerald Wistow** is Professor of Health and Social Care, and Director of the Nuffield Institute for Health, University of Leeds. He has been an adviser to the House of Commons Health Committee and its predecessor, the Social Services Committee, since 1990. He was a member of the 1996 Joseph Rowntree Enquiry into Long-Term Care and the 1995 Mental Health Foundation Enquiry into Community Care. He is the co-author of a dozen books and many other publications on the personal social services, the NHS and community care.

# Author Index